Peachtree® 8 For Dummies®

Cheat Sheet

Debit and Credit Rules

To *increase* an *asset* account, **DEBIT** it.

To *decrease* an *asset* account, **CREDIT** it.

To *increase* a *liability* or *equity* account, **CREDIT** it.

To *decrease* a *liability* or *equity* account, **DEBIT** it.

To *increase* a *revenue* account, **CREDIT** it.

To *increase* an *expense* account, **DEBIT** it.

Important Web Addresses

Peachtree Software: www.peachtree.com

Microsoft Corporation: www.microsoft.com

Hungry Minds, Inc.: www.hungryminds.com

Internal Revenue Service: www.irs.gov

Small Business Administration: www.sba.gov

United States Post Office: www.usps.gov

Table C-1	Keyboard Shortcuts
Press This	*To Get This*
Alt+S	Save or Post
F1	Help
Shift+F1	Field Help
Ctrl+C	Copy selected text to the Windows Clipboard
Ctrl+X	Cut selected text to the Windows Clipboard
Ctrl+V	Paste selected text to the Windows Clipboard
Ctrl+E	Erase the current record
Ctrl+O	Open an existing Peachtree company
Ctrl+N	Create a new Peachtree company
Ctrl+F	Display the Find Transactions W
Ctrl+B	Back up Peachtree data files
Ctrl+R	Restore Peachtree data files

Shortcut to Printing Forms

For a quick way to print your forms in a batch, use the Navigation Aid at the bottom of your screen.

Click the appropriate module (sales, purchases, or payroll) and then click the picture of the form you want to print.

For Dummies: Bestselling Book Series for Beginners

Peachtree® 8 For Dummies®

BESTSELLING BOOK SERIES

Cheat Sheet

Table C-2		**Frequently Used Peachtree Toolbar Buttons**
Button	**Name**	**Function**
ChangeID	ChangeID	Change customer, vendor, or inventory item ID
Close	Close	Close the current window
Convert	Convert	Convert a quote to a sales order or invoice
Delete	Delete	Delete the current transaction/report/form
Edit	Edit	Modify a previously created transaction
Event	Event	Create a customer, vendor, or employee event
Help	Help	Access Peachtree Help system
Jobs	Jobs	Apply payroll hours to jobs for job costing
Journal	Journal	Display the "Accounting-Behind-The-Scenes" journal transaction
Log	Log	View a list of events for a selected customer, vendor, or employee
New	New	Create a new record
Note	Note	Add a note to the current transaction
Post	Post	Save the current transaction and reflect it in the general ledger
Preview	Preview	View a form on screen prior to printing
Print	Print	Print and post or save the current transaction
Recur	Recur	Create a repeating transaction for future months or accounting periods
Save	Save	Store the current transaction
Template	Template	Create and save different task window formats
Void	Void	Void the current transaction

For Dummies: Bestselling Book Series for Beginners

TM

BESTSELLING BOOK SERIES

References for the Rest of Us!®

Are you intimidated and confused by computers? Do you find that traditional manuals are overloaded with technical details you'll never use? Do your friends and family always call you to fix simple problems on their PCs? Then the For Dummies® computer book series from Wiley Publishing, Inc. is for you.

For Dummies books are written for those frustrated computer users who know they aren't really dumb but find that PC hardware, software, and indeed the unique vocabulary of computing make them feel helpless. For Dummies books use a lighthearted approach, a down-to-earth style, and even cartoons and humorous icons to dispel computer novices' fears and build their confidence. Lighthearted but not lightweight, these books are a perfect survival guide for anyone forced to use a computer.

Already, millions of satisfied readers agree. They have made For Dummies books the #1 introductory level computer book series and have written asking for more. So, if you're looking for the most fun and easy way to learn about computers, look to For Dummies books to give you a helping hand.

Wiley Publishing, Inc.

5/09

Peachtree® 8
FOR
DUMMIES®

by Elaine Marmel and Diane Koers

Wiley Publishing, Inc.

Peachtree® 8 For Dummies®

Published by
Wiley Publishing, Inc.
909 Third Avenue
New York, NY 10022
www.wiley.com

Library of Congress Cataloging-in-Publication Data:

Library of Congress Control Number: 00-101841

ISBN: 0-7645-0640-4

Manufactured in the United States of America

10 9 8 7 6 5 4

1O/TR/QZ/QS/IN

About the Authors

Elaine Marmel: Elaine is President of Marmel Enterprises, Inc., an organization that specializes in technical writing and software training. Elaine has an MBA from Cornell University and worked on projects to build financial management systems for New York City and Washington, D.C. This prior experience provided the foundation for Marmel Enterprises, Inc., which helps small businesses implement computerized accounting systems.

Elaine spends most of her time writing; she is a contributing editor to *Inside Peachtree for Windows, Inside QuickBooks for Windows,* and *Inside Timeslips,* all monthly magazines. She also has authored and co-authored over 25 books about software products, including *Quicken for Windows, Quicken for DOS, Excel, Microsoft Project, Word for Windows, Word for the Mac, 1-2-3 for Windows,* and *Lotus Notes.*

Elaine left her native Chicago for the warmer climes of Florida (by way of Cincinnati, Ohio; Jerusalem, Israel; Ithaca, New York; and Washington, D.C.) where she basks in the sun with her PC and her cats, Cato, Watson, and Buddy, and sings barbershop harmony.

Diane Koers: Diane owns and operates All Business Service, a software training and consulting business formed in 1988 that services the central Indiana area. Her area of expertise is providing training and support for Peachtree Accounting software and assisting clients with their other computer software, hardware, and networking needs. Diane has authored over a dozen books on topics such as Windows, Lotus 1-2-3, Corel WordPerfect, and Microsoft Office. She has also developed and written software training manuals for her clients' use.

Active in her church and civic activities, Diane enjoys spending her free time traveling and playing with her grandsons and her three Yorkshire terriers.

Elaine's Dedication

To my mom who's always there for me.

Diane's Dedication

To my dear special friend, Hank. Keep fighting!

Authors' Acknowledgments

We are deeply indebted to the many people who worked on this book. Thank you for all the time, effort, and support you gave and for your assistance.

Oh, where to start? First, thank you Martine Edwards and Laura Moss for your confidence in us, your support in pushing to get this book published, and for listening to us whine throughout the process.

Thank you to all of our many editors and production staff, especially Kelly Ewing for all your patience and guidance, Marla Reece-Hall and Paula Lowell for your assistance in making this book grammatically correct, and Larry Allen for your assistance in making sure that we weren't fibbing about the product.

We'd also like to express our gratitude to Kellie Jones at Peachtree Software for keeping us informed of the latest and greatest happenings at Peachtree Software. We know how frustrating we can be when we nag about things like TAL links and other items. Thanks for listening. . . .

Lastly, thanks to our families, for always being supportive of our stress tantrums and our late-night hours and keeping us supplied with chocolate.

Publisher's Acknowledgments

We're proud of this book; please send us your comments through our online registration form located at www.dummies.com/register/.

Some of the people who helped bring this book to market include the following:

Acquisitions, Editorial, and Media Development

Project Editor: Kelly Ewing

Associate Acquisitions Editor: Laura Moss

Copy Editors: Marla Reece-Hall, Paula Lowell

Technical Editor: Larry E. Allen, Sunbelt Support Centers

Editorial Manager: Rev Mengle

Senior Editor, Freelance: Constance Carlisle

Production

Project Coordinator: Nancee Reeves

Layout and Graphics: Amy Adrian, Joe Bucki, Jason Guy, Gabriele McCann, Julie Trippetti

Proofreaders: Corey Bowen, Vickie Broyles, Susan Moritz, Marianne Santy, York Production Services, Inc.

Indexer: York Production Services, Inc.

Publishing and Editorial for Technology Dummies

Richard Swadley, Vice President and Executive Group Publisher
Mary C. Corder, Editorial Director
Andy Cummings, Vice President and Publisher

Publishing for Consumer Dummies

Diane Graves Steele, Vice President and Publisher
Joyce Pepple, Acquisitions Director

Composition Services

Gerry Fahey, Vice President of Production Services
Debbie Stailey, Director of Composition Services

Contents at a Glance

Cartoons at a Glance

By Rich Tennant

page 341

page 63

page 213

page 7

Fax: 978-546-7747
E-mail: richtennant@the5thwave.com
World Wide Web: www.the5thwave.com

Table of Contents

Introduction

You're not a dummy, even if you think you are. But accounting by itself can be a challenge — and then, when you add the computer part to it . . . well, the whole thing can seem so overwhelming that you avoid it. (What? Never crossed your mind?)

Okay, if you're looking at this book, you've probably decided that you've "avoided" long enough, and now you're going to do it — bite the bullet and "computerize your accounting." We want to help you get the job done as quickly as possible with the least amount of pain. You've got other things to do, after all.

About This Book

Accounting isn't exactly a fun subject — unless, of course, you're an accountant . . . and even then it may not really be all that much fun. You may think that going to the dentist is more fun than playing with accounting software. So, we're going to help you get past the ugly part so that you can start enjoying the benefits quickly.

What benefits? Well, computerizing your accounting can save you time and effort — and can actually be easier than doing it by hand and cheaper than paying somebody else to do it. Oh. We don't mean that you won't need your accountant, because you will. But you'll be able to save money by doing "daily stuff" for yourself — and paying your accountant for advice on making your business more profitable.

Peachtree 8 For Dummies shows you how to set up your company in Peachtree and then use Peachtree to pay bills, invoice customers, pay employees, produce reports about your financial picture, and more. But it's also a real-life situation-oriented book. We try to show you how to use Peachtree using everyday, real-life situations as examples. You know, the stuff you run into in "the real world" that you need to figure out how to handle.

What You Can Safely Ignore

Throughout the book, we include Accounting Stuff tips — you can probably ignore those unless you're interested in that kind of stuff.

Oh, and those gray boxes you see throughout the book? Those are called sidebars, and they contain extra information that you really don't *have* to know but that we thought you might find useful and interesting. So feel free to skip the sidebars as well.

Foolish Assumptions

We'll be honest — we had to assume something about you to write this book. So, here's what we assumed about you:

- ✔ We assumed that you already know a little something about the day to day stuff you need to do financially to run your business — you know, write checks, bill customers, pay employees, and so on. We *didn't* assume that you know how to do all that on a computer.

- ✔ We assumed that you have a PC (that you know how to turn on) with Microsoft Windows 95, Windows 98, or Windows 3.1.

- ✔ Lastly, we assumed that you've bought Peachtree and installed it.

The Flavors of Peachtree

Peachtree comes in three versions: Peachtree First Accounting, Peachtree for Windows, and Peachtree Complete Accounting for Windows. In this book, we cover Peachtree Complete Accounting for Windows, which is the most complete (pardon the pun) of the three products. Peachtree Complete includes a time and billing feature that you won't find in the other two versions, and Peachtree Complete 8 is the only networkable version of Peachtree — make sure, however, that you get the multi-user version. Peachtree Complete contains a job *costing* feature, but you'll find only a job *tracking* feature in the other two versions (if you don't know the difference between job costing and job tracking, you probably don't need either one). And, you can customize reports and forms in Peachtree Complete Accounting for Windows and Peachtree Accounting for Windows, but not Peachtree First Accounting. Throughout the book, when we cover a feature that you won't find in Peachtree First Accounting or Peachtree for Windows, we include notes to let you know.

Peachtree 2002

This book covers both Peachtree 8 and Peachtree 2002, which are very similar products. In most cases, Peachtree 2002 makes working in Peachtree easier and more efficient. Although we based the bulk of the text on Peachtree 8, you'll find cross-references throughout the book to the appendix whenever Peachtree 2002 enhances a process or does things differently than Peachtree 8. And, by browsing through the appendix, you'll be able to easily identify the "new" things in Peachtree 2002.

How This Book Is Organized

Every great book needs a plan. We divided this book into four parts, which are each made up of three to nine chapters, so that you can easily find the information that you need.

Part I: Getting Started

If you're new to Peachtree, then you'll probably want to read this part. We explain how to get around in Peachtree, how to create a company in Peachtree, how to make an effective chart of accounts, and how to set up default information that will save you lots of time later.

Part II: The Daily Drudge

In this section, we cover the stuff you do on a regular basis:

- ✔ Pay the employees (or they won't work!)
- ✔ Bill the customers and collect your money (or you won't be *able* to pay the employees)
- ✔ Buy and pay for goods to sell to your customers (yep, we cover inventory, too)

Stuff like that. We also cover paying for services that keep your business running, and we cover a couple of more esoteric topics, like billing customers for time you spend working and tracking project costs.

Part III: The Fancy Stuff

In this section, we cover a variety of topics — most that you *don't* do every day. First, we show you how to customize Peachtree to make it work your way. Then we show you how to customize forms and produce and modify reports — after all, you put information *into* Peachtree, so you should be able to get it out and see the effects of your business habits. Then we cover reconciling the bank statement and the stuff you do monthly, quarterly, or annually. Our favorite chapter talks about Peachtree and "real-life" situations. (We've got lots more of these, but didn't have space to discuss them.)

Last, we show you how to easily keep your accounting information safe — a *very* important chapter. Why? Because you spend so much time putting stuff into Peachtree that it would be criminal to lose it just because your hard drive crashes or your office is robbed.

Part IV: The Part of Tens

If you've ever read a . . .*For Dummies* book before, then you've seen the Part of Tens. This part contains a collection of "ten-something" lists. Our Part of Tens includes

- Ten common error messages you might see — and what they mean
- Ten things you can get from the Web — not just Peachtree stuff like support and additional information, but fun stuff, too, just in case you've had a bad day and need a laugh
- Ten things you can do (or not do) to make your accountant love you (It's important to keep your accountant happy.)

And in the appendix, we've described the new features you'll find in Peachtree 2002.

Icons Used in This Book

Throughout the book, you'll notice symbols in the margin. These symbols, known as *icons,* mark important points that you'll want to note.

This bull's eye appears next to shortcuts and tips that make your work easier.

When you see this icon, it's not a good thing, but you'll want to make sure that you read the paragraph anyway. This icon warns you of common mistakes and ways to avoid them.

This icon marks any point you'll want to be sure to remember. You may want to reread paragraphs marked with this icon.

This icon identifies information related to accounting in general — not just Peachtree. You can skip this stuff if you don't care about accounting.

When you see this icon, we're identifying a feature that is new to Peachtree 8 and didn't exist in prior versions. If you've never used Peachtree, you won't care. If you have used Peachtree, you'll be interested because you might find the new feature valuable.

Where to Go from Here

Just getting started with Peachtree? Turn the page. Do you have a specific topic of interest? Use the index or the Table of Contents to find the topic and turn to that page.

Part I
Getting Started

In this part . . .

Every project has a beginning point. If you are just getting acquainted with Peachtree, this part is the place
to start. In this part, you find out how to navigate through
the Peachtree screens and how to set up your existing
company records in Peachtree.

Chapter 1

Mastering Peachtree Basics

· ·

In This Chapter

▶ Starting Peachtree

▶ Navigating the Peachtree screen

▶ Getting help

· ·

*W*e know you're eager to get started. Operating a business is a nonstop process, but you have to put first things first.

To work effectively, take some time to get comfortable with some of the features unique to the Peachtree Accounting program. In this chapter, you find out how to navigate in the software as well as open and close companies as needed. We also show you where you can turn for additional assistance. If you're ready, then dig in.

Starting the Program

You can start Peachtree the easy way or the hard way. We prefer the easy way. When you installed Peachtree, it placed an icon on your Windows desktop. Assuming (we know, we're not supposed to assume) that you haven't thrown that icon into the Recycle Bin, you can simply double-click the Peachtree Complete Accounting icon (the one with the peachy little peach on it), and the program starts. Or, if you're using Peachtree Accounting, the icon simply says Peachtree Accounting.

Keep in mind this one informational point. Peachtree comes in three versions: Peachtree First Accounting, Peachtree for Windows, and Peachtree Complete Accounting for Windows. In this book, we cover Peachtree Complete Accounting for Windows, which is the most . . . complete (pardon the pun) of the three products. Throughout the book, when we cover a feature that you won't find in Peachtree First Accounting or Peachtree for Windows, we include notes to let you know.

If you did throw the icon away or you have so many icons on your desktop that you can't see it, okay, you can start Peachtree the hard way. Click Start⇨Programs⇨Peachtree Complete Accounting⇨Peachtree Complete Accounting — for a total of four mouse clicks.

Choosing opening options

After you start Peachtree, what do you do with it? The Peachtree opening screen appears, beckoning you to do one of several things. You can go any of these directions or click Close This Window to exit:

✔ **Open An Existing Company:** Use this option to open a company already existing in Peachtree.

✔ **Set Up A New Company:** Click this one to set up your business with the Peachtree Setup Wizard. (Chapter 2 covers this wizard.)

✔ **Learn About Peachtree Accounting Through An Online Tutorial:** Wander down this path when you've got some extra time and try to spot some of the things you've already seen in this book.

✔ **Explore A Sample Company:** Use this option to explore one of two fictitious companies. One company, Bellwether Garden Supply, is a retail and service company that uses most of the features of Peachtree, including inventory and job costing. The other fabricated company, Pavilion Design Group, is a service business that uses the time and billing features of Peachtree. Pavilion Design Group is only available if you have Peachtree Complete Accounting. You explore one of these in the next set of steps.

✔ **Convert a QuickBooks Company to Peachtree Accounting:** If you have finally come to your senses and want to transfer to Peachtree from *that other software,* click this choice. Peachtree helps to make the conversion pretty painless.

Exploring a sample company

You can best explore Peachtree's features by opening the Bellwether Garden Supply sample company and finding out how to move around in the Peachtree Accounting program. To open a sample company, follow these steps:

1. **Click Explore A Sample Company.**

   If you're using Peachtree Accounting, Bellwether Garden Supply immediately opens.

   If you're using Peachtree Complete Accounting, the Explore A Sample Company dialog box opens.

2. **Continue in Peachtree Complete Accounting by choosing which sample company you want to explore.**

   For this example, click Bellwether Garden Supply.

3. **Click OK.**

   As with other Windows programs, the current open company name appears at the top of the window in the Peachtree title bar.

Getting around town

New to Peachtree Version 8 is Peachtree Today. You can discover it in Chapter 19. For now, click the Close box to close the Peachtree Today window.

The main menu window of Peachtree looks pretty plain. Don't skip too lightly through this "street." The screen actually displays several pieces of information. At the bottom of the screen, the Windows-style status bar (see Figure 1-1) displays information about the field, window, or menu choice you happen to be using, as well as the current date and the current accounting period. In Peachtree 2002, these buttons are interactive. See the appendix for details about the interface changes in Peachtree 2002.

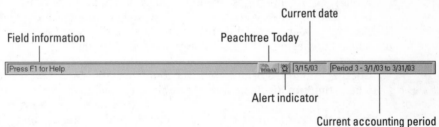

Figure 1-1: The current accounting period appears on the status bar.

Current date

Field information

Peachtree Today

Press F1 for Help | TODAY | 3/15/03 | Period 3 - 3/1/03 to 3/31/03

Alert indicator

Current accounting period

In the Bellwether Garden Supply example, notice a small alarm clock displayed in the status bar. You can tell Peachtree to notify you when certain conditions occur, such as when a bill is past due or inventory on a particular item gets too low. The alarm clock reports to you that the alert condition has been met. You can click the Alarm clock to display the alerts.

You should know, however, that using Alerts and its sister feature, Events, could substantially slow down the response time of Peachtree. (To find out how to turn off the Events feature, see Chapter 13.) From the initial company screen, you need to tell Peachtree what you want to do. You've got the usual two ways to move around in a Peachtree window. Use the traditional "menu method," or check out the pretty navigational aid that comes with Peachtree. Because tradition has been around forever, we start with the traditional Windows method.

Choosing menu commands

The pull-down menus should be a familiar sight from your other Windows programs. Even though the other menu choices are important, you're likely to spend the majority of your time in Peachtree using these three main menu choices: Maintain, Tasks, and Reports.

- ✔ The Maintain menu includes choices for working with data records. For example, you can store vendor, customer, and employee information including names, addresses, and phone numbers.

  A *record* is all the information about one person, product, event, and so on. Every record in a database contains the same fields. A *field* is one item in a record, such as an ID, name, or transaction number. To explore these parts of the information you store in Peachtree, see the "Exploring fields and records" section in this chapter.

- ✔ The Tasks menu is where you do your normal day-to-day work. You can bill your customers, buy materials, and pay your workers by using the Tasks menu.

- ✔ The Reports menu is where it all comes together and where you can see the results of all your hard work.

Using Navigation Aids

Just above the status bar is the fancy graphical Navigation Aid. The Navigation Aid illustrates the flow of information in the various components of Peachtree. When you click one of the Navigation Aid tabs, such as Purchases, a graphical illustration denotes the different tasks that you can use in Purchasing. Figure 1-2 shows you these options.

Clicking Purchases brings up the accounts payable (A/P) tasks, and clicking Sales brings up the accounts receivable (A/R) tasks.

To use the Navigation Aids, simply click the folder category and click the project you want.

Do you need to enter a purchase order? In Purchases, click the icon labeled Purchase Orders. Clicking an icon opens the appropriate window. This is the same window you would get if you made your selection from the Task pull-down menu, which operates by action rather than accounting category. (Refer to Chapter 5 if you're ready to work with Purchase Orders.)

Mastering keyboard shortcuts

Peachtree includes several shortcuts to make entering your data quicker and easier. Using these shortcuts also can eliminate a lot of back and forth movement between the mouse and keyboard. You may recognize some of these shortcuts as standard Windows shortcuts. Table 1-1 lists some shortcuts you're likely to need.

Purchase order icon

Purchases tab

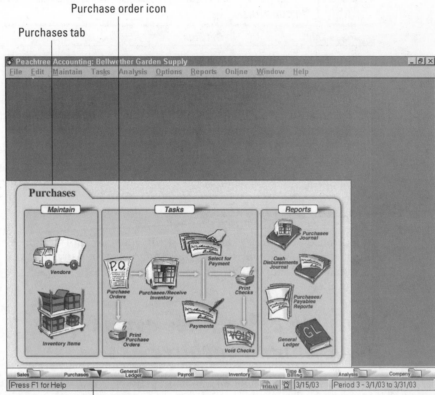

Figure 1-2:
Click
Purchase
Orders if
you just
have to
spend more
money.

Navigation aid folder

Table 1-1	Peachtree Keyboard Shortcuts
Press This	*To Get This*
Alt+S	Save or Post
F1	Help
Shift+F1	Field Help
Ctrl+C	Copy selected text to the Windows Clipboard
Ctrl+X	Cut selected text to the Windows Clipboard
Ctrl+V	Paste selected text to the Windows Clipboard
Ctrl+E	Erase the current record
Ctrl+O	Open an existing Peachtree company

(continued)

Table 1-1 *(continued)*

Press This	To Get This
Ctrl+N	Create a new Peachtree company
Ctrl+F	Display the Find Transactions Window
Ctrl+B	Backup Peachtree data files
Ctrl+R	Restore Peachtree data files

Opening a Company

You can use Peachtree to account for the financial information of more than one company. Although you can open only one company at a time, you can switch back and forth between companies very easily.

Opening a Peachtree company from within Peachtree

The steps to open a company differ, depending on whether you're opening a company while already in a Peachtree company, or whether you're opening a company from the Peachtree opening screen. Discover in Chapter 13 how to turn off the display of the opening screen and have Peachtree open directly to your company. If you're already in a Peachtree company and want to open a different one, follow these steps:

1. **Choose File⇨Open Company (or press Ctrl+O).**

   You get an annoying little message telling you that you're closing the current company.

2. **Click OK to acknowledge the message.**

   The Open dialog box appears.

3. **From the Open dialog box, click the company name and then click OK.**

   If you have Peachtree Complete Accounting, select Pavilion Design Group for this example. The newly opened company name appears at the top of the screen.

Notice the title bar displays Pavilion Design Group as the open company. The menu choices and Navigation Aids are exactly the same for Pavilion Design Group as they are for Bellwether Garden Supply.

Opening a company from the Peachtree opening screen

If you're opening a company from the Peachtree Opening screen, a different dialog box appears. To open a company from the Peachtree Opening Screen, follow these steps:

1. **Click Open An Existing Company to display the Open An Existing Company dialog box.**

   This dialog box lists the companies that you have recently opened in Peachtree. If the company name you want to open does not appear, click the Browse button and make your selection from the Open dialog box.

2. **Click the company name you want to open and then click OK.**

   The selected company opens.

Exploring Peachtree's Windows

Most windows in Peachtree are similar. They have places for you to fill in information and a toolbar across the top containing buttons that you use to take actions in that particular window.

Exploring fields and records

The Maintain Customers window is typical of many other windows you use in Peachtree. For an example, open Bellwether Garden Supply and choose Maintain⇨Customers/Prospects. Take a stroll around this window.

The main part of the window consists of fields. Stop for a moment and talk about these components. When we refer to fields, we're not talking about the place corn grows. *Fields* are pieces of information that fit into a *record,* which is a type of electronic 3 x 5 index card. A record is all the information about one customer, vendor, employee, or inventory part, but a field is one piece of the record such as the ID, name, or phone number. In Figure 1-3, the record is all of the information about Hensley Park Apartments, and Jacob Hensley is in the Contact field.

Lookup list indicator

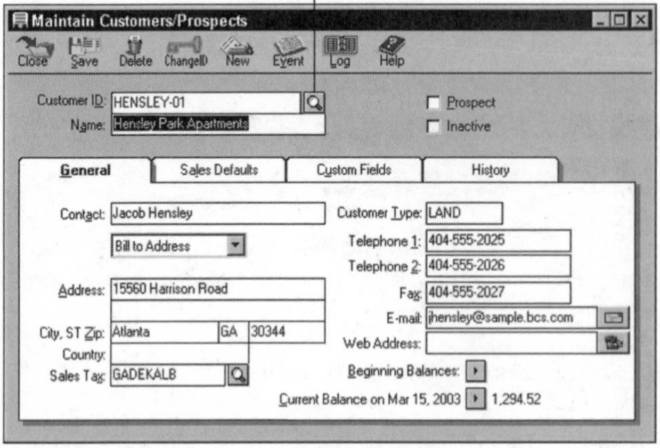

Figure 1-3:
Each record
has many
different
fields.

Looking up information

Some fields, such as Customer ID, have a magnifying glass next to them. These fields contain *lookup lists* that display a list of your customers (or vendors, accounts, employees, inventory items, and so on). You can choose a record from a lookup list. Depending on the global options you have set, a lookup list may automatically appear as you type any character in the field, or you can click the lookup list indicator (magnifying glass) to display the list that is relevant to the current field. (See Figure 1-3.) You can also press the Shift key and the question mark (?) to display a lookup list.

To set the global options that affect lookup lists, turn to Chapter 13.

You can do any of the following while in a lookup list:

✔ Select a customer (vendor, item, and so on), then click OK. Peachtree Accounting selects the highlighted record and closes the lookup list.

✔ Click Cancel to close the lookup list without selecting a record.

✔ Use Find to search for a string of characters. The search covers any text you can see in the displayed list. The Find feature is not case sensitive. Press Enter after you type the lookup text in the entry box. Peachtree highlights the first item that matches your request.

✔ Click Find Next to find the next instance of the previously entered Find text. If there is no next instance, Find skips to the first instance in the lookup list. If there is no instance at all, Find Next does nothing.

✔ Click Sort to sort the displayed list either alphabetically by the ID or name. Numbers sort before letters.

✔ Use the Help option if you need it.

Some lookup lists, particularly the ones in the Task menu selections, have two additional buttons.

✔ Use the New button to add customers, vendors, employees, or inventory items on-the-fly, which means Peachtree adds the record right in the middle of entering a transaction.

In Peachtree 2002, you can use the new Fast Add feature. See the appendix for details.

✔ Click the Edit button to edit the record of a customer, vendor, employee, or inventory item.

Making a date

Many Peachtree windows have date fields where you need to enter data based on the calendar. If you're a keyboard-type person, you can simply type the date. Dates need to be typed as numbers. If you want, you can type the date using the / (slash) key, but the slash isn't necessary. For example, to enter April 13, 2000, type 041300 or 04/13/00. Be aware that Peachtree won't allow you to use a dash in a date.

In most Peachtree date fields, you can get away with entering just the first four digits of a date. Peachtree then enters the year. The year is based on the system date displayed on the Peachtree status bar. This little trick doesn't work in two places: in the Invoice Ship Date field, and when you are entering customer or vendor beginning balances.

Now if you're like us, we need a calendar in front of us to choose dates. Fortunately, Peachtree date fields also include a calendar, shown in Figure 1-4, so you can click that to choose a date. To choose a date from the calendar, follow these steps:

1. **Click the calendar icon next to a date field to display the current month.**

2. **Click the left arrow next to the month name to display a previous month or click the right arrow to display a future month.**

3. **Click the date you want for the date field.**

The small calendar closes, and the date appears in the field.

Calendar

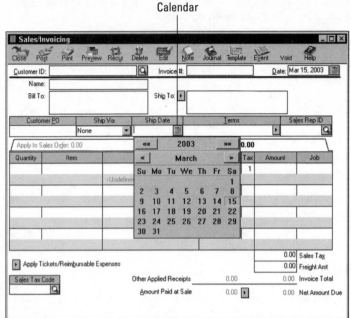

Using the toolbar

Across the top of the window is a toolbar that you use to complete the various tasks involved with the selected window.

The exact buttons vary slightly with the individual window, but most of them have a Close button. You can use either the Close button to get out of a Peachtree window or the Windows Close button (X). The buttons have changed slightly in Peachtree 2002. See the appendix for details.

New to Peachtree Version 8 is the addition of Tool Tips. Tool Tips are great for those "CRS moments" when you look at a button and cannot remember its function. CRS ("Can't Remember Stuff") is a widespread disease that affects people of all ages, races, religions, and hair colors. Position the mouse pointer over any button on the toolbar, and a small yellow box appears to explain the use of the button.

You also use the Post or Save button frequently. The Post button appears if you are using Real Time posting and are using a transaction entry window under the Tasks menu, such as Payroll Entry or Inventory Adjustments. You click the Post button to save and post the displayed transaction to your journals and the G/L. If you are using the *batch* method of posting, Peachtree replaces the Post button with the Save button. You also see the Save button if you are modifying data records, such as customers, from the Maintenance menu. (See Chapter 2 for an explanation of posting methods.)

Post, which you see on the toolbar, is one of those words with many different meanings. It can be a noun like the place you tie your horse, or it can be a verb and mean to send. Of course, the latter is how the word post is used in accounting, and it means to save and send. In Peachtree, you're sending transactions to the general ledger (G/L); then, when you want to find out if you've made any money this month, Peachtree is able to show you.

Getting a Helping Hand

We really hope you get most of the answers you need from this book. However, . . . sometimes you need additional assistance.

What's this all about?

If you're in a Peachtree window and don't quite know what a particular field represents or what you're supposed to enter in that field, you can use the What's This feature, which is similar to what you've probably used in other Windows apps. In Peachtree, use your right mouse button to access this feature when it is available.

Right-click the field where you need a hint. Then, click What's This?. A summary definition of the field appears. To close a pop-up What's This box, click inside it.

Using the Help contents

In Peachtree Version 8, the Help system has been redesigned. It now works in an HTML format, which simply means that it looks and works similar to a Web page. For easier navigation, the help screens now have Back and Forward buttons as well as a Home button. To open the help contents, follow these steps:

1. **Choose Help⇨Contents and Index to open the Peachtree Accounting help windows.**

   The Contents tab appears on top.

   The Help Contents feature presents help information in a book-like format, making it easy for you to browse available topics. If you've used the Help Contents tab in other Windows programs, then you already know how to use the Help Contents in Peachtree.

2. **From the Help Topics dialog box, click the Contents tab to display a list of topics available in Peachtree Help.**

3. **Double-click a book to open that topic.**

4. **Continue opening books until you find the topic you want to read.**

5. **Click the page icon to display the topic.**

    The help information is displayed on the right side of the screen. From this point, you can click the underlined hyperlinks to jump to related topics or print a topic.

Using the Help index

Use the Help Index to look up a keyword or phrase in the extensive online index. The Peachtree Help Index feature works the same as the Help Index in other Windows applications. To use the Help index, use these steps:

1. **Open the Peachtree Accounting Help window.**

2. **Click the Index tab.**

3. **Scroll through the index or type the term you're looking for.**

4. **Double-click a keyword to display a topic that corresponds to it.**

Checking Out New Features in Peachtree 8

Some of the new things added to Peachtree 8 are fairly advanced things — and we won't be covering them in any detail in this book. For example, the technically minded might be interested to know that BTRIEVE 6.1.5 installs to the \PEACHW directory instead of the WINDOWS\SYSTEM directory. And, if you're converting to Peachtree from One Write Plus, you can use a built-in conversion routine.

In Table 1-2, we list the other new features in Peachtree 8 — and the chapters where you can find information about them.

Table 1-2	New Features in Peachtree 8
Feature	*Chapter*
New HTML Help	1
Tool Tips	1
Purchases by Vendor report.	5

Feature	Chapter
Interactive e-mail and Web page addresses for customers and vendors	5, 7
New Recalc button	6
New Void Checks window	6
Write Checks window	6
Void Invoice window	7
Select a name for finance charges	8
New, easier-to-understand statement options	8
Payroll Tax Liability report	10
Pay period starting date	10
Finding Transactions	13
Technology changes to the Forms Designer	14
Print Preview for forms	14
Report styles	15
New ways to summarize the G/L report	16
Financial Report Designer Wizard	16
Peachtree Today, My Business, Peachtree World	19
Copying reports across companies	20
Changes to backup and restore	21
Updating your software online	23

Chapter 2

Setting Up Your Company

. . . .

In This Chapter

▶ Supplying your company information

▶ Specifying an accounting method

▶ Identifying accounting periods

. . . .

*P*eachtree tracks all kinds of information including the names and addresses of your customers, vendors, or employees, and any business transactions that you have made with them. But before Peachtree can do any of that, you have to tell the software about your company. You need to tell it the usual stuff like name and address. (That's so you don't forget who you are. . . .) You also need to tell it when you want to pay Uncle Sam taxes on the money you earn and spend. (Sorry, but "never" is not an option.)

Keep this important fact in mind: Two of the options you set in this wizard are written in stone — no going backward. One is whether you're a cash or accrual business, and the other is the time frame of your accounting year. We talk about these issues in the accounting method and accounting period sections of this chapter.

Starting the New Company Setup Wizard

When you want to create a new company, the New Company Setup Wizard simplifies the task for you. It asks you the basic questions in the order that Peachtree Accounting needs to set up your business. (If you're not setting up a new company but are simply changing settings, see Chapter 4.)

You access the New Company Setup Wizard when you click Set Up A New Company from the Peachtree opening screen. Like most wizards, the New Company Setup Wizard guides you through the process. You've probably used wizards dozens of times (not to mention when you install most apps like Peachtree), so we keep things short and sweet.

If you are already in Peachtree and want to create a new company, choose File⇨New Company to start the New Company Setup Wizard.

When you're done checking out the opening screen, click Next to move to the next screen.

The following sections walk you through each step of the wizard.

Introducing your business to Peachtree

The left half of the wizard screen is pretty self-explanatory. Fill in your business name, address, city, two-letter state name, and, optionally, country. Notice we said *country* — not *county!* Many people misread this line. You see country fields other places in Peachtree Accounting. Use the Tab or Enter keys to fill in or skip through the fields.

The first item on the right side of the screen asks for your business type. To fill in the rest of the screen, follow these steps:

1. **Click the down arrow to display and choose a Business Type.**

   Choices include Corporation, S Corporation, Partnership, Sole Proprietorship, or Limited Liability Company. Selecting a type of business tells Peachtree how to determine equity accounts.

   Equity is what's left after you subtract the company's liabilities from the assets. The equity is the value of a company to its owners. In a corporation, the equity is divided among the stockholders, but if you're a sole proprietorship or partnership, the equity belongs to the individual owners. If you're not sure what type of business you are, talk with your accountant.

2. **Enter your Federal Employer, State Employer, and State Unemployment IDs.**

   If your state doesn't use employer IDs or unemployment IDs, leave these fields blank.

3. **Click Next to move to the Chart of Accounts screen.**

4. **Choose a chart of accounts option and then click Next.**

   If you're not sure what option to select, read the section "Choosing a chart of accounts," later in this chapter.

   What you see next depends on the choice you selected. For example, if you chose to set up a new company based on one of the several sample companies, a list of business descriptions appears. Don't worry if the accounts you select don't match yours completely; you can edit them after you're done with the wizard. (Chapter 3 shows you how to customize the chart of accounts.)

If you choose to copy settings from an existing Peachtree company, a list of existing Peachtree companies appears. Peachtree asks whether you want to copy default information from these other companies. Usually, you do want to copy default information.

5. **Click the sample that most closely matches your business or click the company from which you want to copy and then click <u>N</u>ext.**

   The Accounting Method screen appears.

6. **Click an accounting method and then click <u>N</u>ext.**

   For important information on choosing an accounting method, see "Choosing an accounting method," later in this chapter.

   The Select A Posting Method screen appears.

7. **Select a posting method; then click <u>N</u>ext.**

   To understand posting methods, see "Selecting a posting method," later in this chapter.

   The Accounting Periods screen appears.

8. **Choose an accounting period structure option and then click <u>N</u>ext.**

   See "Selecting accounting periods," later in this chapter, if you're not sure which option to select.

9. **Select the dates as requested and click <u>N</u>ext.**

   The default screen that appears next displays how Peachtree Accounting sets up the standard (default) information for your vendors, customers, and inventory items. Don't worry if you don't plan on using one of these modules, or if the information is incorrect. (See Chapter 4 for information on changing the default information.)

10. **Click <u>N</u>ext and the final setup screen appears.**

    Congratulations! You're almost finished with the New Company Setup Wizard. Optionally, you can have Peachtree display a checklist of steps to continue setting up your company information.

    After you click Finish, you cannot change the accounting method or the accounting periods. If you need to change either of these choices, click the Back button until you reach the screen you need to change.

11. **Choose not to display the Setup Checklist and then click Finish.**

    Peachtree creates a set of data files for your company.

    A message box appears, advising how you can return to the Setup Checklist at any time.

12. **Click OK to close this message.**

    Your company window opens, and the new company name appears at the top of the window.

Choosing a chart of accounts

The wizard also asks you to choose how you want to start your chart of accounts. If you're a new business, you may want to choose one of the samples provided by Peachtree, or you may already have a chart of accounts supplied by your accountant.

The chart of accounts lists the names you use to classify transaction information and categorizes the accounts so that they appear on appropriate financial statements. If you're not sure which chart of accounts to select, you can choose one of the sample charts of accounts supplied by Peachtree. Peachtree has listed dozens of business types (6.25 dozen, or 75, to be exact), and each of those includes accounts typical to the selected business type. For example, the accounts used by a shoe store are different than those used by a drugstore or a dentist.

Accounts are the systematic arrangement of numbers and descriptions to keep records of the business your company transacts. Each time you buy or sell something, you record the transaction and assign it to one or more accounts. Accounts help you organize information by grouping similar transactions together.

Peachtree has several options:

- ✔ **Set Up A New Company Based On One Of Several Sample Companies:** This choice allows you to select from one of the predefined charts of accounts that comes with Peachtree Accounting.

- ✔ **Copy Settings From An Existing Peachtree Accounting Company:** This choice copies the Chart of Accounts from a Peachtree company that is already setup. Use this option if you are starting your Peachtree company books over or starting a second company that's similar to the first one.

- ✔ **Convert A Company From Another Accounting Program:** Choose this option if you are switching from Peachtree Complete Accounting for DOS, Quicken, or Quickbooks.

- ✔ **Build Your Own Company:** Use this choice if your accountant has supplied you with an account list or you are starting with a manual system that uses account numbers.

Choosing an accounting method

At the beginning of this chapter, we mention that two places in this wizard you enter information that is permanent. Choosing your accounting method is one of those two places. Your business can be accrual based or cash based.

Accrual or Cash: What's the difference?

An *accrual*-based business is one that recognizes income in the month an invoice was issued to a customer, regardless of when that customer decides to pay. Also, a purchase is recognized as an expense in the month you make the purchase, not whenever you write the check to your supplier.

A *cash*-based business is one that declares income in the month you receive the payment from your customer and expenses in the month you actually write the check to your supplier.

Dates of customer invoices and vendor bills play no role in a cash-based business.

Say, for example, that you sell a $20,000-product to Smith and Sons on December 13, 1999. You invoice them right away, but they don't pay you until April 2, 2000. Do you declare that $20,000 as part of your sales for December 1999? If the answer is yes, then you're running an accrual-based business. If that $20,000 doesn't show up on your income statement until April 2000, then you're running a cash-based business.

Because you must report your accounting method to the IRS, don't just arbitrarily pick one. If you're not sure, ask your accountant. It might just keep you out of jail.

Selecting a posting method

The posting method determines how Peachtree Accounting processes or transfers the transactions you enter from the individual journals to the general ledger. You have two choices: Real Time or Batch. You can switch posting methods at any time.

Journals are electronic or paper records of accounting transactions. Peachtree has many different types of journals. For example, the Cash Receipts journal stores transactions of money you receive, and the Cash Disbursements journal stores transactions of the money you spend. Through posting, the journals ultimately go into the General Ledger (G/L) where Peachtree sorts the information and reports it to you on financial statements.

If you choose real-time posting, Peachtree posts the transactions to both the individual journals (Cash Receipts, and so on) and to the G/L as you enter and save transactions. This method can save you time. Real-time posting immediately updates the company's financial information. For example, if an accrual-based business enters an invoice to a customer and then prints an income statement, that invoice is included in the income totals. We recommend the real-time posting method.

If you choose batch posting, Peachtree saves the transactions and then posts them in a group. When you use batch posting, you can print registers and check the batch of transactions before posting them to the journals.

Peachtree prompts you to post journals when necessary. For example, before you enter a customer receipt, you need to have all the invoices posted.

Selecting accounting periods

According to a calendar in our office, (the one with the Yorkshire Terriers all over it), a new year starts on January 1. Some businesses, however, start their business year, or *fiscal* year, at different times. You can't watch Dick Clark as the new fiscal year rolls in, but I guess if you wanted to, you could have champagne and throw confetti. (For details on closing a financial year, see Chapter 18.)

It's very important to enter the fiscal periods correctly in Peachtree. Setting the accounting periods is the second of the two permanent items you set in this wizard. After you create fiscal periods, you can't change them.

You can choose from two options on this screen:

- ✔ **Twelve Monthly Accounting Periods:** Each accounting period's starting and ending dates match those of the 12 calendar months. On the next screen you can choose the month to start your fiscal year.

- ✔ **Accounting Periods That Do Not Match The Calendar Month:** Choose this option if you want to set up a custom fiscal year structure. For example, you may want four accounting periods per year or possibly 13 four-week accounting periods per year.

On the next screen, Peachtree prompts you to choose the year and month you want to begin entering data. If you choose to set your own fiscal calendar month, Peachtree also asks you to enter the number of accounting periods you want to use.

Chapter 3

Designing the Chart of Accounts

. . . .

In This Chapter
▶ Understanding account types
▶ Using masking
▶ Modifying the Chart of Accounts

. . . .

*W*e know you're eager to start using the software. But before you dive in, we need to tell you a little about the Chart of Accounts, which serves as the foundation for all your reports. To make sure that you get the reports you want, you may find that a little planning at this stage is wise. Some of the material in this chapter may seem a little dry because it deals with accounting principles and information you need for your big picture financial tracking, but understanding this information helps you set up the Chart of Accounts that produces the business reports you want.

Understanding the Chart of Accounts

You use accounts to keep records of the business your company transacts. Each time you buy or sell something, you record the transaction in the appropriate accounts. Accounts help you organize information by keeping similar transactions together. In today's world, for example, you probably get several different telephone bills for your regular phone, your fax phone, your cellular phone, your pagers, and so on. But when you think of the big picture, all the bills are related to *telephone* expenses. So, when you pay these bills, you record all the transactions in the Telephone expense account.

The Chart of Accounts is nothing more than the list of all your accounts. The Chart of Accounts doesn't show any amounts — just titles and numbers you've assigned to each account. But, like any list, you can, and *should*, organize the Chart of Accounts to make the best use of it. So where *do* you get a list of your accounts and their balances? Use the General Ledger Trial Balance report. See Chapter 15 for details.

Understanding account types

Good accountants and bookkeepers are typically very organized people — they would hate what they do (and probably wouldn't do it for long) if they weren't. So, it should come as no big surprise that they've invented a method to help them organize things further.

To organize the Chart of Accounts, accounting uses *account types*. Usually, accounts are broken down into five general categories:

- **Assets:** Things you own but don't sell to customers. Money in checking and savings accounts, computers, trucks, and money others owe you are all assets.

- **Liabilities:** Debts you owe to others. Bills from your vendors and bank loans are liabilities.

- **Equity:** Also known as *net worth,* equity represents the amount owners have invested in the company. Some people prefer to think of equity as the owner's claim against the assets of the company (as opposed to liabilities, which are outsiders' claims against the business). Basically, if you used your assets to pay off your liabilities, what you'd have left is equity.

- **Income:** The sales you make to your customers. *Income* and *revenue* are interchangeable terms.

- **Expenses:** The cost of staying in business to do business. The wages you pay your employees and the money you spend advertising are expenses.

You can break these five categories down even further into account types, simply to organize them. In Table 3-1, you see the account types available in Peachtree, their general category, and what they represent. The sidebar "Accounting terms for account types" gives the accounting details on these types.

Table 3-1	Account Types and What They Represent	
Account Type	*General Category*	*Represents*
Cash	Asset	Money in the bank that's available for transacting business, as well as undeposited funds (checks, money orders, and so on).
Accounts Receivable	Asset	Money that customers owe but have not yet paid; required for accrual-based businesses.

Account Type	General Category	Represents
Inventory	Asset	The value of the goods you have on hand and available for sale.
Fixed Assets	Asset	The value of things (property and equipment) you own for long-term use (with an estimated life of longer than one year) in your business rather than for resale.
Accumulated Depreciation	Contra asset	The value by which fixed assets are reduced to indicate their decline in value, usually due to age. A truck doesn't last forever, no matter how hard we try to keep it in good running condition.
Other Current Assets	Asset	The value of non-working capital that has a short life (usually less than a year). Employee advances and prepaid expenses, such as deposits made to utility companies, are examples of "*other current assets.*"
Other Assets	Asset	The value of nonworking capital that has a long life (usually longer than one year).
Accounts Payable	Liability	The value of the bills you owe to vendors that are usually due in 30 or 60 days (a short time frame); required for accrual-based businesses.
Other Current Liabilities	Liability	The value of debts that you must pay in less than one year. Short-term loans are "other current liabilities."
Long-Term Liabilities	Liability	The value of debts that you must pay but you have longer than one year to pay them. A three-year bank loan to buy a truck is a "*long-term liability.*"
Equity-doesn't close	Equity	The value of things like common stock that carries forward from year to year. Typically, you use this account type for a corporation that issues stock.

(continued)

Table 3-1 *(continued)*

Account Type	General Category	Represents
Equity-gets closed	Equity	The value of equity accounts that don't carry forward from year to year but instead become part of retained earnings. Use this account type for dividends paid to owners or shareholders.
Equity-Retained Earnings	Equity	The accumulated value of net profits or losses. Peachtree automatically updates this account for you when you close your year.
Income	Income	The value of sales you make to your customers.
Cost of Sales	Expense	The known cost to your business of selling goods or services to customers. Generally, the price you pay for purchased goods for resale or to use in manufacturing goods for resale is the "cost of sales."
Expenses	Expense	The costs your business incurs to operate, such as wages and advertising.

Accrual-based businesses must use an Accounts Receivable account and an Accounts Payable account, but many cash-based businesses also want to use these accounts to produce an aging report of either customers' outstanding balances or bills due to vendors. See Chapter 2 for more on accounting methods.

You need to keep a couple of notes in mind about the account types and equity accounts in your Chart of Accounts:

The account type you choose for an account determines the financial report on which it appears and the placement on the financial report. Consider the three main financial reports: the Income Statement, the Balance Sheet, and the Trial Balance. Income and expense accounts appear on the Income Statement, but not on the Balance Sheet. The Balance Sheet shows all asset, liability, and equity accounts. The Trial Balance shows *all* account types, in the following order: assets, liabilities, equity, income, and expense.

Accounting terms for account types

Nonworking capital is something you own and don't sell to customers, but you could sell it to turn it into cash. Certificates of deposit (CDs) are nonworking capital. The length of time before the CD matures determines whether it is an *other current asset* or an *other asset*. If your company owns CDs or bonds that don't mature for at least one year, you have *other assets*.

Income and *revenue* are interchangeable terms.

Some people call cost of sales, *cost of goods sold* — same thing.

The account type also determines how Peachtree handles the account when you close your year. For example, Peachtree zeroes out income and expense accounts but doesn't zero out asset or liability accounts.

- ✔ You can have only one Equity-Retained Earnings account.

- ✔ You should show the initial investment in the business as either Paid-In Capital, if your business type is a corporation, or Owner's Contributions, if your business type is a proprietorship (sole or partnership). These are Equity-Doesn't Close account types.

- ✔ You should track withdrawals from this investment as Dividends Paid (corporation) or Owner's Draw (proprietorship); these accounts are Equity-Gets Closed account types.

- ✔ The sum of the Equity-Retained Earnings account and any Equity-Doesn't Close accounts (you can have more than one Equity-Doesn't Close account types) equals the net worth of the company prior to the current year.

Numbering accounts

Okay, we've covered account types, which help you organize the appearance of accounts on financial statements. The account numbers you use can also impact the information you can present on financial reports.

First, understand that Peachtree places very few restrictions on the numbering scheme you use:

- ✔ Peachtree sorts account IDs alphabetically — that means numbers first, and you need to use leading zeros to get numbers to sort in numerical order (I know that sounds stupid, but it's true). For example, to get the numbers 1, 27, 100, and 1000 to sort in the order just listed, you'd need to enter them as 0001, 0027, 0100, and 1000.

> ✔ Account IDs can contain any printable character except the asterisk (*), the plus sign (+), and the question mark (?).
>
> ✔ Account IDs cannot contain leading or trailing blanks, but you can use blanks in the middle.
>
> ✔ Account IDs are case sensitive; cash and CASH are two different accounts.

Most people use numbers, not letters for Account IDs; then they use letters for the account's description. The description appears on all reports; the Account ID appears on only some reports.

Because Peachtree places so few restrictions on the Account ID, you can use any scheme you want, but we strongly suggest that you keep it logical. For example, many companies number all assets in the 10000 range, liabilities in the 20000 range, equity in the 30000 range, income in the 40000 range, cost of sales in the 50000 range, and expenses in the 60000 range or higher.

Handling departments or locations

Suppose that your business has multiple geographic locations, and each location generates income and expenses. Or suppose that you don't have geographic locations but you do have multiple departments, and each department generates income and expenses that you want to track. Of course, you want to produce a company-wide income statement, but how do you want it to look?

Perhaps you want a detailed income statement, broken down by department, like the one in Figure 3-1. Or, maybe you want an income statement that summarizes the information for all departments, like the one in Figure 3-2. Or, maybe you want to be able to produce income statements for individual departments, like the one shown in Figure 3-3.

Because we show you all three formats, it's safe to assume that you can produce any of these reports in Peachtree. But, to do so, you must set up the numbering of your Chart of Accounts correctly.

Setting up departmental account numbers

To produce these reports, Peachtree uses a concept called *masking*, which enables you, through the use of account numbers, to easily limit the information that appears on reports. To use masking, you assign one number to an account, say, 40000, and then add a digit or two to represent the department or location. That is, 40000-01 might be income for Department 1, and 40000-02 could be income for Department 2. The implication here is that the same sales account (40000) would appear several different times in your Chart of Accounts, but with a different department number in it. And, you'd set up a 00 level for the account (that is, 40000-00) that Peachtree can use to display the sum of all the departments and represent the company as a whole. You record sales and purchases or payments using the account number that represents the department responsible for the sale, purchase, or payment. You would never record a transaction using the 00 level account. Your expense accounts would work the same way if you want to track costs separately for each department.

Page: 1

Bellwether Garden Supply (BGS)
Income Statement
For the Three Months Ending March 31, 2003

	Current Month			Year to Date	
Revenues					
Sales	$ 0.00	0.00	$	0.00	0.00
Sales - Aviary	3,508.41	13.52		4,608.19	12.19
Sales - Books	89.85	0.35		3,594.70	9.51
Sales - Ceramics	0.00	0.00		0.00	0.00
Sales - Equipment	2,429.72	9.36		7,191.34	19.02
Sales - Food/Fert	349.62	1.35		679.26	1.80
Sales - Furniture	15,000.00	57.81		15,000.00	39.67
Sales - Hand Tools	199.92	0.77		801.64	2.12
Sales - Landscape Services	2,319.37	8.94		3,039.23	8.04
Sales - Miscellaneous	90.00	0.35		90.00	0.24
Sales - Nursery	884.52	3.41		1,122.38	2.97
Sales - Pots	504.59	1.94		574.54	1.52
Sales - Seeds	223.17	0.86		766.24	2.03
Sales - Soil	351.48	1.35		365.46	0.97
Sales - Statuary	0.00	0.00		0.00	0.00
Sales - Topiary	0.00	0.00		0.00	0.00
Interest Income	0.00	0.00		0.00	0.00
Other Income	0.00	0.00		0.00	0.00
Finance Charge Income	0.00	0.00		0.00	0.00
Sales Returns and Allowances	0.00	0.00		0.00	0.00
Sales Discounts	<5.80>	<0.02>		<19.52>	<0.05>
Total Revenues	25,944.85	100.00		37,813.46	100.00
Cost of Sales					
Product Cost	0.00	0.00		0.00	0.00
Product Cost - Aviary	1,407.90	5.43		1,846.80	4.88
Product Cost - Books	3.65	0.01		1,404.75	3.71
Product Cost - Ceramics	0.00	0.00		0.00	0.00
Product Cost - Equipment	1,098.75	4.23		3,161.95	8.36
Product Cost - Food/Fert	138.70	0.53		271.10	0.72
Product Cost - Furniture	0.00	0.00		0.00	0.00
Product Cost - Hand Tools	76.40	0.29		316.45	0.84
Product Cost - Landscaping	0.00	0.00		0.00	0.00
Product Cost - Miscellaneous	0.00	0.00		0.00	0.00
Product Cost - Pots	207.00	0.80		234.75	0.62
Product Cost - Seeds	89.15	0.34		305.30	0.81
Product Cost - Soil	148.92	0.57		156.42	0.41
Product Cost - Statuary	0.00	0.00		0.00	0.00
Product Cost - Topiary	0.00	0.00		0.00	0.00
Direct Labor	0.00	0.00		0.00	0.00
Direct Labor - Landscaping	0.00	0.00		0.00	0.00
Direct Labor - Miscellaneous	0.00	0.00		0.00	0.00
Direct Labor - Nursery	0.00	0.00		0.00	0.00
Direct Labor - Topiary	0.00	0.00		0.00	0.00
Materials Cost	1,352.45	5.21		1,352.45	3.58
Materials Cost - Landscaping	0.00	0.00		0.00	0.00
Materials Cost - Miscellaneous	0.00	0.00		0.00	0.00
Materials Cost - Nursery	229.50	0.88		300.90	0.80
Materials Cost - Topiary	0.00	0.00		0.00	0.00
Subcontractors	0.00	0.00		0.00	0.00
Subcontractors - Landscaping	335.50	1.29		335.50	0.89
Subcontractors - Miscellaneous	0.00	0.00		0.00	0.00
Subcontractors - Nursery	0.00	0.00		0.00	0.00
Subcontractors - Topiary	0.00	0.00		0.00	0.00
Total Cost of Sales	5,087.92	19.61		9,686.37	25.62
Gross Profit	20,856.93	80.39		28,127.09	74.38

Figure 3-1:
An income statement that shows all departments.

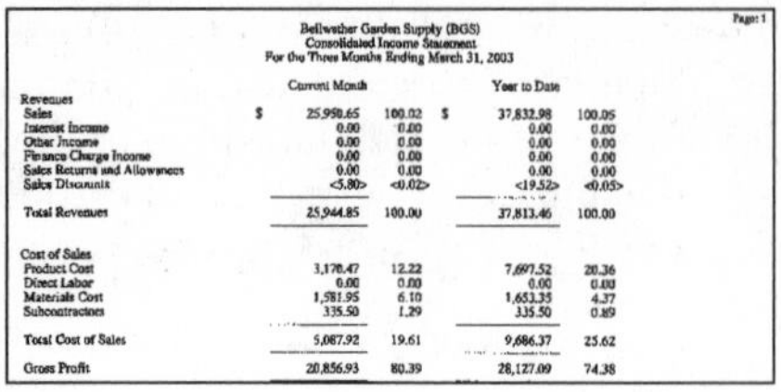

Figure 3-2:
An income
statement
that rolls
up all
departmental
numbers.

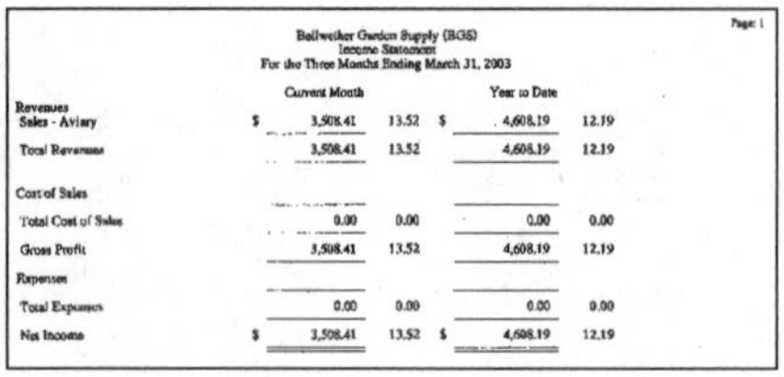

Figure 3-3:
An income
statement
for a single
department.

Or, your situation may be more complex. For example, you may have multiple locations *and* want to track expenses for more than one department at each location. In this case, your account number should include both a location identifier and a department identifier. To track Sales for Location 1, Department 1, your Sales account number might be 40000-01-01, where the first 1 tracks the Location and the second 1 tracks the Department. Table 3-2 shows the various possible combinations for Sales accounts you might find in your Chart of Accounts if you had three locations and three departments:

Table 3-2   Sample Combinations for Accounts Using Locations and Departments

Account Description	Account Number
Sales for Location 1, Department 1	40000-01-01
Sales for Location 2, Department 1	40000-02-01
Sales for Location 3, Department 1	40000-03-01
Sales for Location 1, Department 2	40000-01-02
Sales for Location 1, Department 3	40000-01-03
Sales for Location 2, Department 2	40000-02-02
Sales for Location 2, Department 3	40000-02-03
Sales for Location 3, Department 2	40000-03-02
Sales for Location 3, Department 3	40000-03-03

Be sure to allow the maximum number of characters you need for your departments and locations and keep future growth in mind. For example, if you have ten or more departments, you need two digits for your department number. Don't forget to use a leading zero for department numbers less than ten (for example, 01, 02, 03, and so on).

Consolidating departmental figures

You can extend the department/location scenario one step further. Suppose that you find yourself in the situation where you have two or three geographic locations that each need to use Peachtree — and you're not networked. You *can* set up separate companies in Peachtree, but then, at the end of an accounting period, you won't have a consolidated financial statement to show the true financial picture of your company.

Enter the Consolidation Wizard. This add-on product allows you to use multiple companies in Peachtree and consolidate the information in those companies into one master company. Be sure to follow the masking rules in each subsidiary company to make sure that the master company can produce departmental as well as company-wide financial statements. And, you may find other conditions that prompt you to use separate companies in Peachtree. For example, you may find that your check writing volume exceeds 200 transactions per month. In this case, Peachtree can begin to operate quite slowly; therefore, you may want to consider breaking your company into multiple companies and using the Consolidation Wizard when you need consolidated reports. For more information on the Consolidation Wizard and other add-on products for Peachtree, see the Appendix.

Modifying the Chart of Accounts

Once you understand account types, numbering, and so on, you can dive in and make additions, changes, or deletions to the Chart of Accounts. To make *any* changes to the Chart of Accounts, choose Maintain⇨Chart of Accounts. Peachtree displays the Maintain Chart of Accounts window, shown in Figure 3-4.

Adding new accounts

To add an account, follow these steps:

1. **While viewing the Maintain Chart of Accounts dialog box, type a number for the new account into the Account ID box.**

   Peachtree opens the account list and shows you the number of the account that most closely matches the number you typed. Make sure you type a new number — one that doesn't already exist.

2. In the Description box, type a name for the account as you want it to appear on reports.

3. Open the Account Type list box and select the correct account type for the account you're adding.

4. Click Save.

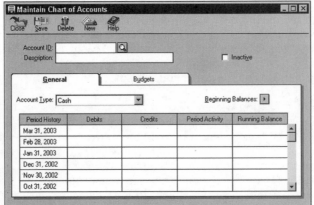

Figure 3-4:
Use this window to make changes to the Chart of Accounts.

Editing accounts

You can edit the description and account type of an account, but you cannot edit the Account ID. To edit the description or account type, follow these steps:

1. Choose Maintain⇨Chart of Accounts to display the Maintain Chart of Accounts window (refer to Figure 3-4).

2. Click the lookup list indicator to the right of the Account ID box or type some characters of the Account ID to display the account list.

3. Highlight the account and click OK or press Enter.

4. Retype the Description or change the Account Type.

5. Click Save.

Deleting accounts

You can delete accounts that have no activity — that is, you haven't used them in any transactions. Choose Maintain⇨Chart of Accounts to display the Maintain Chart of Accounts window. Select the account; then, click the Delete button.

If you try to delete an account that you've used in transactions, Peachtree tells you it cannot delete the account. You can however, set the status of the account to Inactive. If you choose to hide inactive accounts, they won't appear in the list of any transaction window. In addition, hidden accounts don't appear on any report except the Chart of Accounts report. Only people who know the account's number are able to use it. To make an account inactive, display it in the Maintain Chart of Accounts window, place a check in the Inactive box, and click the Save button. You find out how to hide inactive accounts in Chapter 13.

Identifying the rounding account

Peachtree can round numbers on financial statements to either whole dollars or whole thousands of dollars. So, occasionally, when you prepare financial statements, Peachtree needs round numbers. And, Peachtree needs a place to store the difference caused by rounding. Although the account can be any account, Peachtree recommends that you use the Retained Earnings account.

To make sure that Peachtree uses the Retained Earnings account for rounding, follow these steps:

1. **Choose Maintain⇨Default Information⇨General Ledger.**

   Peachtree displays the General Ledger Defaults dialog box, which contains only one field, the Rounding account field.

2. **Confirm that Peachtree has selected the one account you've designated as Equity-Retained Earnings.**

   If necessary, click the magnifying glass next to the account number to display the list. In the unlikely event that Peachtree chooses the wrong account, change it.

3. **Click OK.**

Opening balances

The odds are good . . . very good . . . excellent, in fact, that you've been in business for some time now, and you're starting to use Peachtree after you've done some business. In cases like these, you need to enter beginning balances into Peachtree to represent the business you conducted before setting up your Peachtree company.

Timing the start of using Peachtree

And now is a good time to talk about timing. That is, when should you go live with Peachtree? Well, ideally, try to start using a new accounting package on the first day of your accounting year — January 1, if your business operates on a calendar year; otherwise, the first day of your fiscal year. If you can't wait that long, then start using Peachtree on the first day of a quarter. And, if you can't start using Peachtree on the first day of a quarter, then start on the first day of a month.

Why these target dates? Well, you have the least amount of setup work to do. For example, if your business operates on a calendar year and you start using Peachtree on January 1, you won't need to enter any beginning balances for payroll or any of your income or expense accounts because the balances of these accounts start at zero on January 1. If you start at the beginning of a quarter and you're willing to forego monthly reports preceding the quarter, you can enter summarized information for preceding quarters. And, if you start on the first day of a month, you won't need to play catch-up for the month — which you'd need to do if you started mid-month.

Where do you get the numbers?

If you've used some other accounting package, you can print an Income Statement, Balance Sheet, and a Trial Balance as of the last month you intend to use that accounting package. You can use a combination of the Balance Sheet and the Income Statement, or you can use the Trial Balance: The numbers on these reports in your old software represent the beginning balance numbers of your new Peachtree company.

If you've never used any other accounting package, you should contact your accountant. Provide the date you want to start your company and ask for a Trial Balance, a Balance Sheet, and an Income Statement as of that date. Your accountant probably won't be able to provide the information instantly, especially if you want to start on January 1, 2001, and you ask for the information in December, 2000. Your accountant needs to prepare these reports *after* December 31 so that the reports include all your 2000 transactions.

But don't worry; you can start working in Peachtree without beginning balance numbers; in fact, you may well start working in Peachtree without beginning balance numbers. You just need to remember that year-to-date reports won't be accurate because they won't show the entire picture until you enter beginning balances.

Entering beginning balances

After you get the numbers, entering them into Peachtree is not difficult. If you're going to start using Peachtree at any time other than the beginning of your business year, we suggest you use the alternative method described in the next section. If you're going to start using Peachtree at the beginning of your business year (calendar or fiscal), we suggest that you use Peachtree's Chart of Accounts Beginning Balances window to enter beginning balances. Follow these steps:

1. **Choose Maintain⇨Chart of Accounts to display the Maintain Chart of Accounts window.**

2. **Click the Beginning Balances button to display the Select Period dialog box.**

3. **Select the period from the list.**

   Until you have entered transactions, you can enter beginning balances in Peachtree by month for the year preceding your first open year, for your first open year, or for your second open year. If Period 1 for the company is January 2003, Peachtree makes available each month in 2002, 2003, and 2004; all balances prior to January 1, 2002, would be lumped together into Before 1/1/02.

4. **Click OK to display the Chart of Accounts Beginning Balances window (see Figure 3-5).**

Figure 3-5:
Use this window to enter account balances generated before you started using Peachtree.

| | | | | Liabilities, |
Account ID	Account Description	Account Type	Assets, Expenses	Equity, Income
15400	Leasehold Improvements	Fixed Assets		
15500	Building	Fixed Assets	1,713.00	
15600	Building Improvements	Fixed Assets	325.00	
16900	Land	Fixed Assets		
17000	Accum. Depreciation - Furnitur	Accumulated Depreci		2,613.34
17100	Accum. Depreciation - Equipm	Accumulated Depreci		8,939.10
17200	Accum. Depreciation - Automc	Accumulated Depreci		

The Trial Balance is made up of the balances of all accounts. In order for the Trial Balance to be in balance, the sum of Assets and Expenses should equal the sum of Liabilities, Equity, and Income.

Total: 3,751.00 — 11,552.44
Trial Balance: -7,801.44
[Difference posts to Beg Bal Equity]

Net Income is the difference of Income and Expense account values. The Income and Expense values making up Net Income are already included in the total.

Income - Expenses: 0.00 — 0.00
Net Income: 0.00

5. **Using the numbers you've gotten either from your old accounting system's Trial Balance or from your accountant, enter the balances for each account.**

   If you have an unusual balance in an account (for example, your cash balance is a negative instead of a positive balance), enter a negative number for the account balance.

   When you finish, the Net Income number at the bottom of the window should represent your Net Income for the period. Look for the Net Income at the bottom of your Income Statement.

6. **Click OK to store your beginning balances.**

If you're out of balance . . .

If you're out of balance, the Trial Balance number in Figure 3-5 is *not* zero. In this case, Peachtree wants to post the difference to an Equity-Doesn't Close account called Beg. Bal. Equity. This account doesn't appear in the Beginning Balances window, but it *does* appear on financial statements, general ledger reports, and in the Chart of Accounts list. The chances are good that you're out of balance due to a typing mistake; recheck the numbers you've entered and make sure you've entered *all* the numbers.

If you still can't find the mistake, you can click through Peachtree's warning and let it create the Beg. Bal. Equity account. Your company will then be in balance, and you can safely proceed to enter transactions. If you have to use this workaround, you need to live with the Beg. Bal. Equity account until you find the source of the problem. You can then correct it by clicking the Beginning Balances button in the Maintain Chart of Accounts window. Peachtree displays the Beginning Balances window, if you *haven't* posted any transactions; if you *have* posted transactions, Peachtree displays the Prior Period Adjustment window, which looks and operates just like the Beginning Balances window. When the Beg. Bal. Equity account has a zero balance, you can delete the account.

You can find out more about posting transactions in Chapter 5 — and also in Chapters 6, 7, 8, and 9.

An alternative method for entering beginning balances

If you start using Peachtree at any time other than the beginning of the business year, we suggest that you enter one (or more) journal entries to represent your beginning balances rather than using Peachtree's Chart of Accounts Beginning Balances window. We've found that using journal entries for mid-year starts seems to be less confusing. You'd enter the journal entries to provide balances as of the first day of the first open month.

Because we're trying to avoid using the "d" word and the "c" word this early in the book (debits and credits), we save the discussion of journal entries for Chapter 18.

Chapter 4

Setting Up the Background Information

*B*efore you dive into the day-to-day stuff of managing your company's books, you need to set up preferences. Setting up preferences makes performing daily tasks easier because the preferences save you time. You see, Peachtree uses the default information as a model whenever you create vendors, customers, employees, and inventory items or enter transactions (purchase orders, purchases, invoices, payroll checks, and so on). You can alter this global information when one particular person or item requires something other than the default.

Terminology Alert: Peachtree tends to switch back and forth between two different terms when referring to bills that vendors send you: a *purchase* and an *invoice*. For the sake of clarity, we call vendor bills a purchase; invoices are the things you send to customers so that *you* can get paid.

Setting Purchasing Preferences

"What kind of information do you supply for vendors?" you ask. Well, you set up standard terms. *Terms* describe how long the vendor gives you to hold a bill before you need to pay it and how you want Peachtree to behave if vendors offer you a discount for paying early. You also identify the default account to assign to most vendor bills and vendor discounts. And, you specify how you want Peachtree to age bills that you enter. Last, you can set up custom fields for vendors; you can use custom fields to track information you specify about the people who sell you goods or services.

In Peachtree 2002, you can you can set each general ledger account's treatment of 1099 transactions. See the appendix for details.

Aging is the concept of holding onto a bill for a specified period of time before you apply payment terms to it.

Peachtree applies these preferences to all vendors you create and all purchases you enter. If a vendor or a transaction is unusual in some way, you make a change to the specific vendor or transaction. By using this standard information concept, Peachtree saves you time because you need to change the standard information only for the exceptions to the rule. And let's face it — we *all* like to save time. See Chapter 5 for information on setting up vendors.

Establishing default payment terms and accounts

Efficient bill paying is an art. You don't want to pay your bills either too early or too late. For example, if your bank account earns interest, you don't want to pay a vendor's bill too soon, because you lose interest from the bank. On the other hand, if your vendor assesses late fees or finance charges for bills that you don't pay on time, you don't want to pay a bill too late.

Using Peachtree's Vendor Defaults dialog box, you can establish a typical set of terms to use for most vendors. Chapter 5 shows you how to create vendors and how Peachtree automatically assigns these default terms to each vendor. You need to change terms only for those vendors who *don't* use the typical terms.

To set default payment terms and accounts that most vendors use, follow these steps:

1. **Choose Maintain⇨Default Information⇨Vendors to display the dialog box shown in Figure 4-1.**

2. **From among the Standard Terms option buttons, choose the option that best describes the terms most of your vendors offer you.**

   The terms shown in Figure 4-1 are *"2% 10 Net 30",* which means you can discount the bill by 2 percent if you pay it within 10 days; otherwise, the whole amount of the bill is due in 30 days.

3. **Fill in the appropriate boxes to the right of the terms you select in Step 2.**

   As you select an option button on the left, the boxes on the right change. For example, if you choose C.O.D. (cash on delivery) or Prepaid, only the Credit Limit box on the right remains available because none of the other boxes apply.

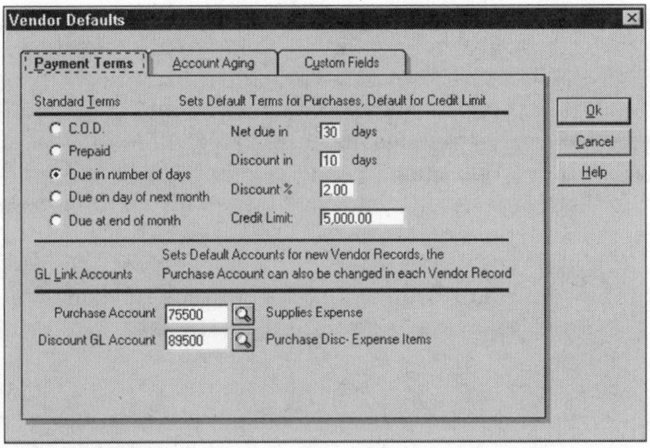

Figure 4-1:
Use the
Vendor
Defaults
dialog box
to define
typical
settings for
vendors.

> **Vendor Defaults**
>
> | Payment Terms | Account Aging | Custom Fields |
>
> Standard Terms   Sets Default Terms for Purchases, Default for Credit Limit
>
> - C.O.D.
> - Prepaid
> - Due in number of days
> - Due on day of next month
> - Due at end of month
>
> Net due in   30   days
> Discount in   10   days
> Discount %   2.00
> Credit Limit: 5,000.00
>
> Ok
> Cancel
> Help
>
> Sets Default Accounts for new Vendor Records, the
> GL Link Accounts   Purchase Account can also be changed in each Vendor Record
>
> Purchase Account   75500   [Q]   Supplies Expense
> Discount GL Account 89500   [Q]   Purchase Disc- Expense Items

4. **At the bottom of the <u>P</u>ayment Terms tab, select the account that you use most often when you post purchases from vendors.**

5. **In the Discount GL Account text box, select the account to which you want Peachtree to post discounts that vendors give you for paying in the specified time.**

   To select the account, type its account number or click the Lookup list indicator to the right of the account number to display a list. In the list, highlight the account number.

6. **Click OK.**

Keep these two points in mind: First, you may never receive discounts from your vendors, but Peachtree expects you to set up the account anyhow. Second, you may want to increase the credit limit. If you exceed the credit limit when buying from a vendor, you are still able to buy from the vendor, but you see this annoying message telling you that you've exceeded the credit limit.

At this point, you can click OK to save the payment terms settings, or you can keep reading; we talk about the Account Aging tab in the next section.

Aging vendor bills

Aging is the concept of holding onto a bill for a specified period of time before you apply payment terms to it. In Peachtree, you can age purchases from either the billing date or the due date; that is, tell Peachtree to count the number of days from either the billing date or the due date.

To set account aging defaults, choose <u>M</u>aintain⇨Default Information⇨<u>V</u>endors. On the Account Aging tab, select a method to age bills: Invoice Date or Due Date. (Optionally, you can change the number of days in each of the four columns on the Aged Payables report.)

You may find the difference between the two aging methods easier to understand if you take a look at two Accounts Payable Aging reports, each prepared using one of the aging methods. For Figure 4-2, we set the Aging option to Due Date and then prepared a customized Accounts Payable Aging report for only one vendor, Arbor Wholesale Suppliers, as of March 31, 2003. In Figure 4-3, we switched the Aging Option to Invoice Date and printed the same report for the same vendor and time frame. (Note that *invoice* here refers to bills your vendors send you.)

Both reports show four outstanding bills for Arbor Wholesale Suppliers listed on four lines. In both reports, you can see the date of each bill and the due date of each bill.

Notice the second bill — the one for $1,250.50. It was posted on February 17, 2003, with terms of Net 30; the bill is due 30 days from the bill date of February 17 — or on March 19. On the first report, it appears to be somewhere between 0 and 30 days old, while on the second report, it appears to be somewhere between 31 and 60 days old. In actuality, according to the first report, on March 31, 2003, the bill is somewhere between 0 and 30 days *past the due date* of the bill. According to the second report, on March 31, 2003, the bill is somewhere between 31 and 60 days *past the invoice date* of the bill.

This report is *not* showing you what is past due. It is showing you the bill's age based on number of days *past* either the *due date* or the *invoice date*.

Many people choose to age vendor bills by Due Date because the bills look "less overdue" on the aging report.

Creating custom fields for vendors

Custom fields are a great way to store information about your vendors when that information doesn't fit anyplace else in Peachtree. Perhaps you want to track details specific to your business or industry. On the Custom Fields tab of the Vendor Defaults dialog box, you can create up to five fields for each vendor. Check a box and, in the Field Labels boxes, type identifying labels for the information you want to store.

When you set up vendors, you can fill in this information for each vendor. (See Chapter 5 for more information on creating or editing vendor information.) On some reports in Peachtree, you can print this information.

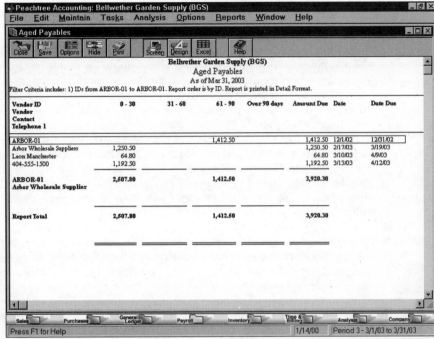

Figure 4-2:
An Aging
report
showing
bills aged by
due date.

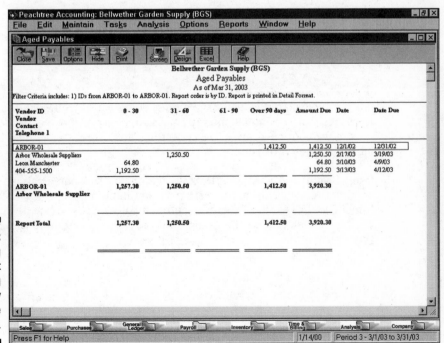

Figure 4-3:
An Aging
report
showing
bills aged by
invoice
date.

Setting Sales Preferences

"What kind of information do you supply for customers?" you ask. Well, you set up standard terms for customers like you do for vendors. Only this time, *you're* the one establishing when payment is due and whether you offer customers a discount for paying early. And, customer terms tell Peachtree how to behave if customers pay early. You also identify the default sales account and discount account where you want Peachtree to assign most customer invoices. You specify how you want Peachtree to age invoices that you prepare. As with vendors, you can set up custom fields for customers to track specific information that may help you increase sales or offer perks. You also can decide whether to charge your customers finance charges for overdue invoices, and you can set their pay methods — cash, check, credit card, anything green.

The concept of aging also applies to invoices you send to your customers; aging still refers to the specified period of time you allow before you apply payment terms to an invoice — and potentially charge the customer finance charges for late payment.

As with vendors, Peachtree applies these preferences to all customers you create and all invoices you enter. If a customer or a transaction is unusual in some way, you make a change to the specific customer or transaction.

Establishing default payment terms and accounts

When customers don't pay you in a timely fashion, you may experience *cash flow* problems. That is, you have money going out of your business for expenses, but not enough money coming in to cover those expenses. To encourage your customers to pay on time, you establish payment terms similar to the ones your vendors set for you.

Using Peachtree's Customer Defaults dialog box, you can establish a typical set of terms to use for most customers. In Chapter 7, when you create customers, you'll see that Peachtree automatically assigns these default terms to each customer. Change preferences for only those customers who *don't* use the typical terms.

To set default payment terms and accounts for most customers, follow these steps:

1. **Choose <u>M</u>aintain⇨<u>D</u>efault Information⇨<u>C</u>ustomers to display the Customer Defaults dialog box (see Figure 4-4).**

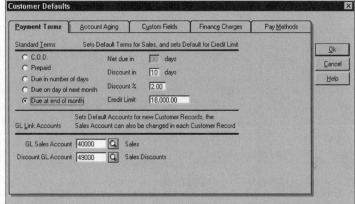

Figure 4-4:
Use the Customer Defaults dialog box to define typical settings for customers.

2. **From among the Standard <u>T</u>erms option buttons, choose the option that best describes the terms you offer most of your customers.**

   The terms shown in Figure 4-4 are 2% 10 Net EOM, which means your customers can discount the invoice by 2 percent if they pay it within 10 days; otherwise, the whole amount of the invoice is due at the end of the month (EOM stands for "end of month").

3. **Fill in the appropriate boxes to the right of the terms you selected in Step 2.**

   The options for customer terms work like the options for vendor terms. As you select an option button on the left, the boxes on the right change. For example, if you choose C.O.D. or Prepaid, only the Credit Limit box on the right remains available because none of the other boxes apply.

4. **Select the GL Sales Account that you use most often when you sell goods or services to customers.**

   To select the account, type the account number or click the lookup list identifier to the right of the account number to display and select from a lookup list.

5. **Select the Discount GL Account you use to track discounts taken by customers.**

6. **If you're done setting payment preferences, click OK to save.**

You may never offer discounts to your customers, but Peachtree expects you to set up the account anyhow. (If you haven't set up a discount general ledger account, see Chapter 3 for information on creating accounts.)

Aging customer invoices

We talk about aging a lot in our society, and now you're getting a whole new picture of wrinkled bills and invoices. Just like you can control the aging process for vendor bills, you can age customer invoices from either the invoice date or the due date.

Accounts receivable aging works the same way accounts payable aging works — that is, you can choose to age by due date or by invoice date. Suppose that you post an invoice on February 20, 2003, with terms of 2% 10, Net 30 Days.

If you set up accounts receivable aging to age by due date, the invoice is due 30 days from the invoice date of February 20, or on March 22. On the Accounts Receivable Aging report, the invoice appears to be somewhere between 0 and 30 days old — that is, on March 31, 2003, the invoice is somewhere between 0 and 30 days *past the due date* of the invoice.

Alternatively, if you set up accounts receivable aging to age by invoice date, on the Accounts Receivable Aging report, the same invoice appears to be somewhere between 31 and 60 days old. That is, on March 31, 2003, the invoice is somewhere between 31 and 60 days *past the invoice date* of the invoice.

This report is *not* showing you what is past due; it is showing you the age of invoices based on number of days *past either the due date or the invoice date*.

Many people choose to age customer invoices by invoice date because the aging report then reflects how old the invoice is. Others prefer to age invoices by due date so that they can see how many days past due the invoice is.

Creating custom fields for customers

The Custom Fields tab of the Customer Defaults dialog box lets you enter labels for up to five fields for each customer. Use these fields to store extra information about customers. For example, you may want to note new customers who found your business on the Web. Simply place a check in any Enabled box, and type the descriptive text in the Field Labels box. When you set up customers, you can fill in this information for each customer. On some reports in Peachtree, you can print this information.

Suppose that you've established a label and filled in information for customers. If you reopen the Customer Defaults dialog box and change the labels, you *won't* affect the information you stored for each customer; you must edit each customer's record and make a change to match the new label you've established. If you simply don't want to show the information you've already entered, you can hide the stored information by removing the check from the Enabled check box in the Customer Defaults dialog box. However, the information reappears if you enable the custom field once again.

Setting up finance charges

Finance charges are fees you charge customers who pay late. Many businesses don't charge finance charges; others believe that charging finance charges encourages customers to pay on time and therefore improves cash flow. Still others believe that charging these fees is necessary if customers continuously ignore payment terms.

If you want to be able to charge finance charges, choose Maintain⇨ Default Information⇨Customers and click the Finance Charges tab of the Customer Defaults box. You must place a check in the Charge Finance Charges box . Then, complete the remaining information to tell Peachtree how to calculate finance charges and then click Ok. This information becomes part of your standard terms.

Placing a check in the Charge Interest on Finance Charges check box tells Peachtree to calculate interest on any unpaid balance as well as unpaid finance charges. Check with your accountant before you check this box; in some states, it is illegal to charge interest on interest. Also, enabling finance charges does *not* make Peachtree automatically assess finance charges. And, you don't need to assign finance charges to *all* of your customers. See Chapter 8 for information on assessing finance charges.

The Finance Charge Warning message at the bottom of the Finance Charges tab actually prints on the bottom of invoices you send to customers. If you're not charging finance charges, you may want to change the message to be more informational; something like, "Happy Holidays" or "See our exhibit at the Business Expo March 16–19."

Establishing payment methods

Pay methods are exactly what they sound like — the various methods of payment that your company accepts. You establish these default settings on the Pay Methods tab of the Customer Defaults dialog box. Choose Maintain⇨ Default Information⇨Customers and click the Pay Methods tab. Then, in the boxes provided, type the names of the payment methods your company accepts.

These payment methods are available when you record payments you receive from customers. And, you can include the Payment Method on reports. For example, you can add this field to the Cash Receipts journal, and you can filter the Cash Receipts journal to see *only* transactions of a particular pay method.

Adding a new payment method after you've already recorded transactions in Peachtree doesn't affect those previously recorded transactions. The new payment method is simply available for new transactions.

Setting Payroll Preferences

To correctly set up and use payroll in Peachtree, you need to identify some basic information, such as the state where your company operates. But understanding payroll is difficult even when you aren't worried about setting up payroll in an accounting program. On the "good news" front, Peachtree uses a wizard to walk you through establishing the defaults for preparing payroll checks and tax-related forms (W-2s, Federal Form 940, and Federal Form 941). Peachtree doesn't prepare most state tax forms, but, Chapter 9 shows you how to use Peachtree payroll reports to find the information you need to complete the forms.

Using the Payroll Setup Wizard

The Payroll Setup Wizard helps you set up basic information about payroll, including payroll fields that Peachtree then uses to calculate payroll checks. *Payroll fields* are things like gross wages and federal income tax (FIT) — those many mysterious abbreviations that appear on your payroll check stub. Chapter 20 describes how to set up a payroll field for some common payroll deductions (or addition — if you're lucky enough to get a bonus) that you want to include on a paycheck.

Effective with Peachtree 8, Peachtree Software Company will *not* be shipping tax tables that calculate federal taxes with the software. To subscribe to Peachtree's Payroll Tax Table Update service, call 1-800-336-1420 Monday through Friday, 8:30 a.m. to 5:30 p.m. eastern standard time. You can use the Payroll Setup Wizard to help you set up payroll either when you first create a company or later, after you've been using Peachtree for awhile. No problem — take your choice. In the paragraphs that follow, we show you how to use the wizard to set up basic payroll information.

The Payroll Setup Wizard also can be useful after you've set up payroll. Suppose, at the time you originally set up payroll, that your company doesn't have a 401(k) plan but later decides to add one. The Payroll Setup Wizard makes this easy. Similarly, if you decide, after setting up payroll, to track vacation and sick leave, use the Payroll Setup Wizard to leave you more time for work! See Chapter 20 for information on setting up a 401(k) plan and tracking both vacation and sick leave.

To start the Payroll Setup Wizard, follow these steps:

1. **Choose Maintain⇨Default Information⇨Payroll Setup Wizard.**

   The first screen of the Payroll Setup Wizard lists the options you are going to set: general ledger accounts, standard payroll fields (taxes, and so on), and optional payroll fields.

2. **When you click Next, you see a screen where you can specify the primary State to receive your payroll taxes, the applicable percentage in the Unemployment Percent for Your Company, and whether you want to record meals and tips for employees.**

   When you enter rates into Peachtree, you must express them as percentages — and many state forms express rates in decimals. For example, suppose the state form shows that your unemployment rate is 0.008. That's a decimal; to express it as a percentage (0.8%), you'd type 0.8 into Peachtree. Yeah, entering these numbers requires that high school math stuff, where you have to divide a decimal by 100 to get the percentage equivalent. Yeah, yeah, yeah. . . .

   Depending on the state you select, Peachtree may ask you for a Locality and Locality Rate.

   If you choose to record meals and tips, Peachtree tracks the amounts for reporting and tax calculation, but it won't post any entries to the general ledger. For more information on recording meals and tips, refer to IRS Publication 15, Circular E, Employer's Tax Guide.

   You can download a copy of the Circular E at the Web site of the IRS:

   `www.irs.gov/forms_pubs/index.html`

   See Chapter 23 to find out about more stuff you can find on the Web.

3. **Click Next to select general ledger accounts to use for payroll (see Figure 4-5).**

   If, when you created your company, you based the chart of accounts on one of the standard companies, Peachtree suggests payroll accounts.

If you don't have payroll accounts set up, you can define them "on the fly." Click the lookup list buttons next to each account box to display a list of existing accounts. Click the New button to create new accounts while still using the Payroll Setup Wizard. Refer to Chapter 3 for information on setting up accounts.

Some people create separate payroll liability accounts for each payroll tax liability. To make your life easier using Peachtree, we recommend that you create payroll liability accounts that correspond to the taxing authority you pay. For example, you pay FIT, FICA, and Medicare to the same taxing authority, so set up only one payroll liability account for all three taxes. If you pay state and local taxes to the same taxing authority, set up only one liability account for both taxes. Check with your accountant if you are unsure. We recommend this approach because it makes writing your payroll tax liability checks easier.

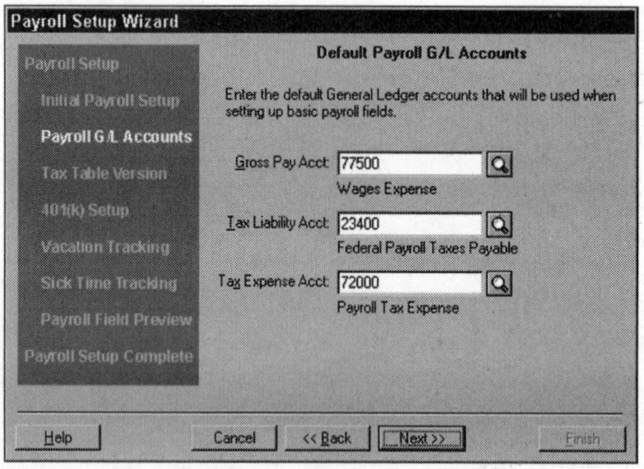

Figure 4-5:
Identify your
payroll
accounts.

4. **Click Next to see the version number of the current global tax table installed on your computer.**

   Peachtree uses tax tables to make calculations related to payroll. The most obvious tax tables calculate the amount of tax to deduct for FIT, FICA, Medicare, and Federal Unemployment Taxes (FUTA).

   To determine whether your tax tables are up-to-date, visit Peachtree's Web site at www.peachtree.com.

   Click the link for Tax Service, select the Peachtree product you're using, and then click the View Tax Update Version History link. Look through this Web page and compare your tax table version to the latest available.

   At this point, you've finished the basic setup for payroll; the remaining choices in the Payroll Setup Wizard enable you to set up payroll fields for a 401(k) Plan, vacation tracking, and sick leave tracking.

5. Click <u>N</u>ext four times to skip setting up the optional payroll fields and see the payroll fields you created.

Peachtree categorizes the payroll fields into employee-related fields or employer-related fields. On the EmployEE Fields tab (see Figure 4-6), you see payroll fields belonging to employees. These include gross wages, FIT, and the employee's share of FICA and Medicare.

Figure 4-6:
On the
EmployEE
tab, you see
payroll
fields
belonging to
employees.

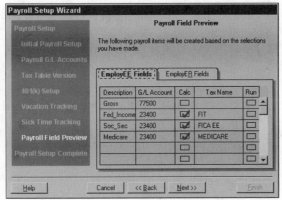

On the EmployER Fields tab, you can view payroll fields paid by the company, including FUTA, state unemployment taxes, and the employer's share of FICA and Medicare.

The payroll field names appear in the Description column, and you see the general ledger account and payroll tax table Peachtree associated with the fields.

6. Click <u>N</u>ext to see the final screen of the Payroll Setup Wizard, which explains that you can modify the setup in the Maintain Employees dialog box.

7. Click Finish to see the Employee Defaults dialog box.

8. Click OK to get rid of the dialog box, or, if you want to establish general employee defaults, see the next section.

Establishing general employee defaults

If you didn't just finish running the Payroll Wizard, choose <u>M</u>aintain⇨<u>D</u>efault Information⇨<u>E</u>mployees to display the General tab of the Employee Defaults dialog box. You can use this tab to change your state or set a locality if necessary and to establish custom fields for storing miscellaneous information about each employee. To make custom fields available, place a check in the Enabled box next to a field.

Peachtree automatically assigns payroll fields to the various boxes on the W-2 form, employee-paid taxes, or employer-paid taxes. You can, however, edit the assignments by clicking the appropriate button in the Assign Payroll Fields For section.

Setting pay levels

Pay levels are names you set for various types of hourly and salary pay. Choose Maintain⇨Default Information⇨Employees and click the Pay Levels tab. By default, Peachtree automatically establishes the pay levels you see. Hourly wage pay levels appear on the left, and salary pay levels appear on the right.

You can create up to 20 different hourly pay levels and 20 different salary pay levels, and you can assign different pay levels to different general ledger accounts. Just type the name for the pay level in the Field Name list and assign the pay level to a G/L account.

To make your general ledger and income statement more meaningful, your accountant may want you to use a different set of pay levels, pointing some or all to different general ledger accounts. For example, you can use pay levels based on your worker's compensation categories as one method of letting Peachtree help you determine your worker's compensation liability.

Employee fields and employer fields

The EmployEE Fields tab and the EmployER Fields tab closely resemble Figure 4-6, which appears at the end of the Payroll Setup Wizard when you review your work using that tool. You can change these settings via the Employee Defaults dialog box. Choose Maintain⇨Default Information⇨ Employees and click the EmployEE Fields tab.

On the EmployEE Fields tab, you can do any of these:

- ✔ Change the G/L Account for a payroll field.

- ✔ Change the tax table Peachtree uses to calculate a particular payroll field. Click in the Tax Name column to view a lookup list box that enables you to choose from a list of available tax tables.

- ✔ Place a check in the Memo column next to a field , such as Tips, to tell Peachtree to calculate that field without updating your general ledger.

✔ Place a check in the Run column next to a field to tell Peachtree *not* to set the balance for this field to zero at the end of the payroll year. For example, if you allow your employees to retain unused vacation from year to year, set up your Vacation field with a check in the Run box.

✔ For fields Peachtree calculates, click the Adjust button to identify the fields you want Peachtree to add when calculating Adjusted Gross Wages for the field. For example, you may want Adjusted Gross Wages to include Gross wages, FICA, and Medicare, but *not* FIT when calculating an auto expense deduction.

✔ For fields Peachtree doesn't calculate, you can supply a default amount. For example, if most employees pay the same amount for medical insurance, you can type that amount in the Amount column, and then supply the appropriate amount for employees who don't pay the standard amount.

If you're entering an amount you want deducted, enter it as a negative amount.

Although you can edit the names of payroll fields, *don't* change the name of a payroll field and *don't* change the order of the payroll fields after you've entered payroll transactions. You'll get inaccurate information on the payroll earnings reports and W-2 forms. And, we recommend that you retain the names of payroll fields Peachtree creates for you because they are often used in payroll tax tables.

On the EmployER Fields tab, you can set these preferences:

✔ Change the general ledger liability and expense accounts for a payroll field.

✔ Change the tax table Peachtree uses to calculate a particular payroll field. Click in the Tax Name column to reveal the lookup list indicator and select from a list of available tax tables.

✔ For fields Peachtree calculates, click the Adjust button to identify the fields you want Peachtree to include when determining Adjusted Gross Wages for the field.

The same warning applies to EmployER field names that applied to EmployEE field names. *Don't* change the name of a payroll field and *don't* change the order of the payroll fields after you've entered payroll transactions. These alterations create inaccurate information on the payroll earnings reports and W-2 forms. And, the names of payroll fields are often used in payroll tax tables.

Setting Inventory Preferences

Before you start filling your virtual shelves in Peachtree, you need to set up the preferences that help track all those wonderful items as they come and go. Inventory items in Peachtree terms are anything that you buy from vendors or sell to customers. You can set these preferences for inventory items:

- ✔ Change the general ledger accounts associated with each type of inventory item.

- ✔ Establish tax types to organize the sales taxes that you remit and report to your state sales tax agency.

- ✔ Establish shipping methods that you use for customers and vendors.

- ✔ Set up custom fields for inventory items.

Inventory items and general ledger accounts

Peachtree uses *item classes* to organize inventory items, and you assign each inventory item to a class when you create it. Chapter 11 includes information on how to create inventory items.

For the purpose of setting defaults, remember that an item's class determines how Peachtree records the cost of the item.

Peachtree allows eight different item classes:

- ✔ *Nonstock,* for items, such as service contracts, that you sell but do not put into your inventory. Peachtree prints quantities, descriptions, and unit prices on invoices, but doesn't track quantities on hand. You can assign a cost of sales G/L account, but it is not affected by a costing method.

- ✔ *Stock,* for inventory items that you track for quantities, average costs, vendors, low stock points, and so on.

   When you've assigned an item to the Stock class, you cannot change the item's class.

- ✔ *Description only,* when you track nothing but the description. For example, you can add comments to sales or purchase transactions using description-only items.

✔ *Assembly,* for items that consist of components that must be built or dismantled.

✔ *Service,* for services you can apply to your General Ledger salary and wages account to bill a customer for services provided by your employees.

✔ *Labor,* for third-party labor costs that you pass on to a customer. You can apply these costs to your G/L salary and wages account.

✔ *Activity,* for recording, using Peachtree's Time & Billing feature, how time is spent when performing services for a customer or job.

✔ *Charge,* for recording, using Peachtree's Time & Billing feature, the expenses of an employee or vendor when working for a customer or job.

See Chapter 10 for more information on Peachtree's Time & Billing feature.

In Peachtree, you can choose the various accounts affected by inventory items in each of these item classes. For stock and assembly items, you also can choose an inventory method. Follow these steps to review (and, if necessary, change) the account assignments for the eight inventory item classes.

1. **Choose Maintain⇨Default Information⇨Inventory Items to display the General tab of the Inventory Item Defaults dialog box, shown in Figure 4-7.**

Lookup list button

Mouse pointer

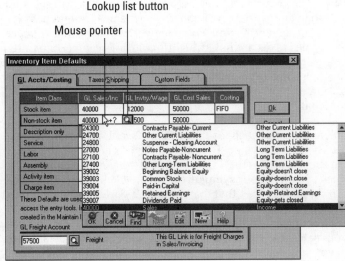

Figure 4-7: Set the default accounts for your inventory items.

2. **Move the mouse pointer over any white box to see the lookup list mouse pointer (arrow + ?).**

3. **Click the lookup list button to open a list of your available accounts.**

4. **Highlight the account you want to use and click OK.**

5. **Repeat Steps 1 through 4 as necessary in any white box on this screen.**

   For the Costing column, choose FIFO, LIFO, or Average as your costing method.

   Check with your accountant to help choose the correct method for your business, but just so you know what we're talking about, turn to the sidebar in Chapter 11.

6. **If necessary, change the GL Freight Account using Steps 3 and 4.**

   You use the GL Freight Account on invoices to assign freight charges to an invoice. Yeah, we know . . . "So what? What's the connection with inventory?" Well, we don't know . . . .

7. **When you finish, click OK or choose another tab and read the related information in the next section.**

Taxes and shipping

Ah, taxes. The government needs to get its cut when you sell something — and so, when appropriate, you must collect sales tax and pass it on to your state's taxing agency. As you would expect with anything connected with government, sales taxes are not straightforward. The government requires that you charge tax on some things but not other things. To take that concept a step further, some organizations (notably charitable agencies) don't pay taxes. And, of course, it's up to you, the seller, to keep straight who pays tax and for what.

If it isn't already open, choose Maintain⇨Default Information⇨Inventory Items to open the Inventory Item Defaults dialog box and click the Taxes/Shipping tab. On the left side of the Taxes/Shipping tab you can define up to 25 different tax types (you have our sympathy if you need all of them). Typically, you want to set up tax types that match the categories you must report on your state's sales tax return. Then, assign a tax type to each inventory item you create. When you sell the item, Peachtree will note the tax type, and when you pay your sales tax, you use a report that segregates your sales by tax type. So that's why you want to set up tax types that match the categories you report on your state sales tax return. See Chapter 7 for information on setting up sales taxes and Chapter 6 for information on paying sales taxes.

You also can use the right side of the Taxes/Shipping tab to set up shipping methods. Remember that shipping methods actually don't have anything to do with inventory items; you assign them to customers and vendors. The shipping methods you assign to customers and vendors will appear on quotes, sales orders, invoices, purchases, and purchase orders. Find out more about setting up vendors in Chapter 5 or customers in Chapter 7.

Custom fields

While you don't assign shipping methods to inventory items, you *do* option-ally assign custom fields to inventory items — notes, alternate vendors, and weight are a few examples of the kind of information you might store in custom fields. Choose Maintain⇨Default Information⇨Inventory and the Custom Fields tab, and you can specify the custom fields you want to use. Place a check in the Enabled box next to any line and then type the name of the custom field into the Field Labels box.

Part II
The Daily Drudge

The 5th Wave   By Rich Tennant

"The first thing we should do is get you two into a good mutual fund. Let me out the 'Magic 8-Ball' and we'll run some options."

In this part . . .

Data entry. It's a dirty job . . . but somebody has to do it. Whether you handle the day-to-day accounting responsibilities associated with your business or have someone in your office do them for you, you'll find this part valuable.

In this part, we show you how to keep up with tasks including billing your customers and collecting money from them, purchasing and paying for goods and services used in your business, and paying employees. We also cover job costing and time and billing tasks.

Chapter 5

Buying Goods

*B*uying things is part of the business of doing business. Some businesses buy goods from vendors and store them in inventory to resell to customers. Some businesses buy goods to use in manufacturing a finished product to sell to customers. And all businesses buy goods and services that they use to stay in business, such as utilities and office supplies.

So, no matter how you look at it, you can expect to receive bills in the mail. And, of course, paying bills isn't fun, but at least Peachtree can make the process easier and save you time — time you can spend earning more money.

This chapter describes the typical actions you take to record and track vendors' bills.

Terminology alert: Peachtree tends to switch back and forth between two different terms when referring to bills that vendors send you: a purchase and an invoice. For the sake of clarity, we call it a purchase unless the screen calls it an invoice. For our purposes, invoices are things you send to customers so that *you* can get paid.

Working with Vendors

If you buy goods or services from a particular vendor on a regular basis, you can save time in the long run if you set that vendor up in Peachtree. In fact, if you *don't* set up the vendor, you'll find it difficult to track how much you've spent with that vendor. There . . . you have two good reasons to set up vendors with whom you do business on a regular basis.

Adding vendors

When you set up a vendor, you supply name and address information, a purchase account to use each time you post a purchase from the vendor, and custom field information. You also can view historical information about your purchases from the vendor for the previous 12 months.

To add a new vendor, follow these steps:

1. **Choose Maintain⇨Vendors to display the Maintain Vendors window, shown in Figure 5-1.**

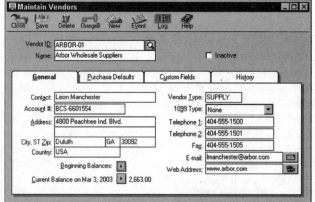

Figure 5-1:
Use this window to add, edit, or delete vendors.

2. **Fill in a Vendor ID and the vendor's name.**

The ID is the number you use to select the vendor when you want to post a purchase or payment, so try to make it meaningful. The ID can be up to 20 characters and numbers long, and it *is* case sensitive. We suggest that you use lower case letters so that your hands don't need to leave the keyboard. By default, Peachtree sorts the vendor list and reports using the Vendor ID. To get Peachtree to sort the vendor list in alphabetical order by default, use characters from the vendor's name as the ID.

Peachtree 8 enables you to store both e-mail and Web addresses for vendors. Both are interactive. So, if you supply an e-mail address and click the icon next to it, Peachtree opens your e-mail program and starts a message to the vendor. Similarly, clicking the button next to the Web address launches your browser and directs it to the vendor's Web site.

3. **On the <u>G</u>eneral tab, fill in contact information — your account number with the vendor and the vendor's address, phone numbers, and, if appropriate, e-mail and Web addresses.**

The account number you supply appears by default on checks you print from the Payment window. Find out more about the Payment window in Chapter 6.

4. **If appropriate, identify the vendor as a 10<u>9</u>9 Type by selecting an option from the drop-down list.**

According to IRS rules, you must issue a 1099 to a vendor who is an independent contractor if the contractor is not incorporated and you pay $600 or more per year to that vendor. Peachtree can print 1099s at the end of the year for vendors you designate as 1099 vendors. Sales representatives might be considered 1099 vendors, based on the IRS definition of employees and independent contractors. See Chapter 9 for more discussion on paying sales representatives who are also employees.

5. **Use the Vendor <u>T</u>ype box to group similar vendors together.**

For example, you may want to distinguish between vendors who supply you with inventory and vendors who provide overhead services such as telephone. Vendor Types can be up to eight characters that are case sensitive. You can limit some reports to specific vendor types.

6. **Click the Beginning Balances button to display the Vendor Beginning Balances window, where you can enter bills you received from vendors *before* you started using Peachtree.**

Technically, you can enter as many beginning balance bills as you want for an individual vendor; however, if you exceed 100 bills, you can enter but not edit or delete any information for the 101st bill and subsequent bills.

7. **Click the <u>P</u>urchase Defaults tab to select a default account for the vendor, a default shipping method, and default terms.**

You need to select a default Purchase account only if it differs from the default account you established in the Vendor Defaults dialog box for the vendor you're creating. (See Chapter 4 for details on global default purchase settings.)

8. **If the vendor is a 1099 vendor, supply the vendor's Ta<u>x</u> ID number, which eventually appears on the 1099.**

9. **Set a shipping method in the Ship Via box.**

   Peachtree creates most of the shipping methods that appear in the Ship Via drop-down list box when you create your company; you can add to or change these methods when you set up defaults for inventory. You can find information on setting up inventory defaults in Chapter 4.

10. **To change the terms for the vendor, click the Terms button.**

    Peachtree displays the Vendor Terms dialog box (see Figure 5-2). Remove the check from the Use Standard Terms check box and set up the vendor's terms.

Figure 5-2:
To change the terms for a vendor, remove the check from the Use Standard Terms check box.

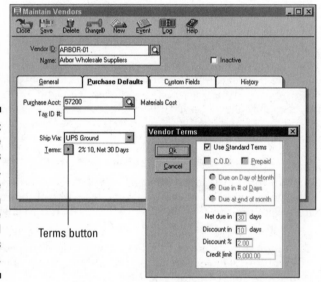

11. **On the Custom Fields tab, fill in the information you established in the Vendor Default dialog box.**

12. **Click the Save button to save the vendor information.**

Changing vendor information

You can change any information you have entered about a vendor, including the vendor ID. If you need to make a change to a vendor's information, follow these steps:

1. **Open the Maintain Vendors window by choosing Maintain⇨Vendors.**

2. **Type a few letters of the vendor's ID — remember, ID's are case-sensitive — or click the lookup list box indicator next to the Vendor ID box to display a list of vendors.**

3. **Highlight the vendor you want to change and click OK.**

   The information you saved previously for the vendor appears.

4. **If you need to change the vendor ID, display the vendor's information in the Maintain Vendors window and then click the Change ID toolbar button.**

   Peachtree displays the Change Vendor ID dialog box. Type the New Vendor ID and click OK. Peachtree changes the vendor's ID.

5. **Click the tab containing the information you want to change.**

6. **Make the change.**

7. **Click the Save button.**

Viewing vendor history

After you have recorded purchases and payments for vendors, Peachtree tracks these transactions by month. Click Maintain⇨Vendors to open the Maintain Vendors window. Type the Vendor ID or highlight your choice from the lookup list and then click the History tab to view a history of your activity with the vendor.

"De-activating" a vendor

If a vendor has gone out of business or you've just decided that you don't want to do business with a particular vendor, you can change the vendor's status to inactive. After you make a vendor record inactive, Peachtree displays a warning if you try to buy something from the vendor.

Although you see a Delete button in the Maintain Vendor window, you can't delete a vendor unless no transactions exist for the vendor. You know, you put somebody in and then realized you didn't want them after all — and you didn't record any transactions. *Then*, you can display that vendor on-screen and click Delete. Otherwise, to "get rid" of a vendor, you must first make the vendor inactive. After closing a fiscal year, you can purge inactive vendors so that they don't appear in lookup lists. See Chapter 18 for information on closing a fiscal year and purging.

To make a vendor inactive, choose Maintain⇨Vendors to open the Maintain Vendors dialog box. In the Vendor ID box, select the vendor you want to make inactive. When the vendor appears on-screen, place a check in the Inactive check box and then click Save. If you need to reactivate the vendor, remove the check mark from the Inactive check box.

An inactive vendor won't appear in the lookup lists if you decided to hide inactive records when you set Peachtree's global options. You can find out how to hide inactive records in Chapter 13.

Working with Purchase Orders

A *purchase order* is a document you use to request merchandise from a vendor. When you enter a purchase order, Peachtree doesn't actually affect any of your accounts — that doesn't happen either until you receive the merchandise or, if you're using cash basis accounting, when you pay the vendor.

Peachtree "takes note" of the transactions — that is, you can print reports that show you the accounts that the purchase orders *will* affect when they are filled. But, the purchase orders don't actually update the accounts when you save the purchase orders.

Entering purchase orders

"If a purchase order doesn't affect any of my accounts, why use it?" you ask. Well, first, you don't *need* to use purchase orders; Peachtree operates correctly if you don't use them. But most people use purchase orders as reminders, particularly when ordering inventory, because the purchase order shows the items they've ordered but not yet received. Others use purchase orders for non-inventory items such as office supplies or contract labor to help track expected expenses.

Purchase orders provide you with a great way of remaining organized and not letting something slip through the cracks. You can use the Purchase Order report to help you stay on top of things.

You can't enter purchase orders in Peachtree unless you have set up a vendor, but you can set up a vendor while working in the Purchase Orders window.

To enter a purchase order, follow these steps:

1. **Choose Tasks⇨Purchase Orders to display the Purchase Orders window shown in Figure 5-3.**

   You can customize the appearance of the Purchase Order window to better suit your needs; if you have changed these settings, your window doesn't look the same as the window you see in Figure 5-3. See Chapter 13 for more information.

2. **Type the Vendor ID or click the lookup list box selector to display the list of vendors.**

   If the vendor exists, Peachtree fills in the vendor's name and Remit To address. Your company's name also appears in the Ship To address box. In Peachtree 2002, you can use the new Fast Add feature to add a vendor. See the appendix for details.

   If you need to add a vendor, click the lookup list selector and then click the New toolbar button. Peachtree displays the Maintain Vendors window. Refer to the section in this chapter on adding vendors. Close the Maintain Vendors window to return to the Purchase Orders window.

Figure 5-3: A typical purchase order.

Purchase Orders							
Close	Post	Print	Preview	Delete	New	Note	Journal Template Event Help

Vendor ID: SOGARDEN-01   PO #: 10302   Date: Mar 3, 2003

Name: Southern Garden Wholesale   ☐ Close Purchase Order   Good thru: Apr 2, 2003

Remit To: 4555 Oakland Park Blvd. Atlanta, GA 30312 USA

Ship To: Bellwether Garden Supply 1505 Pavilion Place Norcross, GA 30093-3203 USA

Ship Via	Discount Amount	Displayed Terms	A/P Account
UPS Ground	12.46	2% 10, Net 30 Days	20000

Quantity	Received	Item	Description	GL Account	Unit Price	Amount	Job
6.00		EQLW-141	Catalog # LM40090: Reel Mo	12000	19.95	119.70	
Reel Mower			Inventory				
6.00		EQLW-141	Catalog # GA44554: Gas-Po	12000	59.95	359.70	
Leaf Blower/Vac			Inventory				
12.00		EQWT-151	Catalog # WT1005280: Sprin	12000	11.95	143.40	
Sprinkler-Impulse			Inventory				

622.80 PO Total

3. **In the PO # box, type a number for the purchase order if you don't intend to print it but just want to post it.**

   If you intend to print the purchase order, leave the PO # box blank, and Peachtree supplies a sequential purchase order number when you print the purchase order.

You can't use the same purchase order number more than once for a particular vendor. You can reuse a purchase order number as long as you assign it to a different vendor.

4. **If necessary, change the date of the purchase order.**

5. **Supply a <u>G</u>ood thru date — the date after which the purchase order should not be filled.**

6. **If necessary, change the shipping method in the Ship Via list box.**

While you *can* change the A/P account, typically, you don't. Although Peachtree doesn't affect any of your accounts when you post the purchase order, later, when you receive merchandise against the purchase order, Peachtree uses the account information on the purchase order to update your company's books.

7. **In the Quantity box, type the quantity you want to order.**

For a whole number such as three, type 3.0. If you type simply 3, Peachtree assumes you want .03.

8. **Click in the Item box.**

The Lookup list box appears so that you can select the item you want to order from the existing inventory items. Peachtree fills in the item description, the general ledger account associated with the item, the item's unit price, and the amount (unit price times quantity). In Peachtree 2002, you can set up general ledger accounts, inventory items, or jobs in the Purchase Order window. See the appendix for details.

Read about setting up inventory items in Chapter 11. If you want to order something that you haven't set up as an inventory item, skip the Item box and provide a description and cost.

9. **Click in the Job box to display the Lookup list box selector and choose a job from the list.**

If you're purchasing a Stock item or an Assembly item, you cannot assign it to a job; however, if you're purchasing any other type of item, you can assign it to a job. You also can assign the line to a job if you don't select any item from the Item list. Chapter 12 covers setting up and assigning types of jobs.

10. **Repeat Steps 7 through 9 for each item you want to order from this vendor.**

Continue to the next section if you want to print the purchase order immediately. Or, you can create a batch of purchase orders and print later. If you don't intend to print or if you want to print a batch, skip to the following section.

Printing a purchase order immediately

You can print a purchase order while you view it in the Purchase Orders window. Make sure you turn on your printer. Follow these steps to finish:

1. **While viewing the purchase order you want to print, click the Print button.**

   Peachtree displays the Print Forms dialog box so you can choose the Purchase Order form you want to use.

2. **Click OK to continue, and Peachtree displays a dialog box asking if you want to print real or practice forms.**

3. **Choose Real to print the purchase order.**

   Peachtree displays a dialog box. Supply the number you want to use when you print this purchase order.

   If you choose Practice, Peachtree prints a form filled with Xs that you can use to check alignment. If you choose Form Design, Peachtree opens the Form Designer window, and you can modify the form. See Chapter 14 for more information on printing and modifying forms.

Posting and printing later . . .
or not printing at all

Posting is the process of saving a transaction and updating your company's books based on the information on the transaction. If you print a large number of purchase orders, you may find it more practical to print them all at once rather than one at a time as you create them. If you don't plan to print your purchase order, assign a PO number to it, and click the Post button. You're done. Peachtree saves the information, and you can refer to it anytime or use it to track incoming shipments.

If you plan to print at a later date, don't assign a PO number to the purchase order; just click the Post button after you've created the purchase order. Peachtree saves the purchase order and assigns a number to it when you print.

For more details on printing forms, see Chapter 14.

You can now preview forms on-screen before printing (see Chapter 14). To print a batch of purchase orders, make sure that you turn on your printer and follow these steps:

1. **Click Purchases in the Navigation Aids.**

2. **Click Print Purchase Orders to display a dialog box from which you can choose a purchase order form.**

3. **Highlight a form and click OK to display a dialog box that asks whether you want to print real or practice forms.**

4. **Choose Real to display a dialog box where you assign the first purchase order number and enter a date.**

   If you choose Practice, Peachtree prints a form filled with Xs that you can use to check alignment. If you choose Form Design, Peachtree opens the Form Designer window, and you can modify the form. See Chapter 14 for more information on printing and modifying forms.

After entering a number for the first purchase order in the batch and a date, click OK. Peachtree prints any purchases that you posted *without* assigning purchase order numbers. After the purchase orders print, Peachtree displays a message asking if the purchase orders printed correctly and if it's OK to assign numbers to them.

When you click Yes, Peachtree assigns numbers to the purchase orders. (That way, if the printer eats one of your pre-numbered forms, you can still make sure that the PO numbers in Peachtree match the hard copy.)

Editing and erasing purchase orders

You can change purchase orders, and you can delete purchase orders. And good accounting practices say you shouldn't ever delete anything. But, because a purchase order doesn't affect your accounts, the offense doesn't seem quite so serious.

You can change or remove items from purchase orders if you have not yet received the items. If you know you'll never receive the items, you can close the purchase order. If the purchase order was simply a mistake and you have not received any items listed on it, why not just erase it? To edit or delete a purchase order, follow these steps:

1. **Choose Tasks⇨Purchase Orders to display the Purchase Orders window.**

2. **Click the Edit button to display the Select Purchase Order window (see Figure 5-4).**

   You can edit any purchase order, even if it isn't open. Look for the Y in the Open? column. If the Open? column is blank, the purchase order has been closed, meaning all the goods have been received and entered, or you got tired of waiting and canceled it.

Show List box

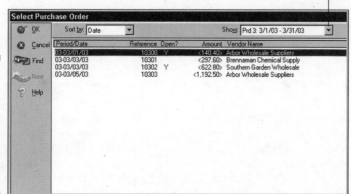

Figure 5-4:
Select a
purchase
order to
view in the
Purchase
Orders
window.

3. **Select a purchase order to view and click OK to display the purchase order in the Purchase Orders window.**

The Select Purchase Order window shows, by default, the period in which you are working. In Figure 5-4, you see the purchase orders entered in March (Period 03). If you don't see the purchase order you want to edit or delete, open the Show list box and select an earlier period.

4. **Make any of the following modifications to the purchase order:**

   • Change the Date or the Good Thru date.

   • Change the Ship Via method, the discount amount, the Displayed Terms, or the A/P account.

   • Adjust the quantity you ordered on any line of the purchase order — even a line you've already received. Find out how to receive items you order in the section on receiving goods against a purchase order in this chapter.

   • Remove any line if you have not received those items. Click anywhere in the line you want to delete and click the Remove button.

   • Close the purchase order by placing a check in the Close Purchase Order check box that appears immediately below the PO #.

5. **Click the Post button to save your changes.**

You cannot delete a purchase order if you have told Peachtree that you have received any of the items listed on the purchase order; the Delete button appears gray (unavailable). If you know you'll *never* receive items remaining on a purchase order, close the purchase order.

Entering Bills

Scenario: A vendor with whom you do business on a regular basis sends you a bill. (Peachtree uses the terms "purchase" and "invoice" interchangeably to represent a vendor bill.) You don't want to pay the bill immediately, but you *do* want to pay the bill in a timely manner. So, enter the bill into Peachtree as a purchase, and Peachtree tracks the bill's age so that you pay it a) when it's still eligible for a discount and b) before the vendor charges you a late fee.

Do you receive a bill on a regular basis from a vendor? Chapter 6 shows you how to create a recurring purchase or payment for things like monthly utility bills or lease payments.

Purchasing without using a PO (or entering a vendor bill)

Unlike purchase orders, purchases update your company's accounts. Whenever any transaction updates your company's books, at least two accounts are affected because of the double-entry bookkeeping concept.

Every purchase you enter automatically updates accounts payable. The other account Peachtree updates depends on whether you record a bill for an inventory item. If you select inventory items in the Purchases/Receive Inventory window, you tell Peachtree to update inventory for the other side of the transaction. If you don't select an inventory item, then, you probably select an expense account, such as your telephone expense account. In that case, Peachtree updates accounts payable and the expense account.

If you're curious about the accounts Peachtree is updating (yes, debiting and crediting), Chapter 18 shows you a neat way to find out what Peachtree is doing.

Peachtree assumes that you wouldn't bother to enter a bill from a vendor you use only occasionally; instead, you'd just pay that bill. Therefore, you can't enter purchases in Peachtree unless you have set up a vendor. For one-time or occasional purchases from vendors you don't expect to use often, use the Payments window or the Write Checks window to pay the bill directly. See Chapter 6 for more information on paying bills.

To enter a purchase (a vendor's bill) that doesn't reference a purchase order, follow these steps:

1. **Choose Tasks⇨Purchases/Receive Inventory to display the Purchases/Receive Inventory window (see Figure 5-5).**

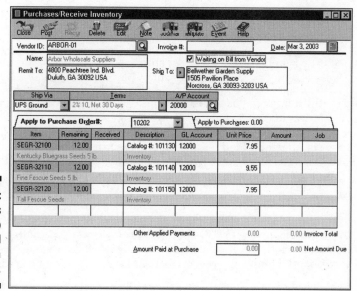

Figure 5-5:
Use this window to record a bill from a vendor.

You can customize the appearance of the Purchases/Receive Inventory window to better suit your needs; if you do, the window doesn't look the same as the window you see in Figure 5-5. See Chapter 13 for more information.

2. **Type the Vendor ID or click the lookup list box and select a vendor from the list.**

   After you select a vendor, Peachtree fills in the vendor's name and Remit To address. Your company's name also appears in the Ship To address box. In Peachtree 2002, you can use the new Fast Add feature to add a vendor. See the appendix for details.

   If you have previously entered purchase orders for this vendor, Peachtree displays the Apply to Purchase Order tab. If you want to receive goods against one of these POs, skip to the next section.

3. **In the Invoice # box, type a number for the vendor's bill.**

   You can't use an invoice number more than once for a particular vendor. You can reuse an invoice number as long as you assign it to a different vendor.

4. **If necessary, change the date of the purchase.**

   Yes, you *can* change the A/P account, but typically, you don't.

5. **In the Quantity box, type the quantity for which you're being billed.**

   For a whole number such as three, type 3.0. If you type simply 3, Peachtree assumes you want .03.

6. **You have two options for entering items that appear on the bill:**

   - If you are recording a bill for an item that you haven't set up as an inventory item, skip the Item box, and just type a description, a general ledger account, and fill in a unit price.

   - If you are recording a bill for an inventory item, select the item in the Item box. Peachtree fills in the item description, the general ledger account associated with the item, the item's unit price, and the amount (unit price times quantity). In Peachtree 2002, you can set up general ledger accounts, inventory items, or jobs in the Purchases/Receive Inventory window. See the appendix for details.

7. **Click in the Job box to display the lookup list button and choose a job from the list.**

   If you're purchasing a stock item or an assembly item, you cannot assign it to a job. However, if you're purchasing any other type of item, you can assign it to a job. You also can assign the line to a job if you don't select any item from the Item list. You can read about setting up jobs in Chapter 12.

   If you assign a line to a job, Peachtree allows you to include it on a customer's bill as a reimbursable expense. Chapter 7 covers information about including reimbursable expenses on bills.

8. **Repeat Steps 5 through 7 for each item you want to order or that appears by the bill you're recording.**

Receiving goods against a purchase order

Scenario: You ordered merchandise using a purchase order, and the merchandise arrives. *Maybe* the bill comes with the merchandise, and *maybe* it doesn't. Either way, you need to update your company's accounts to reflect the receipt of the merchandise so that you know they're available to sell.

You use the Purchases/Receive Inventory window to receive goods against a purchase order. You can, simultaneously, indicate whether you received the bill. Follow these steps:

1. **Choose Tas̲ks⇨Pur̲chases/Receive Inventory to display the Purchases/Receive Inventory window.**

2. **Type the vendor ID or click that handy magnifying glass to display the list of vendors.**

After you select a vendor, Peachtree fills in the blanks for the vendor and your company.

If you have previously entered purchase orders for this vendor, Peachtree displays the Apply to Purchase Order tab, and the window looks like the one shown in Figure 5-6.

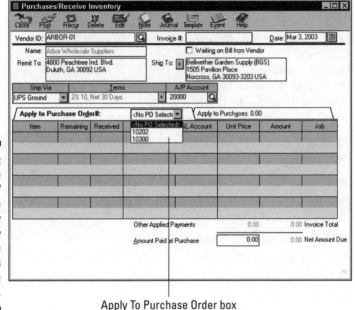

Figure 5-6:
The
Purchases/
Receive
Inventory
window
when you've
entered POs
for the
vendor.

Apply To Purchase Order box

3. **In the Invoice # box, type a number for the vendor's bill.**

   You can't use an invoice number more than once for a particular vendor, so if you get stopped by this, be sure you haven't got an old invoice.

   If you have vendors who don't provide you with an invoice number, your company might have a standard solution for this problem like entering a combination of the vendor ID plus the date or the primary PO number. This usually helps avoid duplications (but not always).

4. **If necessary, change the date of the purchase.**

5. **If only the merchandise arrived but you have no bill from the vendor, place a check in the Waiting on Bill from Vendor box.**

   If you received both goods and a bill, leave the box unchecked.

   As with other transactions, you *can* change the A/P account, but typically, you don't.

6. **Click the drop-down list for the Apply to Purchase Order # box and select the PO number that lists the goods you ordered.**

7. **On each line of the Apply to Purchase Order tab, in the Received box, type the quantity you received.**

   Remember that you have to put the decimal-zero after the whole number, or Peachtree adds the leading decimal: To get 6, type 6.0. Peachtree fills in the amount (unit price times quantity).

8. **Click the Post button to save your work.**

When the bill arrives . . . finally

If you have entered vendor receipts against a PO, but didn't have a bill, you should have placed a check in the Waiting on Bill from Vendor box in the Purchases/Receive Inventory window. When the waiting is over and you've got the invoice, follow these steps to tie up the loose ends:

1. **Choose Tasks➪Purchases/Receive Inventory to open the Purchases/Receive Inventory window.**

2. **Enter the vendor's ID number.**

   Peachtree displays a message indicating that one or more purchases are waiting for a bill from the vendor.

3. **Click OK to close the message.**

4. **Click the Edit button.**

   Peachtree indicates that you started a transaction and asks if you want to save it.

5. **Click No to display the Select Purchase window.**

6. **Find the Vendor Name and then look for a Y in the Waiting? column and Unpaid in the Status columns.**

   Use the Reference column to further help you identify the correct purchase.

7. **Highlight the correct purchase and click OK.**

   Peachtree displays the purchase in the Purchases/Receive Inventory window.

8. **Remove the check from the Waiting on Bill from Vendor box and supply a number in the Invoice # box.**

9. **Click the Post button.**

By making this status change, you indicate to Peachtree that you now consider the bill eligible for payment. See Chapter 6 for information on paying bills.

Shipping Directly to Customers

Suppose that you need to buy something, maybe a special order for a customer, and you want to ship it directly to the customer. No problem. You can specify a customer's address in the Ship To box on either a purchase order or a purchase. Use Tasks⇨Purchase Orders to display the Purchase Orders window or Tasks⇨Purchases/Receive Inventory to make a purchase. In either window, follow these steps:

1. **Type or select the appropriate Vendor ID.**

2. **Click the Ship To button to display the Ship To Address dialog box.**

3. **Place a check in the Drop Ship box.**

4. **Enter the invoice number you're using to bill your customer.**

   You don't need to create the invoice before you set up the drop shipment, but don't forget to bill your customer. For more information about creating invoices for customers, see Chapter 7.

5. **Type the recipient's name and address if you haven't set the recipient up in the Customer List; otherwise, choose a customer from the list and select one of the customer's Ship To addresses.**

   To set up Ship To addresses for customers, see Chapter 7.

6. **Click OK.**

Entering Credits

Suppose that you have a purchase that you no longer need. Should you just erase it? If you want to practice good accounting, the answer is a definite no. Deleting purchases removes the *audit trail* — that "thing" accountants mean when they talk about the list of transactions you enter because your business does business. When accountants can trace transactions from beginning to end, they're really happy people.

Having said that, you need to understand that Peachtree allows you to delete any *unpaid* purchase, even though your accountant won't like it. Display the purchase in the Purchases/Receive Inventory window and click the Delete button.

But Peachtree *won't* let you delete a purchase if you've applied any transactions to it. Suppose, for example, that you accidentally paid a purchase that you later determined you should not have paid. If you try to delete the purchase, the Delete button in the Purchase window is unavailable. In this case, you need to void the check you wrote that paid the purchase, and then you need to enter a credit memo in Peachtree to cancel the effects of the purchase. See Chapter 6 to find out how to void a check. After you've voided the check, follow the steps in this section to finish canceling the purchase.

Besides fixing errors in purchases, don't forget about the times when a vendor issues a credit memo to you for merchandise you return. You need to enter the credit memo into Peachtree to reduce the balance you owe the vendor and match it to the original purchase.

To record the vendor credit, use the Purchases/Receive Inventory window. Fill in the window the same way you would if you were recording a bill, but enter the quantity as a negative number. If you select an inventory item, Peachtree also reduces your inventory. Make sure that the credit memo you enter mirrors the purchase you entered originally; that is, the credit memo should affect the same things (vendor, general ledger accounts, and inventory items) that the original purchase affected.

For the Invoice number, we suggest that you use the original invoice number followed by CM to indicate credit memo. This numbering scheme helps you tie the credit memo to a particular purchase.

The credit reduces the amount you owe the vendor, but it hangs out there unless you match it to a bill. If you print your Accounts Payable Aging report, you can see both the original purchase and the credit memo on the report. To match the credit to a bill and remove *both* entries from the Aging report, use the Payments window. Follow these steps:

1. **Choose Tasks➪Payments to display the Payments window.**

2. **Enter the vendor's ID to display all open invoices for the vendor (see Figure 5-7).**

3. **Find the original bill and the credit memo and place checks in the Pay column next to each entry.**

4. **Enter a number in the Check Number field.**

   Because you're not really writing a check, we suggest that you enter the credit memo number to help you identify the transaction.

5. **Click the Post button to save the transaction.**

These steps effectively write a $0 check and cancel the effects of the purchase.

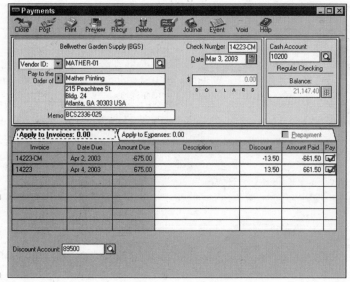

Figure 5-7:
Applying a
credit to a
purchase.

Reporting on Purchasing

To keep things short and sweet, Table 5-1 provides you with a description of the reports that pertain to buying goods. Chapter 15 covers the details on how to print reports.

Peachtree 8 also contains a new report that users having been requesting: the Items Purchased from Vendors report.

Table 5-1	Reports Related to Buying Goods
Report Name	*Description*
Vendor List	For each vendor, lists the ID, the name, the contact name, the telephone number, and tax ID.
Vendor Master File List	Similar to Vendor List but also includes address information and terms.
Vendor Ledgers	Shows the transactions and a running balance for each vendor.
Purchase Order Report	Lists the details of all purchase orders by purchase order number.

(continued)

Table 5-1 *(continued)*

Report Name	*Description*
Purchase Order Register	Lists purchase order numbers, dates, vendor IDs, and amounts; optionally use the PO State on the Filter tab to display only open purchase orders.
Aged Payables	Lists outstanding invoices by vendor and the age of each outstanding invoice.
Purchase Journal	Shows the accounts Peachtree updated for each purchase in the period.
Purchase Order Journal	Listing only purchase orders, this report closely resembles the Purchase Journal.

Chapter 6

Paying Bills

Although we wish things were different, the facts are simple: You can't hold those bills indefinitely . . . eventually, you *have* to pay them. If you prefer to let the bills pile up awhile, you can enter them gradually and pay all bills due by a certain date on your bill-paying day. Occasionally, you may need to pay a single bill or write a check to cover an unexpected expense — you know, the UPS person is standing there waiting for a check to cover the COD package in your hand.

Peachtree helps you pay groups of bills all at once or pay a single bill on the spur of the moment. You can make repetitive payments easily, and, when you have to void checks or pay sales tax on all those goods you've sold, Peachtree helps you keep all the amounts in the right accounts.

Paying a Group of Bills

Most people sit down on a regular basis — say every two weeks — and pay bills. Typically, at that time, they want to pay all bills due by a certain date; they hold bills that are due later until the next bill-paying day. In Peachtree, you can select all bills due by a certain date, or you can select bills for certain vendors or greater than an amount you specify. Then, you can simply tell Peachtree to write the checks and bid your bundle good-bye.

Selecting bills to pay

To pay a group of bills, you use Peachtree's Select for Payment window. Using this window, Peachtree looks for purchases you've entered that are eligible for payment based on information you provide. You can use this window *only* to pay bills you've entered previously. If you receive a bill for a one-time or occasional vendor that you don't want to set up in Peachtree, use the Payments window or the Write Checks window, as we describe in the section on making individual payments, later in this chapter.

To pay a group of bills, follow these steps:

1. **Choose Tasks⇨Select for Payment to display the Select for Payment – Filter Selection dialog box, shown in Figure 6-1.**

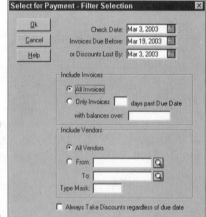

Figure 6-1: Use this dialog box to select bills to pay.

2. **Set the Check Date; most people use today's date.**

You can enter just the month and the day; Peachtree automatically uses the current year established by your computer's clock. If you enter only the day, Peachtree automatically uses the month and year established by your computer's clock. And, Peachtree 8 is Year 2000 compatible. If you type **00**, Peachtree assumes 2000.

3. **Use the Invoices Due Before date to set a cut-off date for invoices you want to pay.**

Peachtree does not select any invoices due after the date you enter in this box.

Peachtree calculates the due date when you enter the bill by using the terms you established for the vendor. So, typically, the due date is *not* the same as the date you entered the bill and is usually 30 days later.

4. **Set a date for the Discounts Lost By box if your vendors offer you discounts for paying by a specified date.**

   If you don't get vendor discounts, this date doesn't matter.

5. **Select the invoices in the Include Invoices section.**

   You can include All Invoices, or you can select the Only Invoices . . . Days Past Due Date option and specify a number of days. You can also add an amount to filter the possibilities in the With Balances Over box.

6. **Make your choices regarding payees in the Include Vendors section.**

   You may want to simply include All Vendors, but you can choose to include a range of vendors by entering either the Vendor ID in the From and To boxes or the Vendor Type in the Type Mask box.

7. **If you always take discounts offered by vendors — even if you're paying later than the discount date — place a check in the Always Take Discounts Regardless of Due Date check box.**

8. **Click OK.**

   Peachtree displays the Select For Payment window you see in Figure 6-2.

Change the order of bills on-screen

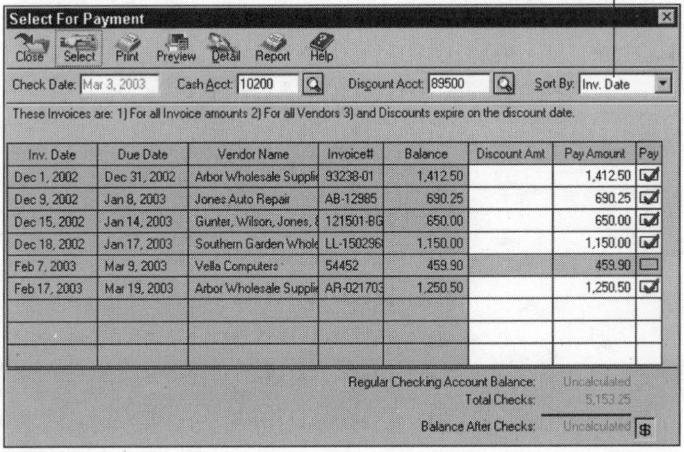

Figure 6-2: This window shows the bills that are eligible for payment based on the choices you made in the preceding dialog box.

Select For Payment

Close Select Print Preview Detail Report Help

Check Date: Mar 3, 2003   Cash Acct: 10200   Discount Acct: 89500   Sort By: Inv. Date

These Invoices are: 1) For all Invoice amounts 2) For all Vendors 3) and Discounts expire on the discount date.

Inv. Date	Due Date	Vendor Name	Invoice#	Balance	Discount Amt	Pay Amount	Pay
Dec 1, 2002	Dec 31, 2002	Arbor Wholesale Suppli	93238-01	1,412.50		1,412.50	✓
Dec 9, 2002	Jan 8, 2003	Jones Auto Repair	AB-12985	690.25		690.25	✓
Dec 15, 2002	Jan 14, 2003	Gunter, Wilson, Jones,	121501-BG	650.00		650.00	✓
Dec 18, 2002	Jan 17, 2003	Southern Garden Whole	LL-150296	1,150.00		1,150.00	✓
Feb 7, 2003	Mar 9, 2003	Vella Computers	54452	459.90		459.90	☐
Feb 17, 2003	Mar 19, 2003	Arbor Wholesale Suppli	AR-02170	1,250.50		1,250.50	✓

					Regular Checking Account Balance:	Uncalculated	
					Total Checks:	5,153.25	
					Balance After Checks:	Uncalculated	$

Peachtree initially displays the bills in Invoice Date order, but you can change to Due Date order or Vendor order using the Sort By list box. Peachtree also selects a Cash account to use to pay the bills and a discount account to use for any discounts you take, but you can select different accounts using the list box selector.

When the entire line for a bill is gray, that entry is a purchase for which you have not yet received a bill (the check remains in the Waiting for Bill from Vendor check box on the purchase). Peachtree won't let you pay purchase orders. If you think the entry should be eligible for payment, close the Select for Payment window and edit the purchase to remove the check from the Waiting for Bill box. See Chapter 5 for more information.

Peachtree assumes that you want to pay all the bills it displays, but you can choose not to pay any bill by removing the check from the Pay column. If you allow Peachtree to calculate balances automatically, Peachtree automatically updates the numbers that appear at the lower right corner of the window.

If you don't allow Peachtree to recalculate balances automatically, you see Uncalculated in the lower-right corner of the window. You can recalculate balances in this window only by clicking the Recalc button ($). If you want to recalculate balances in all windows, see Chapter 13.

The Recalc button containing the dollar sign is new to Peachtree 8; in prior versions, you clicked a Recalc button.

On the toolbar at the top of the window, you can use the Report button to print a report of the bills you've selected to pay; the report sorts the bills by vendor (see Figure 6-3).

2/20/00 at 11:19:17.51   Page: 1

Bellwether Garden Supply (BGS)
Select For Payment Preview Report
As of Mar 3, 2003

Filter Criteria Includes: 1) For all Invoice amounts 2) For all Vendors 3) and Discounts expire on the discount date 4) Bank Account: 10200 5) Invoices Due Before: 3/19/03 6) Discounts Lost By: 3/3/03. Report order is by Vendor ID.

Vendor ID Vendor	Invoice#	Inv. Date	Due Date	Balance	Disc. Date	Discount Amt	Pay Amount
ARBOR-01 Arbor Wholesale Suppliers	93238-01 AR-021703	12/1/02 2/17/03	12/31/02 3/19/03	1,412.50 1,250.50	12/1/02 2/27/03		1,412.50 1,250.50
				2,663.00			2,663.00
GUNTER-01 Gunter, Wilson, Jones, & Smith	121501-BGS	12/15/02	1/14/03	650.00	12/25/02		650.00
				650.00			650.00
JONES-01 Jones Auto Repair	AB-12985	12/9/02	1/8/03	690.25	12/19/02		690.25
				690.25			690.25
SOGARDEN-01 Southern Garden Wholesale	LL-15029684	12/18/02	1/17/03	1,150.00	12/28/02		1,150.00
				1,150.00			1,150.00
	Report Totals:			5,153.25			5,153.25

Number of Checks:	4	
Beginning Account Balance:	0.00	
Total Amount of Payments:	5,153.25	
Ending Account Balance:	-5,153.25	

Figure 6-3:
Printing a report of the bills you're about to pay.

If you highlight any line in the window and then click the Detail button, you can see the details for that line. Click the Select button to change the bills you selected.

Printing checks

As you would expect, Peachtree supports printing checks on your computer's printer. You must order check stock with the correct bank information on it. You can order checks from Peachtree. Look for the check ordering information inside the box with your Peachtree software, in Help (click the Contents tab and open the Peachtree Products and Services book), or on Peachtree's Web site at www.peachtree.com.

Or, you can check with your local forms supplier to see if you can purchase check forms that work with Peachtree and your printer.

Whoever supplies your checks can also supply window envelopes, saving you time when paying the bills because you won't need to use labels or address envelopes in any way.

When you click the Print button in the Select For Payment window (see the last section for details on displaying the Select For Payment window), Peachtree starts the printing process. Follow these steps to complete the process:

1. **Select a check form from the Print dialog box.**

   The form should match the type of check form you purchased for printing checks from Peachtree. You can customize Peachtree's forms; see Chapter 14. In Peachtree 2002, you can choose to use the last form you used or select a form. See the appendix for details.

2. **Click OK and Peachtree displays a dialog box where you choose to print Real checks or a Practice check.**

   If you choose to print a practice check, Peachtree prints a check filled with Xs and 9s that you can use to determine if the form alignment is correct.

3. **Click Real.**

   Peachtree displays a dialog box that suggests a starting check number that you can change, if necessary. Peachtree assigns the starting number to the first check you print and subsequent numbers to subsequent checks when Peachtree posts your checks. If you preprinted numbers on your check stock, you need to make sure that the check(s) you print and the check(s) Peachtree posts both use the same check numbers.

4. **After establishing the starting check number, click OK.**

   Peachtree prints the checks and a message appears on-screen asking if the checks printed correctly. If you choose Yes, Peachtree assigns the check numbers and posts the checks. If you choose No, Peachtree doesn't assign the check numbers or post the checks; you can print them again.

Recording Payments

Occasionally, you need to write one check — only one. You know, you went to the office supply store and bought a box of copy paper, and you paid for it with a check. Now you need to record the check. You certainly don't want to go enter a purchase and then pay the purchase. Well, you don't need to use the Select For Payment window to produce a check; instead use the Payments window.

You also can use the Payments window to pay a single bill. Suppose you enter the telephone bill, intending to pay it on bill-paying day. Then, you change your mind because you're going to be at the phone store anyhow, and you want to bring a check to pay the bill. Use the Payments window.

From the Payments window, you can pay vendors you've set up, or you can write a check to someone you haven't set up in Peachtree. You also can use this window to (heaven forbid) write refund checks to customers. Follow these steps:

1. **Choose Tasks⇨Payments.**

   Peachtree displays the Payments window (see Figure 6-4).

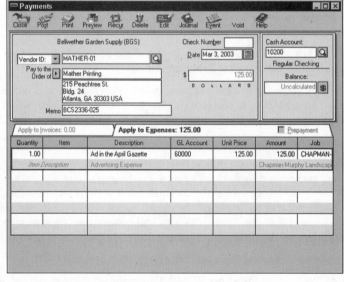

Figure 6-4: Use the Payments window to post (and optionally print) a single check.

2. **Supply a Date for the check.**

3. **Select the Cash Account from which you want to write the check.**

4. **If you *don't* intend to print the check, type the Check Number.**

   For example, if you're recording the check you wrote at the office supply store for the box of copy paper, you have no reason to print the check, but you must enter it. For this situation, enter the check number.

   By default, Peachtree supplies a check number for *any* check you print. If you enter a check number for a check you intend to print, Peachtree prints the word *Duplicate* on the check face — and you don't want that to happen.

   If you're a Type A personality who insists on completing all empty boxes on a screen, you can suppress the printing of the word Duplicate by customizing the check form. See Chapter 14 for details.

5. **Select a vendor and Peachtree displays a window depending on whether that vendor has outstanding bills.**

   If you choose a vendor who has outstanding bills, Peachtree displays the Apply to Invoices tab, listing all the outstanding bills for the vendor (see Figure 6-5). Place a check in the Pay column next to all bills you want to pay. Peachtree displays the dollar amount on the check face. In Peachtree 2002, you can drill down to see the purchase. See the appendix for details.

Figure 6-5:
If the vendor has outstanding bills, check the ones you want to pay.

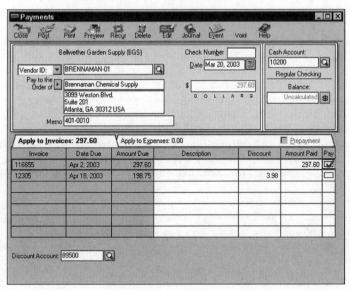

If the vendor doesn't have outstanding bills, or if you don't select a vendor but type a name into the Pay to the Order of box, Peachtree displays the Apply to Expenses tab you saw in Figure 6-4. Fill in the quantity and, if appropriate, select an item. If you don't select an item, fill in the description, supply the GL Account if necessary, and type a unit price. Peachtree calculates the amount. If appropriate, assign the line to a job.

You can include payments that you assign to Jobs as reimbursable expenses on customers' bills. See Chapter 7 for more information.

If you do not select a vendor in Step 5, Peachtree gives you two ways to pay someone you have not set up as a vendor. You can use the Payments window — just don't select a vendor. Instead, type the recipient's name in the Pay to the Order of line immediately below the Vendor ID. If you click the button next to Pay to the Order of, you can supply an address for the recipient, too; that way, you can mail the check in a window envelope. As an alternative, you can write the check in the Write Checks window, which we discuss in the section on writing checks later in this chapter.

6. **Depending on whether you enter a check number in Step 4, continue by clicking Post or Print.**

   If you included a number in the Check Number box, click the Post button to save the check.

   If you didn't include a number in the Check Number box, click the Print button to print the check immediately. Peachtree walks you through the printing dialog boxes we cover in the printing checks section earlier in this chapter. Select real and confirm the print operation. When you finish printing checks, Peachtree assigns the check numbers and posts the checks.

If you prefer to keep working and print a batch of checks later, post your checks without assigning check numbers to them. When you're ready to print checks, choose Reports⇨Accounts Payable. In the Report list, double-click the Disbursement Checks folder and select the check form that matches the check stock you use. Click the Print button to display the dialog box you use to set up batch check printing. Make sure that the First check number, the Cash Account, and the date are all correct; then, click OK. Peachtree prints checks for all the unnumbered payments you created; when printing finishes, Peachtree displays a message asking if the checks printed properly. If they did, click Yes to have Peachtree assign the check numbers to the checks.

You edit payments the same way you edit purchase orders and purchases; click the Edit button in the Payments window to display the Select Payment window. Highlight the transaction you want to edit and click OK. You also can erase checks. We talk more about that in the section on voiding checks later in this chapter.

Handling Repeat Payments and Bills

Suppose that you make a payment — like your rent or your health insurance — every month for the same amount. Peachtree lets you set up recurring purchases or payments. You enter the purchase or payment once and tell Peachtree how often to record the transaction. Recurring transactions save you data entry time. To set up a recurring payment, follow these steps:

Use *recurring purchases* when you expect to print a check to pay a bill. If you *don't* expect to print a check — say that your health insurance company automatically deducts its payment from your checking account — use *recurring payments*.

1. **Choose Tasks⇨Purchases/Receive Inventory to open the Purchases/Receive Inventory window.**

2. **Set up the purchase, but don't assign a check number.**

3. **Click the Recur button on the toolbar.**

   Peachtree displays the Create Recurring Journal Entries dialog box (see Figure 6-6). Don't let the name scare you.

Figure 6-6:
Use this
dialog box
to set up
transactions
that happen
repeatedly.

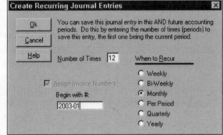

4. **In the When To Recur list, select the frequency you want.**

5. **In the Number Of Times box, type the number of transactions you want to enter for the time frame you chose in Step 4.**

   For example, if you're going to make a payment every week for 7 weeks, type 7 in the Number Of Times box and choose Weekly from the When To Recur list. If you're going to make the payment every month for one year, type 12 in the Number Of Times box and choose Monthly from the When To Recur list.

6. **Assign a starting number for the recurring purchase in the Begin With # box.**

   If you want, set up a prefix for the bill. In Figure 6-6, we added the year and a dash to the number to make Peachtree start each purchase it creates for this recurring transaction with 2003-. Peachtree adds an incremental number, starting with 01. Because we created 12 transactions, Peachtree numbers the last recurring purchase as 2003-12.

   You cannot set up recurring transactions past the last open period. Peachtree allows you to have 24 open periods (usually two years).

7. **Click OK.**

   You can hear some activity on your hard disk while Peachtree creates the transactions. Then, Peachtree redisplays the Purchases/Receive Inventory window, ready for you to enter your next purchase.

If you edit the recurring purchase, take a minute to notice a couple of interesting things:

✔ You can see multiple entries for the recurring transaction in the Select Purchase window. For example, if on April 1, you set up the payment to recur weekly for seven weeks, look for at least four, possibly five entries in April. If you set up the purchase to recur monthly, you need to use the Show list box in the Select Purchases window to display All Transactions or a future period.

✔ When you display the recurring purchase in the Purchases/Receive Inventory window, look for an entry at the bottom of the window, telling you how many more entries exist.

✔ When you click the Edit button in the Payments window to display the Select Payment window, recurring payments don't have reference numbers like recurring purchases do. The Reference number for a payment is the check number. Peachtree leaves the number blank so that you can print a check for the Payment. If you write the check by hand, edit the payment and assign a check number.

Writing Checks

The Write Checks window is new in Peachtree 8.

Suppose that you're writing a check, but you're *not* paying a bill. You can use the Payments window, as we show you in the preceding sections, or you can use the new Write Checks window.

You should be aware of the important fact that you *cannot* use this window to write a check that pays a bill. If you entered a bill for a vendor, pay the bill by using either the Select to Pay window or the Payments window — or you're sure to mess up your accounting.

1. **Choose Tasks⇨Write Checks to display the window you see in Figure 6-7.**

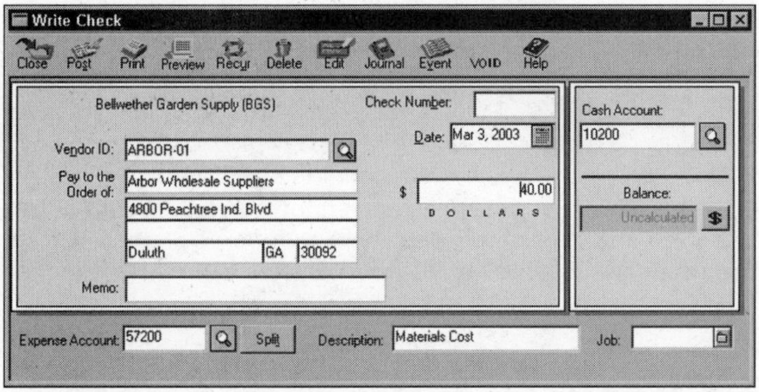

Figure 6-7:
Entering information to write checks that don't pay bills.

2. **You can select a vendor in this window, or you can simply type a recipient's name in the Pay To The Order Of box.**

   If you include the address of the recipient, you can print the check and mail it in a window envelope.

3. **Fill in the check Date and amount.**

4. **Optionally, type an explanation of the purpose of the check in the Memo box.**

5. **If you want to track Job Costing, assign the check to a Job.**

6. **Optionally, choose a different Cash Account.**

7. **Assign the check to an Expense Account; if you need to assign the check to more than one expense account, click the Split button.** Peachtree displays the Split Transaction dialog box (see Figure 6-8).

8. **Click OK to save the information you provide in the Split Transaction window and redisplay the Write Check window.**

9. **Click Print to print the check immediately; otherwise, click Post and print the check later.**

   You can print later by using the steps we describe in the printing checks section earlier in this chapter.

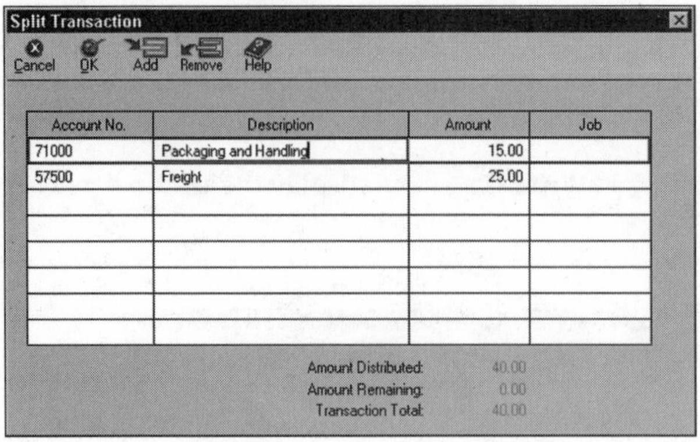

Split Transaction

Cancel OK Add Remove Help

Account No.	Description	Amount	Job
71000	Packaging and Handling	15.00	
57500	Freight	25.00	

Amount Distributed: 40.00
Amount Remaining: 0.00
Transaction Total: 40.00

Figure 6-8:
Be sure to allocate the entire check if you split the check between accounts.

If you've hand-written the check and simply need to record it, follow the preceding steps and also supply the check number; be sure to click the Post button when you finish to avoid printing a check.

Voiding Checks

If you write a check and then discover a problem with the check, you can void it. When you void a check, Peachtree creates a negative check for the same amount as the check you void, but the value of the voided check *increases* your cash account — remember, the original check reduced your cash account. In other words, if you add the two transactions together, you get 0 (accountants say the transactions "Net to 0"); and, of course, a $0 transaction causes no change in your cash balance. The voided check transaction that Peachtree creates has the same number as the original check, but Peachtree adds a V to the number; that is, if you void check 101, Peachtree creates check 101V. You can view (and edit) the voided check in the Payments window the same way you can view and edit any other payment.

To void a check, follow these steps:

1. **Choose Tasks⇨Void Checks, and Peachtree asks you to choose a Cash Account.**

2. **If necessary, click the list box selector to choose the checking account from which you wrote the check that you now want to void.**

3. **Click OK.**

   Peachtree displays the Void Existing Checks window (see Figure 6-9).

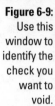

Figure 6-9:
Use this
window to
identify the
check you
want to
void.

> **Void Existing Checks**
>
> Account ID: 10200   Void Date: 3/3/03
>
> | Number | Date | Source | Amount | Payee |
> |--------|------|--------|--------|-------|
> | 10201 | 3/12/03 | AP | 124.68 | Brennaman Chemical Supply |
> | 10202 | 3/12/03 | AP | 360.00 | Gunter, Wilson, Jones, & Smith |
> | 10203 | 3/12/03 | AP | 550.00 | Miller Leasing Corp. |
> | 10204 | 3/12/03 | AP | 335.50 | Duffey Lawn Pro, Inc. |
> | 10205 | 3/14/03 | AP | 147.00 | Gwinnett County License Board |
> | 10206 | 3/14/03 | AP | 274.56 | Jones Auto Repair |
> | 10207 | 3/14/03 | AP | 550.00 | Miller Leasing Corp. |
> | 10208 | 3/14/03 | AP | 250.54 | Southern Garden Wholesale |
> | 10209 | 3/14/03 | AP | 500.00 | Wills Advertising Company |
> | 10210 | 3/15/03 | AP | 530.64 | Safe State Insurance Company |
>
> Void   Close   Help

4. Highlight the check you want to void and click the <u>V</u>oid button.

Peachtree displays a message asking whether you're sure you want to
void the check.

5. Click OK, and Peachtree creates the voided check.

You can sort the checks in the Void Existing Checks window in different ways
to help you find the check you want to void. Click any of the columns in the
window to sort checks by that column heading.

If you accidentally void the wrong check, open the Payments window and
click the Edit button. You can find the voided check in the window — the
check number ends with a V for Void. Highlight that transaction and click OK
to display it in the Payments window. Then delete it by clicking the delete
button.

You can see both transactions in the Account Reconciliation window when
you balance your checkbook, and Peachtree already has marked them both as
cleared. For more information on balancing your checkbook, see Chapter 17.

When you void a check that paid a vendor bill, Peachtree reopens the vendor
bill. That is, Peachtree assumes you still want to pay the bill. If you do want
to pay the bill, simply pay the bill using the Payments or the Select For
Payment window. If, however, you *don't* want to pay the bill, enter a credit
memo for the bill and match the credit memo to the bill. Chapter 5 has more
information.

Paying Sales Tax

Most states expect customers to pay a sales tax on goods they purchase; in some states, customers also pay tax on services. In addition, the county or local government may also assess a tax on customer's purchases. If your business sells taxable goods, you collect the sales tax for at least one taxing authority, and then, of course, you're expected to remit the sales tax to the taxing authority — along with a sales tax return (so that they can make sure that you're not cheating them out of any of the sales taxes you collect).

Paying sales tax in Peachtree is no different than paying any other bill; you can enter a purchase to remind yourself that you owe the money or you can simply write the check. The tricky part? Finding out *how much* to pay because not all sales are taxable in every state. And, when the sales *are* taxable, in some cases, local taxes apply as well. To complicate the issue further, if you operate your business close to a border between jurisdictions, your business may be collecting taxes for more than one jurisdiction — and at different rates.

If you set up your sales taxes correctly (see Chapter 7 for more information), you can use the Taxable/Exempt Sales report (see Figure 6-10) to help you prepare the sales tax return and remit your sales taxes. Choose Reports⇨Accounts Receivable to print this report, which breaks down the taxes you owe by taxing authority.

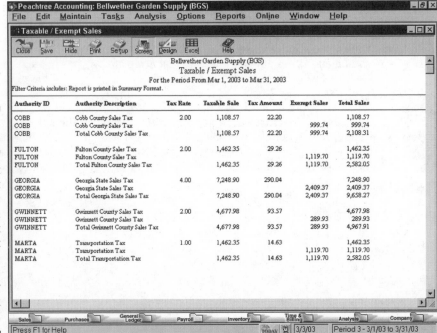

Figure 6-10:
Use the Taxable/Exempt Sales report to fill out the sales tax return that you must include when you make your sales tax payment.

Tracking Money You've Paid with Reports

When you need to track the outflow of money, Peachtree offers some reports that help you. Table 6-1 provides you with a description of the reports that pertain to paying bills. See Chapter 15 to find out how to print reports.

Table 6-1	Reports Related to Paying Bills
Report Name	*Description*
Check Register	Lists each check with the check number, payee, and the amount.
Cash Requirements	Lists all unpaid purchases and their due dates for the date range you specify.
Cash Disbursements Journal	Shows the accounts that Peachtree updated for each check you wrote in the period.

Chapter 7

Selling Products and Services

. . . .

In This Chapter

▶ Setting up sales tax authorities and codes

▶ Creating customer defaults

▶ Entering quotes, sales orders, and invoices

▶ Managing sales transactions and invoices

. . . .

*W*hat treasures we have in our customers! (Well, most of them anyway.) After all, we wouldn't be in business without them would we?

Peachtree operates under an assumption that you might generate a quote to a customer, convert that quote into a sales order, and then when you produce the goods or service, you can turn that sales order into an invoice. You do not, however, have to use either quotes or sales orders to use Peachtree's invoicing feature.

Even if you don't use quotes or sales orders, we suggest you read this entire chapter. Peachtree's steps for creating and editing quotes, sales orders, and invoices are almost identical. Therefore, to eliminate redundancy, we explain most of the details in the Quotes section. We show you the differences between entering quotes, sales orders, and invoices in the individual sections of this chapter.

In addition to talking about the forms you use to sell things to your customers, we're going to talk about another important selling issue — sales taxes.

Working with Sales Taxes

Everyone hates to pay sales tax; taxes make us feel like we're paying more for our purchase than we should. Like it or not, though, most states expect customers to pay sales tax, usually on goods, but occasionally on services as well. Some states even charge other types of sales tax, such as a local or city tax. If your state has sales taxes, you, as the seller, are obligated to collect the sales tax from your customer.

Yielding to the authorities

If your business sells taxable goods or services, you collect the sales tax for the taxing authority. Peachtree calls the taxing "authority" the agency that has the right to tell you to collect sales tax from your customers. That authority could be only your state government. Frequently though, other local agencies are involved.

For example, your state charges a tax, but so do several of your counties. If so, you need to set up Sales Tax Authorities for your state and for each county as well.

Suppose that your business is located in the state of Georgia and that the state charges a 4 percent sales tax for goods. You pay the tax to the Georgia Department of Revenue. Now, if you have a branch of your business located in Brown County, Georgia, you have to charge those customers an additional 2 percent which, in turn is paid to the Brown County Treasurer's office. If another branch is located in Green County, Georgia, the customers at that store have to pay an additional 2.5 percent to the Green County Treasurer's office. In this situation, you have three different taxing authorities, the State of Georgia, Brown County, and Green County.

What if you pay two or more of your taxes to the same payee? What authorities should you create? In that situation, you still should set up three different authorities. Doing so allows you to determine the exact amount of tax collected for each county tax on the Sales Tax report.

Before you set up the Sales Tax Authorities codes, you must set up a vendor to whom you remit the sales tax. You can find out how to set up a vendor in Chapter 5. To follow this exercise, you must have a vendor set up; use Georgia Department of Revenue as the vendor name.

To set up Sales Tax Authorities, follow these steps:

1. **Click Maintain⇨Sales Taxes⇨Sales Tax Authorities to display the Maintain Sales Tax Authorities dialog box.**

2. **Type an ID for the authority.**

   You can use up to eight letters or numbers (alphanumeric characters). For our example, use **GEORGIA**.

3. **Type a description of the authority.**

   Here you've got up to 30 characters of space. Type **Georgia State Sales Tax** for our example.

4. **Enter the tax rate.**

   If your state charges 4 percent, type 4.00; if it charges 5.5 percent, type it as 5.50. Peachtree automatically converts this value to a percentage.

Chapter 7: Selling Products and Services *103*

5. **Type or select the vendor ID to which you remit this sales tax.**

   This step assumes that you have set up the tax payee as a vendor as mentioned at the beginning of these steps. Choose the Georgia Department of Revenue.

6. **Enter the G/L liability account to which you want to post the sales tax you collect.**

7. **Click Save.**

8. **Repeat Steps 2 through 7 for each authority you need.**

   Figure 7-1 shows the three authorities for our sample.

Figure 7-1:
Create a separate authority for each sales tax you want to track.

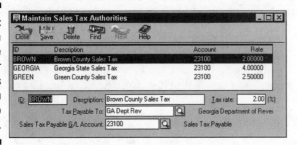

Creating Sales Tax Codes

After you determine the Sales Tax Authorities, you need to set up the Sales Tax Codes. The Sales Tax Codes are made up of combinations of Sales Tax Authorities. Because your customers in Brown County have to pay a Georgia State and Brown County tax, those two taxes together make up one sales tax code for your Brown County branch. The customers in Green County pay Georgia State tax and Green County tax, so that combination generates the need for a second sales tax code. You also need a third sales tax code for those customers who simply pay the Georgia State tax with no county tax included.

Follow these steps to set up a Sales Tax Code:

1. **Click Maintain⇨Sales Taxes⇨Sales Tax Codes to display the Maintain Sales Tax Codes dialog box.**

2. **Type an ID in the Sales Tax Code box and a Description.**

   Use a maximum of eight alphanumeric characters for the ID. We suggest you use some type of description. Call your first code **GABrown** as an ID with the description **Georgia, Brown County**.

3. **Click the box in the ID column and enter the first taxing authority ID for this tax code.**

   Peachtree fills in the description, tax rate, and G/L account you assigned to the selected authority.

   This ID text box reveals a little quirk in Peachtree. Generally, if a field has a lookup list available, the field displays a magnifying glass for you to click. This one doesn't. We don't know why . . . but it doesn't. So, if you don't remember the taxing authority ID, you can right-click the ID field to display the Sales Tax Authority lookup list. If you double-click the ID field, the Maintain Sales Tax Authority window opens, allowing you to create new sales tax authorities.

4. **If your state requires you to charge sales tax on the freight you charge to your customers, place a check in the Tax Freight box.**

   When you create an invoice to your customer, if you add a freight amount in the invoice freight box, Peachtree calculates tax on the freight.

5. **Enter any remaining tax authorities for this sales tax ID and then click Save.**

   See Figure 7-2 for an example.

6. **Repeat Steps 2 through 4 for each sales tax code you need.**

7. **Click Close.**

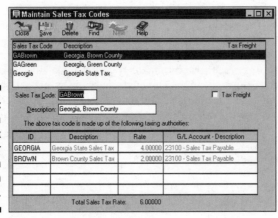

Figure 7-2:
Create a
sales tax
code for
each
combination
of tax.

Working with Customers

Before you can generate quotes, sales orders, or invoices, you need to set up your customer defaults and enter the individual customers. In Chapter 4, we show you how to create the defaults you use here. Peachtree identifies each customer by a unique ID that allows Peachtree to track any transactions related to the customer.

Adding customers

When you set up a customer, you supply name and address information, a sales account to use each time you post a sale to the customer, and any custom field information you set up in your defaults. You also can view historical information about your sales to and receipts from your customers over the previous twelve months.

To add or modify customer information, choose Maintain⇨Customers. Peachtree displays the Maintain Customers/Prospects window with four tabs, as shown in Figure 7-3. The following sections examine what you can do with each tab in this dialog box.

General tab   Customer Type field

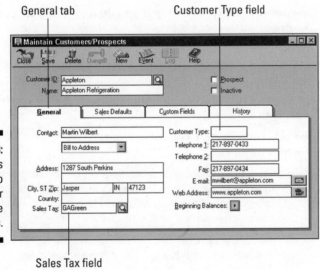

Figure 7-3:
Use this
window to
add, edit, or
delete
customers.

Sales Tax field

The General tab

Peachtree supplies the General tab for basic customer identification information such as ID, name, address, and phone numbers.

Use the ID as the identification to select the customer when you create a customer transaction. Enter up to 20 alphanumeric characters (except the characters *, ?, or +) for a customer's ID. Peachtree sorts the customer reports by customer ID. Numbers sort before letters, and, because the field is case sensitive, capital letters sort before lowercase letters.

We suggest that you use lowercase letters so that your hands don't need to leave the keyboard. Peachtree sorts the Customer list and many other reports by default using the Customer ID. To get Peachtree to sort the customer list in alphabetical order by default, use characters from the customer's name as the ID.

Choose Maintain⇨Customers. Peachtree displays the Maintain Customers/Prospects window. Fill in the General tab by following these steps:

1. **Type a Customer ID for the customer and the customer's Name.**

   Enter up to 30 alphanumeric characters for the customer's name.

   IDs are case sensitive, so that the IDs Baker, BAKER, and baker are treated as three different Customer IDs.

2. **Click the Prospect check box only if you do *not* want this customer ID included on any customer reports.**

   If you generate an invoice for the prospect or clear the check box, the prospect becomes a regular customer, and Peachtree includes the ID on customer reports.

3. **Fill in the contact information, phone numbers, and, if appropriate, e-mail, and Web address.**

   Peachtree Version 8 enables you to store interactive e-mail and Web addresses for customers.

   If you enter an e-mail address and click the icon next to it, Peachtree opens your e-mail program and generates a message to your customer. Clicking the button next to the Web address launches your Web browser and directs it to the customer's Web site.

4. **Click the drop-down arrow for the Bill to Address box, choose the shipping address you want to enter, and enter the shipping information.**

   You can store up to nine different shipping addresses for each customer. Whenever you create a quote, sales order, or invoice, you can pick from the stored shipping addresses, thereby saving data entry time.

Two additional fields exist on this window that we need to discuss: the Customer Type field and the Sales Tax field.

- ✔ **Customer Type:** Use the Customer Type field to group similar customers together. You can then limit the information on most A/R reports to a specific customer type. For example, you may want to distinguish between commercial customers and retail customers. Being consistent when entering the customer type is the secret to using the Customer Type field effectively. The Customer Type field is case sensitive.

  Don't want to charge finance charges to all your customers? No problem. Consider using the Customer Type field to identify whether you charge finance charges. Then, when you need to assess finance charges, you can select customers by customer type.

- ✔ **Sales Tax:** You need to choose the sales tax code that applies to this customer. Either type the applicable sales tax code or click the lookup list button.

The Sales Defaults tab

From the Sales Defaults tab, you can define several additional pieces of customer information. Peachtree relates many of the fields on this window to the inventory and payroll modules.

1. **Choose Maintain⇨Customers and click the Sales Defaults tab.**

2. **If applicable, select a default Sales Rep for this customer and type the Sales Rep ID or select one from the lookup list.**

   See Chapter 9 for information on creating Sales Reps.

3. **Define a G/L Sales Account for the customer if different from the default account established in Customer Defaults.**

   For more information about Customer Defaults, see Chapter 4.

   When you create an inventory item, you specify a sales account for the item. When you generate an invoice, the sales account associated with inventory items overrides the customer sales account. You can find out how to establish inventory items in Chapter 11.

4. **Enter a purchase order number in the Open P.O. # box if your customer has given you a standing purchase order number to use for all purchases from you.**

   This purchase order number defaults to the customer purchase order field on the Quotes, Sales Orders, and Sales/Invoicing windows.

5. **Choose a preferred shipping method.**

   Establish shipping methods in the Maintain Inventory Item Defaults window. If necessary, you can override the preferred method when you generate a customer invoice. You established shipping methods in Chapter 4.

6. **Enter the Resale number if the customer does not have to pay sales tax.**

Most states require a customer to provide you with their resale number for tax-exempt purchases.

7. **Choose the pricing level most often associated with this customer.**

Pricing levels are tied to inventory items.

See Chapter 11 for details on how to assign up to five prices to each inventory item. Peachtree then automatically charges this customer the price shown in the pricing level you specify here.

8. **If you want to change the default terms for the customer, click the Terms button.**

Unless you specify terms, Peachtree assumes this customer gets the default terms established when you set up Customer Defaults. When Peachtree displays the Customer Terms dialog box (see Figure 7-4), remove the check from the Use Standard Terms check box and set up the customer's terms.

Use Standard Terms check box

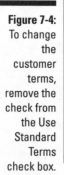

Figure 7-4:
To change the customer terms, remove the check from the Use Standard Terms check box.

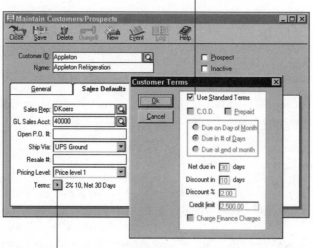

Terms selection button

Remove the check from the Use Standard Terms and the Charge Finance Charges check boxes if you know you won't charge this customer finance charges. To learn about finance charges, see Chapter 8.

Custom customer information fields

When you set up default customer information (see Chapter 4), you establish the custom fields for the Maintain Customers/Prospects window. To enter custom information, choose Maintain⇨Customers. Click the Custom Fields tab and type the available information for the customer in each custom field box. Click the Save button to save the customer information.

Historical facts

When you first set up a customer, the History tab doesn't have any information. However, after you've recorded customer sales transactions, the History tab gives you a month-by-month summary of both sales and receipts.

To view customer history, click Maintain⇨Customers then click the History tab.

Modifying customer information

Customers move around, so you may find the information you have stored on a customer to be outdated. You can change any information you entered in the Maintain Customers/Prospects window.

Follow these steps to modify customer information:

1. **Click Maintain⇨Customers to open the Maintain Customers/Prospects window.**

2. **Type the customer's ID or click the lookup list to display a list of customers.**

3. **Highlight the customer you want to change and click OK.**

   The information you saved previously for the customer appears.

4. **Click the tab containing the information you want to change and make any necessary changes.**

5. **Click Save, and Peachtree updates the customer's file.**

Changing customer IDs

In this era of acquisitions and mergers, you have customers who change their business names. If you create your customer IDs based on the business name, you may find it difficult to locate a customer in Peachtree's lookup lists. Keep your customer records easily accessible by changing the Customer ID.

1. Choose <u>M</u>aintain⇨<u>C</u>ustomers and in the Maintain Customer/Prospects window, display the customer you want to change.

2. Click the ChangeID button to display the Change Customer ID dialog box.

3. Type the ID in the Enter <u>N</u>ew Customer ID box and click <u>O</u>K.

Remember, customer IDs are case sensitive.

Saying good-bye when a customer is no longer a customer

If a customer has gone out of business or you've just determined you don't want to do business with a particular customer, change the customer's status to Inactive. An inactive customer doesn't appear in the lookup lists if you elect to hide inactive records from Peachtree's global options. When you've inactivated a customer record, Peachtree displays a warning if you try to make a sale to the customer. Chapter 13 shows you how to hide inactive customers.

After closing a fiscal year, you can purge inactive customers from your Peachtree customer list. See Chapter 18 for information on closing a fiscal year and purging.

To make a customer's status inactive, choose <u>M</u>aintain⇨<u>C</u>ustomers and in the Maintain Customer window, display the customer you want to inactivate. Click the Inactive check box and then click Save.

If you need to reactivate a customer, remove the check mark from the Inactive check box.

If you need to see the inactive customer information, you have to type the ID in the customer ID or turn off the hide inactive records feature from Peachtree's global options.

Where to begin? Beginning balances

Chances are, you've been selling your goods and services for a while. And . . . you probably haven't been paid yet for all the work you've done. You've probably given your customers a specified amount of time to pay their invoices to you; you specified your terms when you set up your default customer information in Chapter 4.

Although some invoices aren't due yet, others may be past due. Either way, the customer owes you money. When you begin using Peachtree, you need to tell Peachtree about those unpaid invoices, especially if your business is accrual based. Enter these as customer beginning balances.

Entering the invoices as beginning balances does not affect the general ledger. In an accrual-based business, the sales figures apply to your general ledger when you originally create the invoices. You can see how to enter G/L beginning balances in Chapter 3.

To enter customer beginning balances, follow these steps:

1. **Choose Maintain⇨Customers.**

2. **Click the Beginning Balances button to display the Customer Beginning Balances dialog box.**

3. **Double-click the first customer for which you need to enter a beginning balance invoice.**

   Did you think you'd have to recreate your invoices? You don't. You did that when you originally sent the invoice to your customer. Provide Peachtree with a few key pieces of information.

4. **Enter the invoice number and the date of the original invoice.**

   The date is important for Peachtree to age the invoice properly.

   You must enter the entire date, including the year. The easiest method is to enter a date as mmddyy. For example, to enter an invoice dated April 13th, 2001, type 041301.

5. **Optionally, enter the customer's Purchase Order Number.**

6. **Enter the invoice amount.**

7. **Click the lookup list button and choose your A/R Account number.**

   The A/R Account translates to the Accounts Receivable account. Notice we say, "Accounts Receivable." We're not talking about the Sales account. It's a common mistake to enter the sales account number.

8. **Repeat Steps 4 through 7 for each outstanding invoice for the selected customer.**

   Figure 7-5 shows a sample list of outstanding invoices.

   Technically, Peachtree has no limit to the number of beginning balance invoices you can enter for an individual customer; however, if you exceed 100 invoices, you can enter but not edit or delete the 101st invoice and subsequent invoices.

9. **Click Save and then click the Customer Balances tab and select the next customer to enter beginning balances.**

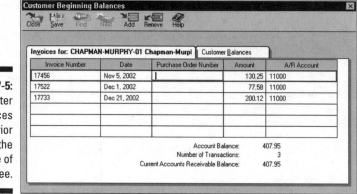

Figure 7-5:
Enter
invoices
dated prior
to the
usage of
Peachtree.

10. Click the Close button once to finish entering beginning balances and again to close the Maintain Customers/Prospects window.

We recommend that you print an Aged Receivables report to verify the invoice information and dates.

Bidding with Quotes

Many businesses let their customers know how much a product or service costs by producing a *quote* before the customer decides to buy. Peachtree allows you to create a quote; then when the customer determines he or she *does* want to make the purchase, you can convert that quote to a sales order or an invoice.

Quotes are optional in the Peachtree sales process.

Entering quotes

The top part of the quote window contains header information such as customer name, address, quote number, date, and other such information. Enter the actual products or services you supply in the body of the quote. In Chapter 13, you can find out how to modify the appearance of certain Peachtree windows by using templates.

The steps to create, edit, and print quotes, sales orders, and invoices are almost identical.

To create a quote in Peachtree, follow these steps:

1. **Click Tas_ks_⇨Quotes/Sales Orders⇨Quotes to display the Quotes window, as shown in Figure 7-6.**

Post button

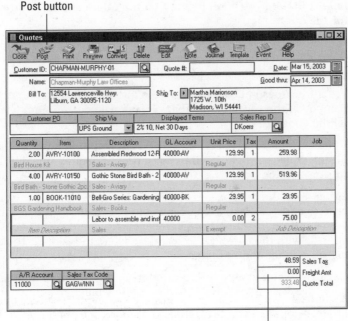

Figure 7-6:
Quotes
inform your
customer in
advance the
price of a
product or
service.

Freight Amount box

2. **Type or select the _C_ustomer ID.**

   You can't enter a quote in Peachtree unless you have set up a customer.

   If you begin typing the Customer ID, only to find you haven't yet entered the customer into Peachtree, press the Plus (+) key while the insertion point is in the ID box. Peachtree opens the Maintain Customers/Prospects window, allowing you to create the customer record. When you close the Maintain Customers/Prospects window, Peachtree redisplays the Quote window. This same procedure works for any lookup list you open in Peachtree. Pressing the Plus (+) key opens the Maintain window for whatever field you need: Vendors, Customers, Inventory, Payroll, or Chart of Accounts. In Peachtree 2002, you can use the new Fast Add feature to add a customer. See the appendix for details.

3. **Optionally, enter a Quote Number.**

   If you're going to print the quote (and usually you do), don't enter a quote number. When you print the quote, Peachtree assigns the number. If you have already assigned the quote a number, perhaps from a verbal quote, enter the quote number.

4. **Enter the Date you want printed on the quote and an expiration date for the quote.**

   Peachtree assumes the quote is valid for a period of 30 days and prints the ending date on the quote form. If you are giving your customer a longer period of time, choose a different date in the Good Thru date box.

   Peachtree doesn't do anything to the quote if the customer doesn't respond in the specified number of days. The date is simply for printing on the quote form.

5. **If the customer has specified a different shipping address than the billing address, click the Ship To button to display the Ship To Address dialog box.**

   Either open the list box and choose a shipping address, or type a custom address. Peachtree doesn't store a custom address permanently in the customer record; however, Peachtree *does* store the custom address with the current quote and transfers the address to the resulting sales order and/or invoice.

6. **Click OK when you've finished entering the shipping information.**

   It's unlikely your customer has given you a purchase order number for a quote. After all, if you're quoting it, it's not yet a purchase. You can leave the Customer PO field blank.

7. **Optionally, type a shipping method or choose a shipping method from the Ship Via list box.**

8. **Enter the Displayed Terms for this order.**

   By default, Peachtree displays the terms you chose when you set up this customer in Maintain Customers.

9. **Optionally, select a Sales Rep ID.**

   Take a look at Chapter 9 for information on how to set up a sales representative.

10. **In the body of the quote, enter a quantity for the first item on the quote.**

    When you enter the body of the quote, keep a couple of things in mind. A number of variables exist here. You enter data one way if you're using inventory items and another if you're not.

    If you're quoting a service or product that doesn't have a quantity, you can leave the quantity blank.

11. **If you're selling an inventory item, select the Item ID.**

    Peachtree fills in the item description, the G/L sales account, the item's unit price, and tax status. Then Peachtree multiplies the quantity times the unit price for the amount. In Peachtree 2002, you can set up general ledger accounts or inventory items in the Quotes window. See the appendix for details.

    If you're quoting or selling a nonstock item or you don't use inventory, leave the Item box blank and fill in the Description, G/L Income Account and Unit Price.

    Quotes do not affect the general ledger, but whenever the quote becomes a sale, Peachtree then uses the G/L account numbers to update your financial information.

    Remember, if you have the Hide General Ledger Accounts global option activated, Peachtree does not display G/L Account fields in the Quotes window. To modify G/L accounts used for this transaction, you must click the Journal button in the window toolbar.

12. **If you're quoting or selling a nonstock item, select the Tax status.**

    The Tax box refers to the tax types you determine when setting inventory defaults. Peachtree uses default tax types of 1 f or Taxable and 2 for Exempt. If you're using inventory items, Peachtree determines the tax type from the inventory item. You can find out how to set up inventory items in Chapter 11.

13. **You probably won't have a job number assigned yet because this is still a quote, so skip the job box.**

14. **Repeat Steps 10 through 13 for each item you want to quote.**

15. **If you're going to charge shipping charges and you know the amount, enter it in the Freight Amt box.**

16. **If your business is an accrual-based company, you can select the A/R Account for this potential sale, although typically, you don't change the default.**

    If yours is a cash-basis company, this field displays `<Cash Basis>`, and you can't access the account box. If you have elected to hide general ledger accounts in A/R, you won't even see an A/R Account box.

We're assuming that you need to print the quote; however, if don't need to print the quote, click the Post button. Peachtree saves the quote for future reference. To print your quote, see Printing Forms in Chapter 14.

Converting quotes to a sales order or invoice

Congratulations! You got the sale! Now, you're ready to generate a sales order or an invoice from the original quote.

To convert a quote to make the sale, follow these steps:

1. **Click Tas_ks_⇨Quotes/Sales Orders⇨Quotes to display the Quotes window.**

2. **Click the Edit button to display a list of previously created quotes.**

3. **Choose the quote to be converted and then click _O_K.**

   You may have to click in the Show list to display quotes from a different time period.

   If you don't remember what month you created the quote, try this: Choose All Transactions (it's at the top of the list) from the Show list. Then, click Find and enter a few characters of your customer's name. When you click OK, Peachtree locates the first quote for the customer you specify. If this still isn't the one you're searching for, click Next. Peachtree locates the next occurrence.

4. **Change the date on the quote to the Sales Order or Invoice date you want to use.**

   The date you choose must fall within or later than the current accounting period.

5. **Click the Convert button to display the Convert Quote dialog box.**

   You can convert the quote to a sales order or an invoice. If you select invoice, you have the option of printing immediately or not printing at all.

6. **Choose a conversion option.**

   The options that display depend on your selection as follows:

   • If you choose Sale/Invoice, you get a text box prompting you for an invoice number. If you elect not to enter an invoice number, the quote turns into an invoice, but you need to print it at a later time.

   • If you choose Sale/Invoice and Print Now, you're prompted for a beginning invoice number and other print options after you click _O_K.

   • If you choose Sales Order, a text box appears with the next sales order number displayed. You can change this sales order number if desired.

7. **Click _O_K.**

After you convert a quote, it no longer exists if you click the Edit button in the Quote window. You can, however, access it as a sales order or invoice from the Edit window of sales orders or invoices.

Working with Sales Orders

Why should you use sales orders? Why not just create an invoice? Well, this choice is really a matter of timing. If your business receives a customer order and ships the product or provides the service within a day or two, you could skip the sales order step and wait to enter the invoice. If, however, a lapse exists between the time you take the order and the time you provide the product or service, you may find the sales order feature very helpful. The sales order feature lets you enter items for a customer and then invoice and ship the items as they become available, tracking the backorders in the system.

By viewing inventory and sales order reports, you know the number of items backordered for your customers to help you plan purchases from your vendors.

Sales orders are optional in the Peachtree sales process.

You may find entering data in the Sales Order window very similar to creating a quote. Also, like a quote, even though you reference G/L accounts when you create the sales order, Peachtree doesn't affect the general ledger until you create an invoice.

To create a Sales Order, follow the steps for creating a quote, as shown in the previous section — but make these changes:

1. **Click Tasks⇨Quotes/Sales Orders⇨Sales Orders to display the Sales Orders window.**

2. **Fill in the Customer information in the header or select the Customer ID from the lookup list.**

   In Peachtree 2002, you can use the new Fast Add feature to add a customer. And, if you try to sell something you don't own, you'll see an "Out of Stock" warning. See the appendix for details.

3. **Fill in the body of the Sales Order, keeping these variations in mind:**

   • Peachtree automatically assigns a number in the SO# (Sales Order Number) field.

   • A Sales Order does not have a Good Through field.

   • Your customer may (but not necessarily) supply you with a customer purchase order number.

- If you're using Peachtree's job costing, you may have already assigned a job number to the customer order. If so, be sure to indicate the Job ID and optionally the Phase Code and Cost Code to each sales order line item.

Peachtree can play a visual trick on you here. When you click the Job box, the Job box expands backward and covers up the amount box (see Figure 7-7). At first glance, it appears the Amount has disappeared, but it's only hidden. When you move the insertion point past the Job box, Peachtree redisplays the Amount. Read about setting up jobs in Chapter 12.

Job box

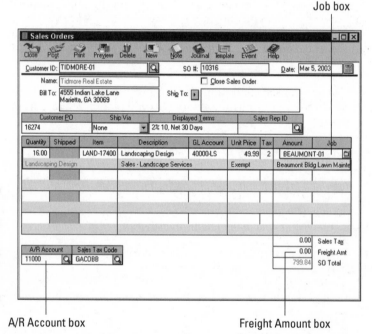

Figure 7-7:
The amount is not gone, just temporarily hidden.

A/R Account box

Freight Amount box

- If you're going to charge shipping charges and you know the amount, enter it in the Freight Amount box.

- The Shipped quantity box is unavailable for you to edit. As the ordered goods ship, whether partially or completely, Peachtree tracks the quantity shipped and enters it in this column of the sales order.

Sales orders do not affect the general ledger, but whenever the sales order becomes an invoice, Peachtree then uses the G/L account numbers to update your financial information.

4. **When you've finished entering the sales order, click the Post button to save the transaction or the Print button to print it.**

   See Printing Forms in Chapter 14 for instructions on printing sales orders.

Generating an Invoice

Finally! Your company has produced the product or performed the service, and you are now ready to collect your money. Most businesses generate an invoice as proof of the sale to give or send to their customers.

If you read the preceding sections on creating quotes or creating sales orders, then you know quite a bit about creating an invoice. As with quotes and sales orders, you enter the invoice header information and the body information. The difference is that when you *do* use sales orders, you enter the information a little differently from the way you enter data if you *don't* use sales orders.

Invoicing against a sales order

Only one sales order can apply to an invoice. However, you can create multiple invoices from a single sales order.

To create an invoice and apply it to a sales order, follow these steps:

1. **Click Tasks⇨Sales/Invoicing to display the Sales/Invoicing window.**

   The Sales/Invoicing window is very similar to the Quotes and Sales Order windows.

2. **Type or select the Customer ID.**

   You can't enter an invoice in Peachtree unless you have set up a customer through Maintain Customers.

   Remember, with the insertion point in the ID field, you can press the Plus (+) key to open the Maintain Customers/Prospects window. In Peachtree 2002, you can use the new Fast Add feature to add a customer. See the appendix for details.

   Here's where things get a little different. When you select your Customer ID, Peachtree looks for any open sales order for that customer. If an open sales order exists, Peachtree automatically brings the Apply to Sales Order # tab to the front of the window.

   If the invoice you want to enter does not apply to a sales order, click the Apply to Sales tab and proceed according to the Invoicing Against Sales section below.

3. **Click the arrow on the Apply to Sales Order # tab to display a list of open sales orders.**

4. **Choose the sales order you want to invoice against.**

   Peachtree fills in the information you supply when you create the sales order including Ship To, Purchase Order Number, Sales Rep, and the Items Ordered.

5. **Enter the invoice <u>D</u>ate and change any header information.**

   Inventory Item numbers on a sales order cannot be edited from an invoice. To change item numbers, you must edit the original sales order. You can however, change the quantities or item description. To add additional items or charges to the invoice, click the Apply to Sales tab and add the items there.

6. **Enter the quantities shipped in the Shipped column, or if the entire order has been filled, save time by choosing <u>E</u>dit⇨Ship <u>A</u>ll.**

   Peachtree then fills in the remaining quantities of the order.

   Well okay, this feature is not really new, but it has been changed. On versions of Peachtree prior to Version 8, notice the Ship All and Ship None buttons on the toolbar. These buttons provide the same feature as the choices under the Edit menu.

7. **Type or verify the Freight Amount.**

   If you enter freight information when you create the sales order, it appears automatically on the invoice only if you use the Ship All feature. If you make a partial shipment and need to charge freight, enter the freight amount manually.

8. **Click Po<u>s</u>t or Print.**

   You probably want to print the invoice, but if you are not going to print it or if you want to continue entering invoices and print them later in a batch, click the Post button to save the invoice. To print your invoices, see Printing Forms in Chapter 14.

When you post or print the invoice, if the current invoice total plus any unpaid invoices for this customer exceed the credit limit you establish when you set up the customer, you see a warning message. Peachtree doesn't stop you from exceeding a customer credit limit; it simply warns you. You make the decision to proceed with the sale or not. Click OK to accept the invoice and continue posting or printing.

Invoicing against sales

Your business doesn't use sales orders? You don't need these optional features because you can create an invoice without a sales order.

To create an invoice, follow these steps:

1. **Click Tasks⇨Sales Invoicing to display the Sales/Invoicing window.**

2. **Enter the invoice header information.**

   To review how to enter the header information, see the section on creating quotes earlier in this chapter. The header information includes the invoice date, shipping address, the customer's purchase order number (if available), shipping method, terms, and sales rep ID. In Peachtree 2002, you can use the new Fast Add feature to add a customer.

3. **Fill in the line items for the invoice based on the following options:**

   Just like quotes and sales orders, a number of variables exist here, depending on whether or not you use the Peachtree inventory module. Keep these steps in mind for creating the body of the invoice:

   - Enter a quantity for the first item on the invoice. You can leave the Quantity field blank when invoicing a service or product that doesn't have a quantity.

   - If the product is an inventory item, select the Item ID. Peachtree fills in the item Description, the G/L Account, the item's Unit Price, and Tax status. Then Peachtree multiplies the quantity times the unit price for the amount. In Peachtree 2002, you can set up general ledger accounts, inventory items, or jobs in the Sales/Invoicing window. See the appendix for details.

   - If your product is a nonstock item or you don't use inventory, leave the Item box blank and enter a Description, G/L Account, and unit price.

   - The Tax box refers to the tax types you determine when setting inventory defaults. If you're using inventory items, Peachtree determines the Tax type from the inventory item.

   - Optionally, if you're using Peachtree's job costing feature, click in the Job box to display the magnifying glass and choose a job from the list.

   - If you're going to charge shipping charges and you know the amount, enter it in the Freight Amount box.

4. **Post or Print the invoice.**

   You probably want to print the invoice but, if you are not going to print it or if you want to continue entering invoices and print them later in a batch, click the Post button to save the invoice. To print your invoices, see Printing Forms in Chapter 14.

As with sales orders, when you post or print the invoice, if the current invoice total plus any unpaid invoices for this customer exceed the credit limit you established when you set up the customer, you see a warning message. Peachtree doesn't stop you from exceeding a customer credit limit; it simply warns you. You make the decision to proceed with the sale or not. Click OK to accept the invoice and continue posting or printing.

Editing a Sales Transaction

Like most transactions you enter in Peachtree, quotes, sales orders, or invoices are not written in stone. Peachtree makes it quite easy for you to modify anything on the transaction — even after it has been printed.

1. **Click the Tasks menu and select the type of document you wish to edit: Quote, Sales Order, or Sales/Invoicing.**

   In our example, you edit a sales order.

2. **Click the Edit button.**

   For this example, the Select Sales Order window opens and lists previously created sales orders.

   The Select Sales Orders window displays sales orders generated in the current period. If you don't see the transaction you want to edit, open the Show list box and select a different period.

3. **Choose the transaction you want to edit and then click OK.**

   Peachtree displays the transaction on the screen.

4. **Make any desired changes to the transaction and then click Print to reprint the transaction or click Post to save the transaction without reprinting it.**

Voiding an Invoice

If you generate an invoice and then discover the invoice needs to be canceled, use the new Void Invoice feature.

Peachtree has the ability to quickly void invoices now in Peachtree Version 8.

Although technically you could delete an invoice to get rid of it, deleting an invoice is not good accounting practice. When you delete transactions, you lose your audit trail of the actions you've taken. And, if the original invoice occurred in a previous month, you could hurt the integrity of your reports. Your accountant would not be a happy camper.

When you void an invoice, Peachtree creates several transactions. First, Peachtree creates another invoice with the same invoice number as the original, except it adds a V to the invoice number. That invoice amount is a negative dollar amount equal to the amount of the original invoice. For example, if you generate invoice number 1234 for $150.00 that you must cancel, Peachtree generates another invoice 1234V for –$150.00 to void the original.

If the original transaction involves inventory items, Peachtree restores to inventory the items sold. In the general ledger, Peachtree creates a reversing entry, affecting sales and accounts receivable, and if applicable, cost of sales and inventory. If the original invoice does not come from a sales order, negative values appear for the quantities *sold;* however, if the original invoice does come from a sales order, negative values appear for the quantities *shipped.* Peachtree then reopens the sales order.

Peachtree then creates a zero-dollar receipt to pay both the original and voided invoice. This receipt clears both transactions from the aged receivable report. In other words, if you add the two transactions together, you get zero and, of course, a $0 transaction causes no change in your cash balance. You can view the zero-dollar receipt by clicking the Edit button from the Tas<u>k</u>s⇨<u>R</u>eceipts window and selecting the appropriate receipt.

To void an invoice, follow these steps:

1. **Click Tas<u>k</u>s⇨<u>S</u>ales/Invoicing.**

2. **Click the Edit button and double-click the transaction you want to void.**

   The transaction must appear on the screen before you can void it.

   Optionally, choose a different period from the Show drop-down list to find the invoice you want.

3. **Click the Void button.**

   Peachtree opens a Void Existing Invoice dialog box like the one in Figure 7-8.

4. **Type the date you want — usually the current date — in The Following Invoice Will Be <u>V</u>oided As Of box.**

5. **Click <u>O</u>K.**

   Peachtree lists the word "Void" beside both the original and reversing invoices and uses the invoice number as the receipt reference number.

If you determine you voided the wrong invoice, before you can delete the voided invoice, you need to delete the receipt.

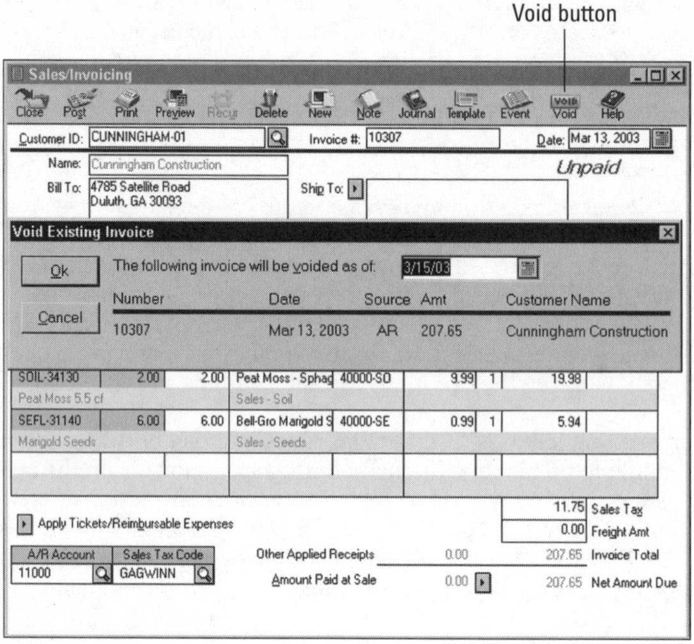

Void button

Figure 7-8: Peachtree displays the invoice number, date, amount, and customer.

Recurring Invoices

In some businesses, you have customers you bill the same amount every month for the same products or services. By setting up recurring entries, you can save a great deal of time entering these invoices. Even if the amount differs next time, it's helpful to have all the other information filled out for you. Then, you only have to change the amount.

Recurring entries cannot be created if you generate the invoice using a sales order.

You also can create recurring purchases, payments, and general journal entries. You can adapt the following steps for the other types of tasks.

To create recurring invoices, follow these steps:

1. **Click Tas**k**s⇨Sales/Invoicing to display the Sales/Invoicing window.**

2. **Enter the invoice information as you usually would, but do *not* enter an invoice number or click Post, Save, or Print.**

3. **Click the Rec**u**r button to display the Create Recurring Journal Entries dialog box, shown in Figure 7-9.**

Recur button

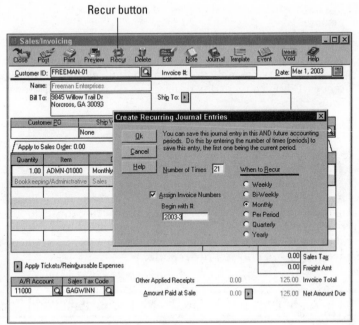

Figure 7-9:
Save data
entry time
by creating
recurring
entries.

4. **Enter the Number of Times to create the entry, including the current transaction.**

   You can enter any number up to 24. The maximum number of times depends on the transaction's original date and the current accounting period. You can enter recurring transactions only within the two open fiscal years of Peachtree Accounting.

5. **Under When to Recur, select a time frame for the recurring invoice.**

   You can choose Weekly, Bi-Weekly, Monthly, Per Period, Quarterly, or Yearly.

6. **Optionally you can assign a beginning invoice number, by clicking the Assign Invoice Numbers check box.**

   Peachtree displays a box to enter a beginning invoice number. All of the transactions are numbered incrementally. A number of our clients use a system involving the current year. For example, if you enter a transaction that starts in January 2000, you might use a starting invoice of 2000-1. Peachtree then numbers the next invoice 2000-2, and so forth.

   Peachtree doesn't automatically print recurring invoices. If you leave the invoice number blank, you can print the recurring transactions when you use Peachtree's batch printing method or edit the transaction and click Print. Chapter 14 discusses how to print batches of forms.

7. Click <u>O</u>K for Peachtree to post all transactions in the appropriate periods.

If you need to edit or delete a recurring transaction, Peachtree prompts you with the Change Recurring Journal Entries dialog box. You can edit the current invoice only or the current invoice and all future occurrences. Editing a recurring transaction does not affect previous transactions.

Reviewing Customer Reports

Peachtree offers several useful reports that you can use for listing customer information, compiling tax information, and tracking those quotes you want to turn into sales. In Tables 7-1, 7-2, and 7-3, we provide you with a description of the reports that pertain to selling your goods and services. See Chapter 15 to learn how to print reports.

Table 7-1 Reports Related to Quotes and Customers in General

Report Name	Description
Customer List	For each customer, lists the ID, name, contact name, telephone number, and resale number
Customer Master File List	Similar to Customer List, but also includes address information, tax codes, and terms
Customer Sales History	Summarizes, by customer, how much each has purchased
Prospect List	Lists each prospect with contact and telephone number
Quote Register	Lists each quote with quote date, expiration date, customer name, and quote amount
Sales Tax Codes	Lists each sales tax code with all corresponding authorities, tax rates, and vendor information

Table 7-2 Reports Related to Sales Orders

Report Name	Description
Picklist Report	Lists open sales order items such as item ID and description, quantity to ship, and warehouse location
Sales Backorder Report	Lists open order items, such as item ID, description, and quantities on order, on hand and on purchase orders
Sales Order Journal	Lists sales orders in journal entry format
Sales Order Register	Lists each sales order and its status
Sales Order Report	Lists the details of all sales orders by sales order number

Table 7-3 Reports Related to Customer Invoicing

Report Name	Description
Customer Ledgers	Shows the transactions and a running balance for each customer
Invoice Register	Lists each invoice number with date, quote number, customer name, and invoice amount
Items Sold to Customers	Lists quantity, amount, and profit of inventory items sold to customers
Sales Journal	Lists transactions as reported to the general ledger
Sales Rep Report	Lists total sales by Sales Rep ID
Taxable/Exempt Sales	Lists all taxable and exempt sales per tax authority

See Chapter 5 for information on how to use the Taxable/Exempt Sales report to pay your sales tax.

Chapter 8

Collecting the Money

. . . .

In This Chapter

▶ Receiving your customers money

▶ Tracking accounts receivable

▶ Issuing credit memos

▶ Charging finance charges

▶ Printing statements

. . . .

*O*ne of our favorite sayings is, "As much fun as I'm having doing what I'm doing . . . I'm still doing it for the money."

Most people *do* find that their preferred part of being in business is collecting the money. Peachtree not only provides you with an easy way to track the money your customers owe you, it also provides you with a few ways to encourage the customer to pay up.

Peachtree refers to the money you receive from your customers as *receipts*. That sounds logical enough, doesn't it?

Recording Receipts

Peachtree's Receipts feature allows you to enter all checks, cash, and credit card slips you receive and deposit them in your checking account. Peachtree provides two ways to account for receipts. The method you use is mostly determined through timing.

One method is used when you receive the customers' money *at the time of the sale*. You enter the receipt right on the invoice and when you print the invoice, it can also show the funds received.

The other and most commonly used method is to apply the receipt through the Receipts window. You can use this method either if the customer pays you at the time of the sale, or if the customer pays you at a later date.

Applying receipts to an invoice

Take a look at the Receipts window first to apply a receipt to a customer invoice:

1. Choose Tasks⇨Receipts to display the Receipts window.

2. Enter a Deposit Ticket ID.

The deposit ticket ID lumps receipts together for account reconciliation. If you want this transaction to be reconciled as a separate item, enter a unique deposit ticket ID. For more information about deposit ticket IDs, see the sidebar later in this section. You can find out more about Account Reconciliation in Chapter 17.

3. Select the Customer ID.

If this customer has unpaid invoices, Peachtree lists them on the Apply To Invoices tab (see Figure 8-1). If the customer has paid up, Peachtree displays the Apply To Revenue tab. In Peachtree 2002, you can drill down to see the invoice. See the appendix for details.

Pay box

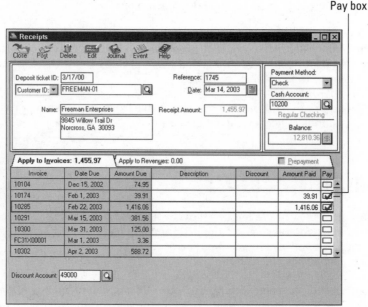

Figure 8-1: Peachtree lists the customer's unpaid invoices (and credits).

4. Enter a Reference number that helps identify the receipt.

You must enter a reference number for Receipt transactions, usually the customer's check number. If the receipt was transmitted electronically, you might enter the EFTS confirmation number or the date.

5. **Enter the Date of the receipt.**

   This refers to the date you *received* the check, not the date *on* the check.

6. **Select a Payment Method: Cash, Check, Charge, and so on.**

   You set up payment methods in the Customer Defaults screen. You can find out how to set Customer Defaults in Chapter 4. You can run some reports based on payment methods. Chapter 15 shows you how to filter reports.

7. **Verify, in the Cash Account list, the bank account into which you're depositing the receipt.**

   If you make a direct sale that doesn't require an invoice, click the Apply to Revenues tab and specify a Sales account and an amount.

8. **Check the Pay column beside each invoice being paid in full by this receipt.**

   If the amount of the receipt doesn't match the invoice amount, enter the actual amount received in the Amount Paid column.

   If the amount paid is less than the amount due, Peachtree assumes the customer still owes the difference. The next time you open the Receipts window for the customer, Peachtree displays the remainder due on the invoice.

   If the amount paid is less than the amount due and you're going to write off the difference, enter the full amount of the invoice in the amount box and then click the Apply to Revenues tab and enter a negative amount for the amount you're writing off. (Make sure the amount is not taxed.) Choose your write-off account for the G/L account. This process clears the invoice from A/R, posts the correct amount received to cash, and debits the Write Off account (because the entry is negative).

   If the amount paid is over the invoice amount, Peachtree automatically creates a credit balance against the specified invoice. The next time you display the Receipts window for this customer, you see a credit balance. If you're going to absorb the overpayment (usually for small amounts), click the invoice as paid in full and then click the Apply to Revenues tab and enter the overpayment amount. This clears the transaction from Accounts Receivable.

   The amount Peachtree displays in the Receipt Amount box should match the total amount received from your customer.

9. **Click Post or Save to record the receipt.**

The Receipts window also gives you a handy way to write off an entire invoice as a bad debt. In the Receipts window, enter a unique reference number that helps identify the receipt as a write-off. For example, we typically use the letters WO (for write-off) or BD (for bad debt) and the original invoice number as the reference number (BD12345). Click the Cash Account

What's a deposit ticket ID?

Peachtree uses deposit ticket IDs to make account reconciliation easier to manage. You should assign the same deposit ticket ID to all transactions that you deposit on the same deposit ticket. All receipts that use the same deposit ticket ID appear as one lump sum in account reconciliation.

By default, Peachtree automatically enters the deposit ticket ID as a representation of the current date. The date is not an actual deposit date, and this method may not be appropriate for the way you do business. It depends on how and when you actually make your bank deposits.

Suppose you go to the bank daily, perhaps March 16th. Using Peachtee's default method, all transactions you enter into Peachtree that same day would have a deposit ticket ID of 3/16/00. If you receive five checks for a total of $1,525.32, when you move to the Account Reconciliation screen, Peachtree displays a reference of 3/16/00 for $1,525.32. So far, no problem.

The problem arises if you receive checks daily, enter them into Peachtree daily, but do not go to the bank until you've accumulated several days worth of checks. The following list illustrates what happens if we split the receipt dates of the five checks totaling $1525.32:

Date	Check Amount	Deposit Ticket ID
March 16	$125.75	3/16/00
March 16	$28.41	3/16/00
March 17	$722.01	3/17/00
March 18	$549.10	3/18/00
March 18	$100.05	3/18/00

When you go to the bank you make one deposit of $1,525.32 (which also is the amount that appears on your bank statement). However, in the Account Reconciliation window, Peachtree displays the following three transactions:

3/16/00	$154.16
3/17/00	$722.01
3/18/00	$649.15

Using the default deposit ticket ID, you'd have to sit and figure out which transactions match up to total the ones listed on your bank statement. Complicate this scenario by adding lots of receipts, and you can see the dilemma.

Okay, we've discovered the problem, now how can we remedy it, you ask? Again, it depends on your banking methods. If you have a routine where you go to the bank only on Fridays, for example, then, when you enter the receipts, use Friday's date as the deposit ticket ID.

However, if you hold your checks until whenever you're good and ready to go to the bank, try this method:

Take your bank deposit ticket book and sequentially number each deposit slip. As you enter your daily receipts, use the number on the top deposit slip as your deposit ticket ID. When you're preparing your deposit for the bank, you tear out the top ticket, leaving the next deposit ticket number exposed and ready to enter for the next batch of checks. Using this method allows Peachtree to lump the receipts together for easier account reconciliation.

box to select the Bad Debt Expense account. Click the Pay check box for the invoice you wish to write off as a bad debt and then click Post. The transaction gets cleared from Account Receivable and increases the Bad Debt Expense account.

Our clients frequently ask, "Can I print a copy of this receipt for my customer?" The answer is no. Sorry.

In Peachtree 2002, you can print the receipt. You also can print a deposit ticket report based on receipts you enter. See the appendix for details.

Entering receipts from nonestablished customers

Occasionally, you receive money from a customer you haven't invoiced. If the customer isn't set up in your Customer list, you can still record a receipt.

The procedure is the same as applying receipts to an invoice, except you won't enter a Customer ID. Skip this field and enter the customer's name in the Name text box. Because you haven't entered an invoice for this customer, Peachtree displays the Apply to Revenues tab. Enter the sales account and the receipt amount, as shown in Figure 8-2, and then Post the transaction.

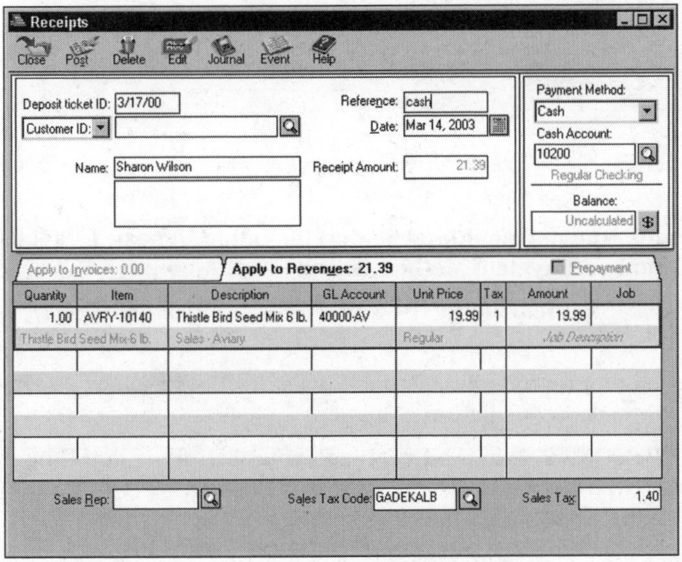

Figure 8-2:
Recording receipts for nonestablished customers.

Applying receipts at the time of sale

You can also apply a receipt by recording it at the time of sale as you create the invoice. You can see how to create an invoice in Chapter 7. Using this method allows Peachtree to print the amount received on the invoice.

To apply a receipt at the time of the sale, follow these steps:

1. **Set up the invoice in the Tasks⇨Sales/Invoicing window.**

2. **Click the Amount Paid at Sale button to display the Receive Payment dialog box, as shown in Figure 8-3.**

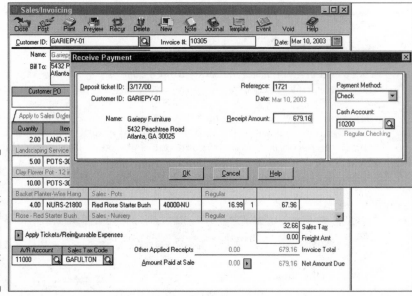

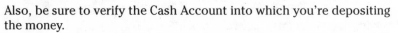

Figure 8-3:
Enter
receipt
information
in the
Receive
Payment
window.

3. **Enter the payment information including Deposit Ticket ID, Reference number, Payment Method, and Receipt Amount.**

   Also, be sure to verify the Cash Account into which you're depositing the money.

   Don't forget to enter a deposit ticket ID that ties your deposits together for bank reconciliation.

4. **Click OK to close the Receive Payment window and then Post or Save the transaction.**

Boing! Handling Bounced Checks

One of those nasty facts of life, now and then, is that customers write us bad checks, sometimes by accident, and sometimes not. In Peachtree, you handle checks returned for nonsufficient funds (NSF) in two steps:

1. **Create and post a new invoice to charge the customer the NSF fees.**

2. **Create a receipt and apply a negative amount for the same amount as the original check.**

   For example, suppose the original (bounced) check is for $82.10. In the example you see in Figure 8-4, we create a NSF invoice number 23501NSF for $20.00. Then, on the receipt window, we apply a negative $82.10 against the open invoice.

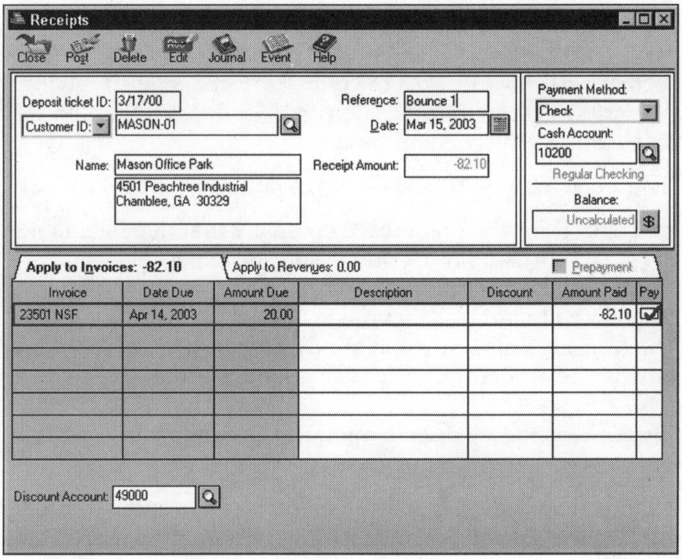

Figure 8-4:
Create a negative receipt to adjust your bank balance.

Two things happen in Step 2. Peachtree updates the customer balance for the money he or she now owes again against the original invoice and corrects the bank account balance.

Finally, Peachtree creates a new receipt when the customer writes you a second check or instructs you to redeposit the original check. If the customer writes a second check for the original amount plus the NSF fee, Peachtree clears the invoice in full. If however, the customer instructs you to redeposit the original check, Peachtree enters the amount of the check only. After all, they still owe you the NSF fee.

We really hope you don't have to use this section of our book.

Handling Credit Card Receipts

If your business accepts credit card payments from customers, you can enter and track these transactions in Peachtree Accounting. Assuming (we know, we know, there we go again) you have to wait for that time lapse before you receive the money from the credit card company, you can begin recording credit card transactions in Peachtree Accounting, but you need the following first:

- ✔ One (or more) G/L accounts in your Chart of Accounts to use for the credit card receivable amount. To obtain this, create an account in the Accounts Receivable area of your Chart of Accounts, giving it an ID and a description to identify it, such as VISA Receivable. Choose Accounts Receivable as the account type.

  Chapter 3 shows you how to create new accounts.

- ✔ A vendor ID for the credit card company that deposits money. This way you can record and track processing fee expenses.

To record a credit card transaction, you must follow two sets of steps, one when the transaction occurs and another when you know the credit card company has deposited the money in your account.

1. **Choose Tasks➪Receipts to open the Receipts window (refer to Figure 8-1).**

   When you record credit card receipts, always enter customer payments using Tasks➪Receipts. You can apply the customer credit card receipts to open invoices or to revenue. You cannot manage credit card receipts effectively when using the Amount Paid field in Sales/Invoicing.

2. **Record the receipt information.**

   Use the techniques shown in the "Applying receipts to an invoice" section or the "Entering receipts from non-established customers" section earlier in this chapter. *However,* you must use this exception: Enter the credit card receivable G/L account as the Cash account.

3. **To keep the customer's ledger accurate and up-to-date, record the amount paid in the Receipts window as the Full amount of the credit card charge, regardless of how the bank handles processing fees.**

   You add the processing fees as an expense when your bank statement arrives.

After the credit card company has notified you that the money has been deposited into your account, you need to create another receipt that transfers the funds from the credit card receivable account to your bank account.

1. **Create a receipt in the Tasks⇨Receipts window just like any other Peachtree receipt, with the following exceptions:**

   • Skip the customer ID field and enter the credit card company name in the Name field. Because you're not using a customer ID, Peachtree automatically displays the Apply to Revenues tab.

   • On the line item G/L Account field, enter the Credit Card Receivable account number.

2. **Post or save the transaction as usual.**

Giving Credit Where Credit Is Due

Unfortunately, sometimes, (and hopefully, infrequently), your products get returned, or you need to make an adjustment to a customer invoice. In these situations, you need to create a credit memo to reduce the amount of money your customer owes. If you owe money to a customer for overpayment or because you apply a credit memo to an invoice, you can write a check to the customer for the refund amount you owe.

Creating a credit memo

To Peachtree, a credit memo is simply a negative invoice. (Refer to Chapter 7 to discover how to create invoices.) You enter a credit memo in almost the same manner you create a regular invoice, except you need to make these adjustments:

✔ Enter noninventory items as negative currency amounts, with a leading minus sign (–). The total of the invoice becomes a negative amount.

✔ Enter negative quantities for returned inventory items. The amount is calculated as a negative. Peachtree returns the goods to inventory and, if applicable, adjusts cost of goods.

The credit memo must have an invoice number to be later reconciled in the Receipts window. We recommend you use the original invoice number, if there is one, with the letters CM at the beginning or end. For example, if the returned goods were originally billed on invoice 1234, you might number the credit memo CM1234 or 1234CM. You may want to include a line describing why the credit memo is being issued (returned, damaged, adjustment, and so on). You can print the credit memo; just click the Print button.

For information on how to customize forms, see Chapter 14.

If the credit memo is for the exact amount of an invoice, you need to apply them together to update the Accounts Receivable accounts.

1. **Choose Tasks⇨Receipts to display the Receipts window.**

2. **Select the customer ID.**

   The credit memo appears in the invoice listing along with the original invoice.

3. **Click the Pay check box for both the invoice and the credit memo.**

   The amount of the receipt displays zero (0.00). Therefore, no money is being applied to the general ledger.

4. **Enter a receipt reference number.**

   For example, you might use the credit memo number or the invoice number.

5. **Click Post or Save.**

   Both transactions clear from Accounts Receivables.

Issuing refund checks for a credit memo

If you owe money to a customer for overpayment or because you applied a credit memo to an invoice, you can write a check to the customer for the refund amount owed.

Issuing a refund check is actually a two-step process. First, you write the check from the Payments window, and then you apply the check and credit memo or overpayment together in the Receipts window. This process is based on the assumption that you've already created a credit memo or applied the overpayment. See the previous two sections for more information.

Although Peachtree's new Write Checks feature is similar to Payments, you cannot issue a check to a customer (and have it tie back to Accounts Receivable) from the Write Checks window. So, don't write the refund check from the Write Checks window. Instead, follow these steps to issue a refund:

1. **Click Tasks⇨Payments to display the Payments window.**

2. **Choose Customer ID from the first drop-down list indicating that the check goes to a customer rather than a vendor (see Figure 8-5).**

3. **Choose the Customer ID of the customer receiving your refund.**

   As with generating A/P checks, don't enter a Check Number if you're going to have Peachtree print the check for you. Enter a check number only if you're (heaven forbid) hand writing checks.

4. Verify the check **D**ate and Cash Account from which you are writing the check.

5. On the Apply to Customer Account tab, enter a description for the refund like the one you see in Figure 8-5.

6. Enter or select the G/L account to which you want to post the refund amount.

   Typically, this is your Accounts Receivable account.

7. Enter the amount of the refund, and print the check as you would print any Accounts Payable check.

   If you're not going to actually print the check, click Po**s**t.

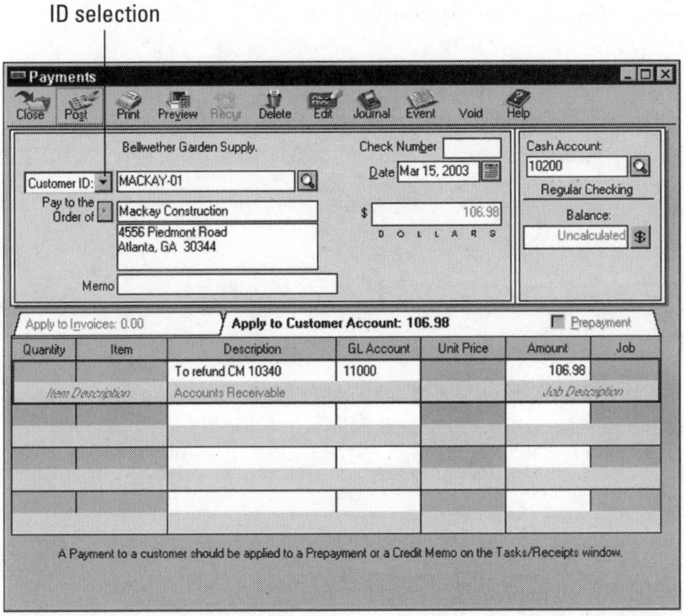

ID selection

Figure 8-5:
After you select Customer ID from the drop-down list, Peachtree displays customer IDs in the lookup list box.

Next, you need to apply the refund check to the credit memo or overpayment. You use the same method as when you apply a credit memo to an invoice.

1. From the Tas**k**s⇨**R**eceipts window, select the customer ID.

   The credit memo appears in the invoice listing along with the refund check.

2. Click the Pay check box for both the credit memo and refund check.

   The amount of the receipt displays zero (0.00). Therefore, no money is being applied to the general ledger.

3. **Enter a receipt reference number such as the check number you wrote to the customer.**

4. **Click Po̲st or S̲ave.**

   Both transactions clear from Accounts Receivables.

Entering Finance Charges

Sometimes you want to nudge your customers into paying their bills on time by charging them a late fee or a finance charge if they pay later than the due date. Peachtree can calculate finance charges for all customers who have not been excluded from finance charges and who do meet the filter criteria you determine when it's time to apply the finance charges.

If you have customers who you *don't* want to charge finance charges, you must alter the default terms for that customer. In the Maintain Customers/Prospects window, click the Terms button on the Sales Defaults tab. Then, remove the check from the Use Standard Terms and the Apply Finance Charge boxes.

How do finance charges work?

Just who does Peachtree charge finance charges? Well, only customers who have a check in the Apply Finance Charge box, mentioned in the preceding paragraph. Okay, that's obvious, but *then* who gets charged finance charges?

Peachtree calculates finance charges using the following formula for *each* overdue invoice:

```
Finance Charge = Number of Days Past Due multiplied by The
                 Daily Rate multiplied by The Outstanding Invoice
                 Amount
```

The formula uses these definitions:

✔ Number of Days Past Due is the number of days between the date that you calculate finance charges and one of the following:

- The invoice date if aging is set to Invoice Date in Customer Default Information.

- The due date if aging is set to Due Date in Customer Default Information.

- The date of the last finance charge calculation.

- Daily rate is the percentage you set divided by 365 days.

To clarify this, consider an example: Today is July 15, and you want to calculate charges for an invoice dated 5/1/00 (due 5/31/00) in the amount of $200.00.

Your company charges an 18 percent finance charge for invoices 30 days overdue. You age your customer invoices by due date.

First, the invoice is overdue by 44 days (From May 31 to July 15).

```
(.18/365) x 44 x 200.00 = 4.34
```

The .18/365 is the annual percentage rate divided by 365 days. Multiply that by the 44 days the invoice is past due, and then multiply that times the $200.00 invoice amount. Therefore, a finance charge applied on 7/15/00 would be $4.34.

Who and how much does Peachtree charge?

Chapter 4 shows you how to set up the finance charge default information. Here, we'll review your defaults to see the figures Peachtree uses to calculate finance charges.

Click Maintain⇨Default Information⇨Customers to display the Customer Defaults dialog box and then click the Finance Charges tab. You need to make sure you've selected the following settings:

- ✔ The Charge Finance Charge box must be checked.

- ✔ Enter the number of days overdue. The invoice needs to be overdue before you charge finance charges. This safeguard allows a grace period for your customers, but it also depends on the method you use to age invoices: by invoice date or due date.

- ✔ Some companies charge two different percentage rates — one percentage rate for past due invoices under a certain amount and another percentage rate for past due invoices over a certain dollar amount. If you are charging two different rates, enter the ceiling amount in the Up To text box. If you're not using two different rates, you leave the default entry of $10,000.

- ✔ Enter an *annual* percentage interest rate. If you are using two different rates, this one is for amounts that are up to the amount you enter in the Up To box. Enter the rate as a regular number. For example, if you charge 18.5 percent, enter 18.5 in the rate box.

- ✔ Enter an annual interest rate for amounts higher than the Up To entry box. If you charge only one interest rate, this rate is the same as the first percentage you enter.

✔ Optionally, enter a minimum finance charge amount. If the calculated amount is less than the minimum, Peachtree increases the amount to the minimum you specify here.

Suppose that your company charges your customers a $5.00 per month late fee, regardless of the invoice dollar amount. To make Peachtree apply the charge for you, set the percentage amounts to .01 percent. (That's one tenth of a percent — the calculation doesn't work if you enter just a zero, so you have to enter something.) Enter a minimum charge of $5.00.

✔ Select Charge Interest on Finance Charges if you want to compound late charges.

✔ Select a G/L account to apply the finance charges. (Typically, an income account.)

Peachtree Version 8 allows you to choose how the finance charge appears on the statement.

✔ Select to have your statement print the phrase `Late Charge` or `Finance Charge` as a description.

After you have your defaults customized, click OK to close the Customer Default dialog box.

Applying finance charges

Okay, now that you understand how the finance charge process works, you can actually apply the charges.

When you determine to apply a finance charge, Peachtree creates but does not print an invoice for the amount due. The charges do appear on customer statements, so you need to apply finance charges before you print customer statements.

1. **Click Tasks⇨Finance Charge to display the Calculate Finance Charges dialog box.**

2. **Optionally, select a range of customers for whom you want to calculate finance charges.**

   If you leave the options blank, Peachtree assumes you want to calculate charges on all eligible customers (by way of the Charge Finance Charges check box).

3. **Enter the date you want Peachtree Accounting to use to calculate finance charges and then click OK.**

   The Apply Finance Charges dialog box appears.

4. **If you'd like to review the finance charges before Peachtree actually applies them, click No to Apply Finance Charges.**

   If you'd prefer to just go ahead and apply the charges, click Yes to the Apply Finance Charges section dialog box.

   You can review finance charges before applying, but you need to repeat these steps to actually apply the charges.

5. **Choose a Report Destination: Screen or Printer and then click OK.**

   The Finance Charge Report Selection appears. You don't *have* to print the report, but we recommend that you do.

6. **Click OK to print the report in detail.**

7. **If you elected to review the charges before Peachtree applied them, repeat Steps 1 through 6 but choose Yes in Step 4.**

   Peachtree applies the actual finance charges to the customer.

   The finance charge entries are generated with a reference number that begins with the letters FC (for Finance Charge). Therefore, never enter a customer invoice with a reference number that begins with FC, or Peachtree uses this transaction when recalculating finance charges.

Producing Statements

Before you print statements the first time, you may want to determine statement default preferences. Choose Maintain⇨Default Information⇨ Statements/Invoices to display the Statement/Invoices Defaults dialog box. For statements to print, you must select at least one of the check boxes in the Print Statements for Customer Accounts With section.

In the Statement/Invoices Defaults dialog box, specify

- ✔ The minimum customer balance necessary to print a statement.
- ✔ Whether to print statements to those customers with negative or zero balances.
- ✔ Whether to print your company name, address, phone, and fax number.

Select your preferences and click OK.

Now you're ready to have Peachtree print customer statements. The fastest method is to use Peachtree's Navigation Aid.

To print statements, follow these steps:

1. Click the Sales tab on the Navigation Aid, as shown in Figure 8-6.

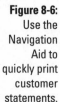

Sales tab   Customer Statement

Figure 8-6:
Use the
Navigation
Aid to
quickly print
customer
statements.

2. Click Customer Statements.

If you don't have the Navigation Aid available, use the menu. Choose
Reports⇨Accounts Receivable. Scroll down the Accounts Receivable
report list until you see a folder marked Customer Statements and
double-click the folder.

3. Double-click a form to print.

The Statement dialog box appears.

**4. Choose from one of the two statement types: Balance Forward or
Open Item.**

- Balance Forward statements consolidate a customer's unpaid balance from month to month. The total balance from the previous
statement is shown as a single balance forward amount, and any
new invoices or receipts display beneath it (sort of like the credit
card statements you receive each month).

- Open Item statements do not consolidate open invoices on the
next statement. Peachtree lists each invoice, and shows receipts
against the invoice for either full or partial payment in the time
since the last statement.

5. Select a statement date.

6. **Optionally, select a From and To Customer ID or Customer Type and then click OK to print the statements.**

When the statements finish printing, you see a message box that asks if they printed properly. When you click Yes, Peachtree records the statement date in the customer record, which is then used as the balance forward date the next time you print statements.

Reporting on Money Your Customers Owe

Although Peachtree can't guarantee that you make a profit every month, it does give you some ways to show yourself (or your investors) your various financial reports. We're sure you especially like to track the money you're taking in to plan your budget or keep your banker happy. So, in Table 8-1, we provide you with a description of the reports that pertain to collecting your money.

See Chapter 15 to learn how to print reports.

Table 8-1	Reports Related to Collecting Your Money
Report Name	*Description*
Aged Receivables	Lists each customer with their outstanding invoices or credits in aging categories.
Cash Receipts Journal	Lists the date, amount, description, and general ledger account number of all receipt transactions created during a specified period.

Chapter 9

Paid Employees Are Happy Employees

● ●

In This Chapter

▶ Setting up employee defaults

▶ Writing and printing paychecks

▶ Paying commissions or bonuses

● ●

They call it *work* for a reason, some people say. And we can't think of too many people who are willing to work without being paid. If you aren't using an outside payroll service, then you may want to consider using Peachtree's payroll features.

Peachtree's payroll features mimic the functions you perform when you prepare payroll checks by hand. But, after you've set up basic background information for each employee (yes, you still need to know the employee's gross wages and number of exemptions), we think that preparing payroll in Peachtree is much easier and faster than preparing payroll checks manually. Why? Because you don't need to look up payroll taxes in the Circular E flyer, and you don't need to subtract the taxes to determine the net payroll check. Furthermore, you don't need to keep track of the payroll tax liability amounts you, as the employer, must pay. And, if you allow Peachtree to print the checks, you don't need to write them. In this chapter, we show you how to set up your employees and produce paychecks.

Even if you prepare payroll in Peachtree, you're going to have questions about handling various types of situations. The Circular E booklet that you get from the government every December is your bible for payroll questions. If you don't understand the Circular E, contact your accountant.

If you use an outside payroll service, you may want to consider using Peachtree's payroll features to keep your general ledger up-to-date. That way, you can accurately report your company's financial picture. If your outside payroll service provides you with journal entries, you can ignore Peachtree's payroll features and simply enter the journal entries (see Chapter 18). However, if your outside payroll service doesn't provide you with journal entries, you may want to use Peachtree's payroll features to match your records with theirs.

Understanding Payroll Basics

Before you start setting up employees and paying them, you really need to consider some basic information: whom you pay and when you should start using payroll in Peachtree.

Peachtree uses *payroll tax tables* to calculate the amounts you deduct for taxes (Federal Income Tax, Social Security, Medicare, and so on). Effective with Peachtree 8, Peachtree Software Company is instituting a new policy: They will *not* be shipping tax tables that calculate federal taxes with the software. To accurately calculate payroll, you must either subscribe to Peachtree's Payroll Tax Table Update service or create your own tax tables. To order tax table updates, call 1-800-336-1420 Monday through Friday, 8:30 a.m. to 5:30 p.m. eastern standard time.

Employees and sales representatives . . .

We should begin by clarifying that, in this chapter, we're talking about paying people who work for you. You can rule out vendors for this discussion. Vendors don't work for you — they just provide you with goods or services. We're not talking about vendors because you pay vendors from the Payments, Write Checks, or Select for Payment window, as you do in Chapter 6.

Both employees and sales representatives work for you. As you see in this chapter, you pay employees from the Select for Payroll window or the Payroll Entry window. Although employees are always employees, sales reps might be employees, or they might be independent contractors. So, the window(s) in Peachtree that you use to pay sales reps depends on their employment status: employee or independent contractor.

If you are uncertain about an individual's status, check with your accountant.

Employees work for you, so, in this chapter, we're talking about them. And sales representatives who are also employees work for you, so we're talking about them. We aren't talking about sales representatives who you treat as independent contractors; you pay them as 1099 vendors from the Payments,

Write Checks, or Select for Payments windows. See Chapter 5 for information on designating a vendor as a 1099 vendor. See Chapter 6 for information on paying vendors.

Most sales reps, whether they are employees or independent contractors, earn commissions. If you want to track commissions to make paying sales reps easier, you need to specifically identify sales reps (both employees and independent contractors) in Peachtree. Interestingly, Peachtree has you set up a sales representative in the same window where you set up employees, even though the sales representative might be an independent contractor and not an employee.

So, of course, being the logical individual that you are, you ask, "If a sales rep *isn't* an employee, *why* should I set up a sales rep in the same window where I set up employees?" Peachtree has you set up sales reps in the Maintain Employees/Sales Reps window for two related reasons:

✔ If you set up sales representatives in the Maintain Employees/Sales Reps window, you can include the sales rep on invoices.

✔ If you include a sales rep on an invoice, you can produce the Sales Rep report, which shows commissioned and noncommissioned sales amounts per sales rep.

Including a sales rep on an invoice *does not* automatically generate a commission amount for the sales rep. The inventory items sold on the invoice must be subject to commission. In the section "Writing and Printing Payroll Checks" in this chapter, we tell you how to pay sales representatives who are also employees. In the section "Determining commission amounts," you see a sample of the Sales Rep report. See Chapter 7 for more information about including sales representatives on invoices. See Chapter 11 for information on making an inventory item subject to commission.

When should you start to use payroll?

You can start using Payroll at any time during a calendar year, but you may find it easiest to start using Payroll on January 1. Why? Because, if you start using Payroll on January 1, you won't have to enter any beginning balance information — information to account for paychecks you've already produced this year that need to be included on payroll tax forms and W-2s at the end of the year.

If you can't start using Payroll on January 1, try to start on the first day of any payroll quarter: January 1, April 1, July 1, or October 1. Payroll tax laws require that you file payroll tax returns quarterly, and you need to include information only for the current quarter. So, if you start using Payroll at the beginning of a quarter, you can enter beginning balance information as lump sums for each quarter of the current year in which you've produced payroll checks.

As a final resort, if you can't start using Payroll on the first day of any payroll quarter, then start using Payroll on the first day of a month. You need to enter beginning balance information for the other months in the current payroll quarter, but you can enter quarterly amounts for other payroll quarters of the current year in which you've produced payroll checks.

Working with Employee Information

In Chapter 4, we show you how to set up payroll default information for your company. After you have the default information in place, you need to set up your employees, establishing specific information for each of them. For example, different employees claim different withholding exemptions. And, some employees may participate in a company retirement plan, but others may not. Or, some, but not all, may receive a health insurance benefit. To set up employees, choose Maintain⇨Employees/Sales Reps. Peachtree displays the General tab of the Maintain Employees/Sales Reps window (see Figure 9-1).

Withholding information   Type field

Figure 9-1:
Just as
you might
expect,
you supply
general
employee
information
on the
General tab
of the
Maintain
Employees/
Sales Reps
window.

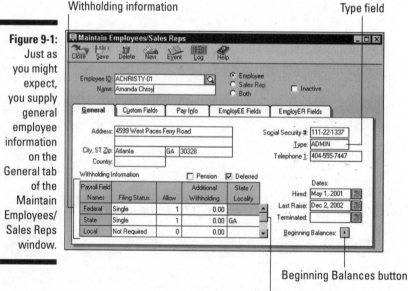

Beginning Balances button

Scrollbar to see additional fields

At the top of the window — not associated with any of the tabs in the window — you assign an ID and type in a name. Notice that you can set up each person as an employee, a sales rep, or both. Typically, you deduct payroll taxes for employees, and you don't deduct payroll taxes for sales representatives. If you select Sales Rep, three of the five tabs in the window become gray, and the individual doesn't appear in the Payroll windows when you are paying employees. Choose Both if the individual is both a sales representative and an employee.

Because the window has five tabs, we discuss the tabs individually.

General employee information

You use the General tab (refer to Figure 9-1) of the Maintain Employees/Sales Reps window to give Peachtree general information about each employee — things like the employee's name, address, and social security number (you need those when you produce W-2s at the end of the year). You also provide withholding information in the lower-left corner of the window: the employee's marital status and the number of exemptions he or she claims for federal, state, and local withholding. Notice in Figure 9-1 that the first three payroll fields in the Withholding Information section appear, but that you can scroll down to find additional payroll fields.

On the right side of the tab, you supply additional personal information about the employee, much of which is self-explanatory (that is, social security number, telephone number, date of hire, and so on). Peachtree provides the Type field to give you a way to group employees. In Peachtree 2002, you can store employee e-mail addresses. See the appendix for details.

The Type field can be particularly useful if your company pays worker's compensation insurance. You might want to use the worker's compensation categories in the Type field to make it easier to produce a report that helps you pay your worker's compensation liability.

In the lower-right corner of the tab, you see the Beginning Balances button. Click this button if you are starting Payroll on any day other than January 1 and you have already produced paychecks in the current year. Peachtree displays the Employee Beginning Balances window (see Figure 9-2).

Use the boxes in this window to enter payroll amounts you've paid already this year. You specify the pay period each column represents; a column can represent a pay period, a month, or a quarter, or even multiple quarters. For example, suppose that you want to start entering payroll as of July 1, which is the beginning of the third payroll quarter. In the Beginning Balances window, you can enter one column of numbers that represents all the payroll amounts you've paid for the first six months (two quarters) of the year.

Although you can enter amounts for each pay period, we don't recommend that approach simply because it's cumbersome and time-consuming.

At the top of each column you intend to use, type the ending date of the time-frame represented by the amounts. Then, in the boxes below the date, type in the appropriate amounts for each payroll field, entering deductions as negative amounts and earnings as positive amounts. Based on the information in Figure 9-2, we're starting Payroll on May 1. In the first column we include the quarterly amount for the first quarter of the year. In the second column, we include the monthly amount for April, the first month of the second quarter.

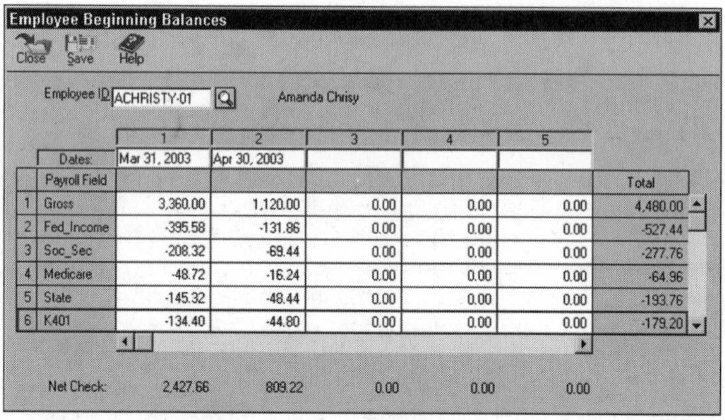

Figure 9-2:
Record amounts for paychecks you've written this year prior to using Peachtree.

Click the Save button when you finish, and Peachtree redisplays the Maintain Employees/Sales Reps window.

Custom fields

If you choose Maintain⇨Default Information⇨Employees, you can view the screen where you establish the custom fields that appear in the Maintain Employees/Sales Reps window. When you click the Custom Fields tab, you can type the appropriate information for the employee in each custom field box. Custom field information is optional.

Payroll information

On the Pay Info tab of the Maintain Employees/Sales Reps window (see Figure 9-3), you tell Peachtree the method and frequency you use to pay the employee. We cover both of these in this section, starting with frequencies.

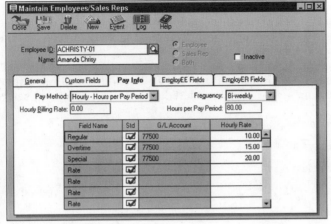

Figure 9-3:
Tell
Peachtree
how often to
pay your
employees.

Setting payroll frequency

Peachtree allows you to pay your employees using any of five frequencies:

✔ Weekly

✔ Bi-weekly

✔ Semi-monthly

✔ Monthly

✔ Annually

You don't need to pay all your employees using the same frequency; that is, you can pay some employees weekly, some bi-weekly, and some monthly. The choice is yours. Most companies tend to pay all employees at the same time, but Peachtree doesn't have that requirement.

Determining pay method

Pay methods tell Peachtree how to calculate wages — and you set up the pay methods your company uses in Chapter 4. When you open the Pay Method list box (click the drop-down arrow to the right of the box), you see that you can choose Salary, Hourly – Hours per Pay Period, or Hourly – Time Ticket Hours:

✔ Choose Salary to pay your employees a flat rate, regardless of the number of hours they work in a pay period.

✔ Choose Hourly – Hours per Pay Period to pay your employees based on hours they work in a pay period.

✔ Choose Hourly – Time Ticket Hours to pay your employees based on Time Tickets they submit.

You use Time Tickets when you intend to bill your customers for the time your employees work on projects for them. You can, but don't have to, pay employees based on the Time Tickets they submit. You can find out more about this pay method in Chapter 10.

When you choose Hourly – Hours per Pay Period, Peachtree displays the standard number of hours associated with the frequency you select:

- ✔ Frequency: Standard Hours
- ✔ Weekly: 40
- ✔ Bi-weekly: 80
- ✔ Semi-monthly: 88
- ✔ Monthly: 176
- ✔ Annually: 2112

Last, you indicate the amount, per pay period, that you want to pay the employee. In Figure 9-3, we're paying the employee time-and-a-half for overtime, and double-time for special occasions (maybe Sundays). For salaried employees, you typically don't see an Overtime field.

Employee fields

You really need to understand only one thing about EmployEE Fields tab of the Maintain Employees/Sales Reps window (see Figure 9-4). You use it to indicate anything about the employee that *doesn't* follow the defaults you set up for the company back in Chapter 4.

For example, you may change the G/L Account to send wages to a different account than the default account. Or, as in Figure 9-4, Amanda doesn't participate in the company's 401(k) plan. Therefore, we removed the checks from the STD column (STD represents *standard,* as in the company default) and also from the Calc column.

You remove the check from the STD column so that Peachtree allows you to remove the check from the Calc column. What's the Calc column? Well, when you place a check in the Calc column, Peachtree expects to use a payroll tax table to calculate the amount for the field. You remove the check from the Calc column under two conditions:

- ✔ When you're not going to use a calculation to figure the amount for the employee; instead, you want to supply a fixed amount in the Amount column.
- ✔ When you don't want to calculate the field for the employee at all.

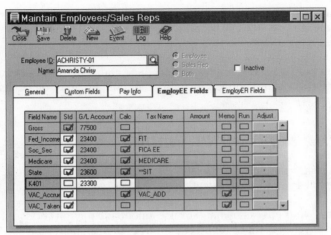

Figure 9-4:
Use this tab
to indicate
any
nonstandard
information
about
employee
fields for the
selected
employee.

If the employee's calculation is different from the standard (default) calculation, and you remove the check from the STD column, but you don't remove the check from the Calc column, select a different calculation for the employee by clicking in the Tax Name column and selecting a different calculation from the lookup list.

If you don't intend to calculate the field for the employee at all, you must remove the checks from both the STD column and the Calc column, or Peachtree still calculates an amount based on the formula in the payroll tax table.

Employer fields

Like its counter part, the EmployER Fields tab in the Maintain Employees/ Sales Reps window closely resembles the same tab in the Employee Defaults dialog box — and for the same reason. Peachtree gets the information it displays in the Maintain Employees/Sales Reps window from the information you enter in the Employee Defaults dialog box.

You need to understand the same thing about the EmployER Fields tab that we say about the EmployEE tab: You use it to indicate anything about the employee that *doesn't* follow the defaults you set up for the company.

Writing and Printing Payroll Checks

Now you come to the part that your employees like most — the part where you produce paychecks. Peachtree enables you to pay employees en masse or one at a time; we discuss both methods. Typically, you pay groups of employees at the same time, so we think you can make more use of the group method.

We recommend that you let Peachtree print paychecks for you. You can save *lots* of time, and reduce the possibility of introducing errors because you won't be typing in information.

In this section, we show you how to produce and print paychecks and how to pay commissions and bonuses — two other common payroll needs.

Paying a group of employees

Paying a group of employees is similar to paying a group of vendors. This process walks you through selecting employees to pay and printing paychecks.

If you write your checks by hand or use an outside payroll service, plan to print the paychecks that Peachtree produces to plain paper because Peachtree posts the information to the general ledger when you print the checks.

Follow these steps:

1. **Choose Tasks⇨Select for Payroll Entry.**

   Peachtree displays the Select Employees – Filter Selection dialog box you see in Figure 9-5. Use this dialog box to select the majority of employees you want to pay.

   Try to make the selection include everyone you want to pay, even if the selection includes more people than you intend to pay. After you make choices in this dialog box, you have another opportunity to exclude employees.

2. **In the Pay End Date box, select the date that represents the last day of the pay period.**

3. **In the Include Pay Frequencies section, check the boxes that represent the pay frequencies you want to include.**

   For example, include employees you pay weekly. As you can see from the dialog box, you can include all pay frequencies; if you don't have any monthly or annual employees, you can leave the boxes checked without affecting anything.

4. **In the Include Pay Methods section, choose to pay hourly employees, salaried employees, or both.**

5. **Use the Include Employees section to limit the range of employees you pay.**

   If you want to pay all employees who meet the other criteria you establish in this dialog box, simply choose All Employees. Otherwise, select the first employee you want to include in the From box. Then, in the To box, select the last employee you want to include.

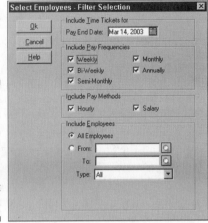

Figure 9-5:
Use this
dialog
box to
identify the
employees
you want
to pay.

6. **Click OK, and Peachtree displays the Select Employees to Pay window (see Figure 9-6).**

If you don't like the selection you see, click the Select toolbar button to redisplay the Select Employees – Filter Selection dialog box (refer to Figure 9-5).

Figure 9-6:
Use this
window to
confirm that
the payroll
checks
you're about
to print are
the ones
you want to
produce.

Employee ID	Employee Name	Check Amount	Field Names	Hours	Salary	#Weeks	Pay
ACHRISTY-01	Amanda Chrisy	774.22	Regular	80.00		2	☐
			Overtime				☐
			Special				☐
AKORNYLAK-01	Alex Kornylak	810.06	Regular	80.00		2	☑
			Overtime				☐
			Special				☐
DBECKSTROM-01	Dorothy Beckstrom	470.77	Regular	60.00		2	☑
			Overtime				☐
			Special				☐

The Select Employees to Pay dialog box has some options to keep in mind:

✔ An asterisk next to an employee's name signifies that you've set up the employee's pay method as Hourly – Time Ticket Hours — and that employee's paycheck is based on the number of Time Ticket hours in the current pay period. Find out more about Time Tickets in Chapter 10.

✔ An (e) next to an employee's name signifies that you've set up the employee to use electronic time and attendance.

✔ You can change the number of hours worked for hourly employees or the salary for salaried employees; Peachtree recalculates the check amount.

✔ You can change the number of weeks in the pay period. Typically, you see 1, 2, 12, or 52; these numbers indicate the frequency with which you pay employees (weekly, bi-weekly or semi-monthly, monthly, or annually). Changing the number of weeks in the pay period affects the pay period beginning date on the paycheck stub. Peachtree calculates the beginning date by subtracting the number of weeks from the Pay Period Ending Date.

Starting in Peachtree 8, you can print the Pay Period Beginning Date on a paycheck stub. You need to customize the payroll check form to add the field. See Chapter 14 for information on customizing forms.

✔ You can avoid paying an employee by removing the check from the Pay column.

Viewing the details

You can view and make changes to the details of any employee's check. Highlight the employee and click Detail on the toolbar. Peachtree displays the Select Employees to Pay – Detail window. When you finish, click OK to redisplay the Select Employees to Pay window.

Don't change Social Security or Medicare amounts. If you do, you'll find discrepancies on your payroll tax reports, and the 941 quarterly payroll tax return won't be accurate. You can, however, change Federal Income Tax and state income tax with no side effects. Make changes to the hours/salary first and the taxes second, or Peachtree won't make your tax changes.

Allocating time to Jobs

If you use Jobs and want to allocate an employee's time to various Jobs, follow the steps in "Paying a group of employees" to display the Select Employees to Pay window. Then follow these steps:

1. **Highlight the employee in the Select Employees to Pay window.**

2. **Click the Jobs button to display the Labor Distribution To Jobs window (see Figure 9-7).**

3. **Click in the Job column on the line displaying the type of pay you want to allocate — Regular, Overtime, or Special — and Peachtree inserts a blank line with a lookup list button.**

4. **Select a Job using the lookup list indicator.**

5. **In the Hours column, assign hours to that job.**

6. **Click OK when you finish to redisplay the Select Employees to Pay window.**

Labor Distribution to Jobs

Cancel · OK · Add · Remove · Help

Job	Hourly Field	Hours	Amount
BEAUMONT-01	Regular	60.00	540.00
None	Regular	0.00	0.00
None	Overtime	0.00	0.00
None	Special	0.00	0.00
Total for check		540.00	

Figure 9-7:
Allocate
employee
hours to
Jobs.

Listing the checks that you plan to print

Wouldn't it be nice to know how many checks Peachtree is planning to print? (You may have noticed that you don't see that number in the window anyplace.) Well, if you click the Report button, Peachtree prints a report that shows you the details and the number of checks you're printing.

Want to preview the check on-screen? Thanks to the new Print Preview feature in Peachtree 8, now you can preview checks on-screen (see Chapter 14).

Printing checks

If you choose the Print button in the Select Employees to Pay window, Peachtree first displays a dialog box so that you can select a check form. Then you see a dialog box that asks if you're printing real or practice checks. (You can print practice checks to see Xs and 9s on the form where words and numbers will appear.) Click Real, and you see a dialog box that asks you to confirm the first check number. When you click OK, Peachtree prints the checks and displays a dialog box asking you to confirm that the checks printed properly.

Paying employees individually

Do you need to pay only one or two employees? Use the Payroll Entry window and follow these steps:

1. **Choose Tasks➪Payroll Entry to display the Payroll Entry window (see Figure 9-8).**

2. **When you use the lookup list next to the Employee ID field to select an employee to pay, Peachtree fills in the employee's regular payroll information.**

   In Peachtree 2002, you can set up an employee from the Payroll Entry window. See the appendix for details.

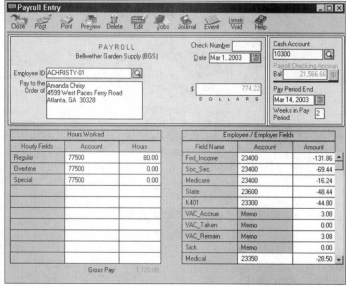

Figure 9-8:
Use this
window to
pay an
individual
employee.

3. If necessary, change the information.

For example, if an hourly employee doesn't work all of the hours in the pay period, adjust the number of hours.

Don't change Social Security or Medicare amounts. If you do, you'll find discrepancies on your payroll tax reports, and the 941 quarterly payroll tax return won't be accurate. You can, however, change Federal Income Tax and state income tax with no side effects. Make changes to the hours/salary first and the taxes second, or Peachtree won't make your tax changes. Any changes that you make affect the current check *only*.

4. Use the Jobs and Preview buttons at the top of the screen to assign the employee's hours to a Job and to preview the check.

In Peachtree 2002, you can set up jobs in the Payroll Entry window. See the appendix for details.

5. Click the Print button to print the check, and Peachtree displays the Print Forms dialog box so that you can select a check form.

Don't assign a check number before printing; because Peachtree assigns the check number to the check, Peachtree prints Duplicate on the check if you also assign a check number.

If you don't print checks, you can post (save without printing) the check. If you post the check instead of printing, assign a check number.

6. Highlight the appropriate check form and click OK.

Peachtree displays the dialog box where you choose to print Real or Practice checks.

7. **Click Real, and Peachtree displays the dialog box where you confirm the first check number.**

8. **Click OK.**

   Peachtree prints the check and updates the employee's record and the general ledger.

Paying commissions, bonuses, or other additions

Many companies pay employees bonuses at the year of the year. And, employees who act as sales representatives usually earn commissions. It may seem strange to you that we're talking about two very different situations in the same breath, but Peachtree handles both situations the same way. In fact, you can use the technique we show you here to handle any form of additional lump sum income that you must pay through payroll — jury duty, maternity leave, and so on. We refer to these lump sum income amounts as payroll additions.

Setting up a payroll item

You can use a Pay Level to record a bonus or commission, but we recommend that you use the technique we describe here for three reasons:

✔ You can control whether to include the payroll addition in gross pay when calculating payroll taxes or other payroll fields, such as retirement contributions. (Peachtree automatically includes Pay Levels in gross pay when calculating payroll fields.)

✔ The payroll addition appears as a separate item on payroll reports, making it easier to track.

✔ Setting up a payroll addition item is less work than setting up a Pay Level.

Follow these steps to set up a payroll addition item for commissions:

1. **Choose Maintain⇨Default Information⇨Employees to display the Employee Defaults dialog box.**

2. **Click the EmployEE Fields tab and scroll down to find a blank line.**

3. **Type the name of the payroll addition in the Field Name column — the name you use will appear on the paycheck stub.**

4. **Assign the line to a general ledger account — usually your wage expense account.**

Because commissions (and bonuses, jury duty pay, maternity leave pay, and so on) vary from employee to employee, you don't check the Calc column and create a payroll tax table to calculate the amount. You also don't need to supply an amount in the Amount column. You need to tell Peachtree only whether to include additional pay when Peachtree calculates gross wages for each tax. For example, you may want Peachtree to *include* commission pay in gross wages when calculating FIT, Social Security, and Medicare. At the same time, you may want Peachtree to *exclude* commission pay in gross wages when calculating a pension plan deduction.

Suppose that you want Peachtree to include additional pay in gross wages when Peachtree calculates Federal Income Tax. Follow these steps:

1. **Choose Maintain⇨Default Information⇨Employees.**

2. **On the EmployEE Fields tab of the Employee Defaults dialog box, scroll up to find Federal Income Tax (it's probably called Fed_Income).**

3. **Click the button in the Adjust column for Fed_Income to display the Calculate Adjusted Gross dialog box (see Figure 9-9).**

Figure 9-9: Use this dialog box to identify the amounts Peachtree should add together to calculate adjusted gross income before calculating the selected tax.

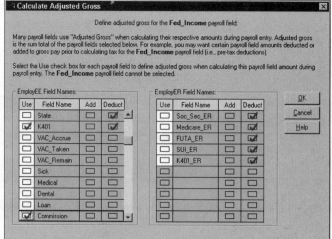

4. **If necessary, scroll down in the EmployEE Field Names area on the left side of the dialog box until you see Commission.**

5. **Place a check in the Use column to have Peachtree add commission pay to gross wages before calculating Federal Income Tax.**

   If you're not sure whether you want Peachtree to include a payroll addition when Peachtree calculates adjusted gross wages, contact your accountant.

6. **Click OK to redisplay the Employee Defaults dialog box.**

   You need to repeat these steps for each payroll field for which Peachtree's calculation of adjusted gross wages should include commission pay — at a minimum, Social Security and Medicare.

If you adjust the gross wage calculation for Social Security and Medicare, be sure that you click the Adjust button for these payroll fields on *both* the EmployEE Fields tab and the EmployER Fields tab.

7. Click OK to close the Employee Defaults dialog box.

To actually pay an employee a commission, simply fill in the amount in the field on the employee's paycheck. Peachtree adjusts appropriate taxes, based on settings you establish in the Calculate Adjusted Gross dialog boxes.

Don't change Social Security or Medicare amounts. If you do, you may find discrepancies on your payroll tax reports, and the 941 quarterly payroll tax return won't be accurate. You can, however, change Federal Income Tax and state income tax with no side effects.

The W-2 Form and payroll additions

You can, if you want, show commissions in Box 14 on the W-2. The assignment is entirely optional; that is, Peachtree includes the commission wages in Boxes 1 (gross wages), 3 (Social Security wages), and 5 (Medicare wages) automatically. Showing the wages in Box 14 simply identifies the component of Gross Wages (Box 1) that were commissions. Be aware that you can assign only one payroll field to Box 14.

To include commissions in Box 14, follow these steps:

1. **Choose Maintain⇨Default Information⇨Employees to display the Employee Defaults dialog box.**

2. **Click the General tab of the Employee Defaults dialog box.**

3. **Click the W-2s button to display the Assign Payroll Fields for W-2's dialog box (see Figure 9-10).**

4. **In the text box next to number 1̲4, type the name of the payroll field.**

5. **From the list box, select the appropriate field to print in Box 14 — commissions, in this example.**

6. **Click OK to redisplay the Employee Defaults dialog box.**

Determining commission amounts

With respect to commissions, one burning question pops immediately to mind: How do you know how much commission to pay an employee?

When you produce an invoice that contains items that are subject to commission *and* you assign a sales rep, Peachtree's Sales Rep report shows you the commissioned sales for each sales rep. Choose Reports⇨Accounts Receivable. From the Report List on the right, choose Sales Rep Reports. You can print this report (see Figure 9-11) for any date range. See Chapter 7 for more information on invoicing.

W-2s button

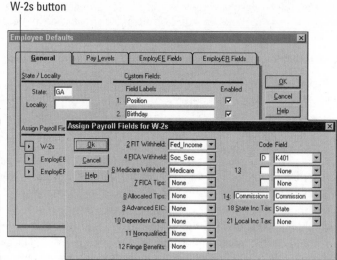

Figure 9-10:
Use this
dialog box
to report
commissions
in Box 14 of
the W-2
form.

In Figure 9-11, Dorothy Beckstrom made three sales that contained commissioned inventory items, and one sale that contained no commissioned inventory items. As her employer, you'd multiply the commissioned amount by Dorothy's commission rate and pay her the resulting number.

Customer returns usually affect commissions due. So, we have a few recommendations concerning paying commissions:

✔ Print the Sales Rep report only once each month and pay commissions only once each month for the *preceding* month — to make sure that you've processed all invoices for the month.

✔ Hold back a specified amount from each rep's commissions and pay that amount when the sales rep decides to leave your company. This practice protects you if you pay a commission for a sale that you later determine you won't collect. Be sure to include this policy in your employee information packet because you can be sure your employees are tracking the commissions due to them.

✔ Reversing a commission for a merchandise return is *not* a problem. Simply enter a credit memo and assign the sales rep to the credit memo. Reversing a commission for a return where you don't get any merchandise back is a little trickier. We suggest that you set up a nonstock inventory item that you assign to your Sales Returns and Allowances account, making sure to set the item up as subject to commission. When you issue the credit memo, use the nonstock inventory item.

Dates for credit memos should be in the period when you enter the credit memo — which is *not* necessarily the period in which you sell the item. That way, you are always able to pay commissions for a specified period, and you pay a net amount.

Sales Rep Reports

Close Save Options Hide   Print Setup   Preview Design Excel   Help

Bellwether Garden Supply (BGS)
Sales Rep Report
For the Period From Mar 1, 2003 to Mar 31, 2003
Filter Criteria includes: Report order is by Sales Rep ID. Report is printed Summarized by Customer.

Sales Rep ID	Name	Comm Amnt	Non-Comm Amnt	Total Sales	% of Total	Last Inv Date
DBECKSTROM-	Coleman Realty		267.78	267.78	1.20	3/11/03
	Cunningham Construction		160.00	160.00	0.72	3/13/03
	Gariepy Furniture	1,149.92		1,149.92	5.15	3/10/03
	Hensley Park Apartments	259.97	299.94	559.91	2.51	3/15/03
	Totals for DBECKSTROM-01 Doro	1,409.89	727.72	2,137.61	9.58	
DGROHS-01	Ertley Bulldog Sports		179.90	179.90	0.81	3/3/03
	Totals for DGROHS-01 Derrick Gro		179.90	179.90	0.81	
MMARKLEY-01	Freeman Enterprises		571.81	571.81	2.56	3/3/03
	Totals for MMARKLEY-01 Marian		571.81	571.81	2.56	
SPEACHY-01	Holt Properties, Inc.		159.40	159.40	0.71	3/4/03
	Totals for SPEACHY-01 Susan Peac		159.40	159.40	0.71	

Figure 9-11:
Use the
Sales Rep
report to
help you
identify
commission
amounts
to pay.

Writing the Payroll Tax Liability Check

You have to pay the payroll tax liability, and the IRS frowns greatly if you don't pay it in a timely fashion. The IRS classifies each employer as either a semi-weekly or monthly depositor, and your classification determines when your payroll tax deposit is due after a payday. You make your federal tax deposit at any bank, and you complete Form 8109 as your deposit ticket. On Form 8109, you specify the amount of the deposit, the type of tax, such as 941, and the period for which the tax applies: 1st quarter, 2nd quarter, 3rd quarter, or 4th quarter.

For simplicity's sake, we strongly urge you to write your federal payroll tax liability check and make your payroll tax deposit *at the same time* that you generate paychecks. That way, you just can't get into trouble.

You write your payroll tax liability check from either the Payments window or the Write Checks window. There's nothing tricky to it except, perhaps, determining how much you owe.

Peachtree 8 contains a new Payroll Tax Liability report to help you easily determine the amount of your payroll tax liability. Choose Reports⇨Payroll, and from the Report List on the right, choose Tax Liability Report. If you print the default version of the report, you see each tax name listed and each employee under that tax name, along with the amount withheld and the liability amount for one month.

For those of you who have used Peachtree's 941 Worksheet in the past, the Tax Liability amount on this report ties back to the 941 Worksheet. If you are a monthly depositor, this report is easier to read to determine your liability. If you are a semi-weekly depositor, you don't need to mess with the 941 B form anymore; simply use the new Tax Liability Report for the specified timeframe.

If you prefer, you can print a much shorter version of the report by printing it in summary format. Or, you can print the report for only one kind of tax: federal, state, or local. If you're viewing the report on-screen, click the Options button, and Peachtree displays the options dialog box for the report. Use the Tax list box to choose not to print all taxes but only federal, state, or local taxes. Place a check in the Print Report in Summary Format box to produce a report that looks like the one shown in Figure 9-12.

Use the totals in the Tax Liability column for each tax to determine the amount of money you owe for each of your payroll tax liabilities. Then, open the Write Checks window or the Payments window and write a check to your local bank. In the Write Checks window, set the Expense Account to your payroll tax liability account and the Cash Account to a payroll checking account (if you have a separate account) or to your operating checking account. In the Payments window, set the G/L Account on the Apply to Expenses tab at the bottom of the window to your payroll tax liability account(s) and the Cash Account to a payroll checking account (if you have a separate account) or to your operating checking account.

Figure 9-12: A summarized version of the Tax Liability Report.

Tax Liability Report

Close Save Options Hide   Print Setup   Preview Design Excel   Help

Bellwether Garden Supply (BGS)
Tax Liability Report
For the Period From Mar 1, 2003 to Mar 31, 2003
Filter Criteria includes: Report order is by Employee ID. Report is printed in Summary Format.

Tax Description	Gross	Taxable Gross	Tax Liability
FUTA	8,371.64	8,371.64	66.99
940 Total			66.99
FIT	7,958.85	7,958.85	697.18
FICA EE	8,371.64	8,371.64	519.05
FICA ER	8,371.64	8,371.64	519.05
Medicare EE	8,371.64	8,371.64	121.40
Medicare ER	8,371.64	8,371.64	121.40
941 Total			1,978.08
GA State Taxes			
GASUI ER	8,371.64	8,371.64	251.15
GASIT	7,958.85	7,958.85	292.12
GA State Total			543.27
Report Total			2,588.34

Paying your payroll tax liability doesn't affect the numbers that appear on the Tax Liability Report. The report shows what you *should* pay and doesn't consider what you may have already paid, which is *another* good reason to pay your tax liability at the same time you generate paychecks.

Exploring Payroll Reports

Besides the Payroll Tax Liability report, Peachtree offers several reports that you can use for a variety of tracking needs. Table 9-1 shows you a description of the reports that pertain to payroll. See Chapter 15 to learn how to print reports.

Table 9-1	Other Reports Related to Payroll
Report Name	*Description*
Employee List	For each employee, lists the ID, name, contact name, address, Social Security number, and pay type.
Check Register	Lists each paycheck with the check number, payee, and the amount.
Current Earnings Report	Shows, for the current period, much of the same information on the Payroll Register: breakdowns (by payroll field) of each paycheck. The Current Earnings report, however, subtotals each employee.
Quarterly Earnings Report	Shows the same information as the Current Earnings Report but for the current quarter.
Yearly Earnings Report	Shows the same information as the Current and Quarterly Earnings Reports but for the year.
Payroll Register	Lists every paycheck in the specified time period; provides the same information as the Current Earnings report, but without subtotaling each employee.
Payroll Journal	Shows the accounts Peachtree updated for each paycheck in the period.
Payroll Exception Report	Shows the difference between the tax amount Peachtree calculates and the tax amount withheld for each specified payroll tax.
Payroll Tax Report	Shows, for the selected tax, each employee, Social Security number, the number of weeks worked, the gross, the taxable gross, the excess gross, and the tax amount. You can print this report for every payroll tax for which you've set up a calculation and marked the Appears on Payroll Tax Report Menus check box.

Chapter 10

Billing for Your Time

. . . .

In This Chapter

▶ Setting up time and expense items

▶ Entering Time and Expense Tickets

▶ Paying employees for hours worked

▶ Creating customer invoices

. . . .

Some companies, particularly service-oriented professionals like accountants, consultants, lawyers, and architects, bill their customers for the time spent to complete projects. These companies often have employees track time and expenses, such as travel, for each of their projects. Then, the employer bills the customer for the employee time and expenses. In some cases, the companies also pay employees based on time worked.

In this chapter, we show you how Peachtree supports these billing functions — complete with a clock that lets you time your activities.

See Chapter 12, to find out how you can use jobs in Peachtree to create reimbursable expenses — expenses you incur that may have nothing to do with any time spent by anyone, but you want to include them on an invoice to a customer. Using time and expense tickets provides an alternative — and possibly better — method for creating reimbursable expenses if you don't need jobs for any other reason. (Chapter 12 lists information concerning the restrictions imposed if you use Peachtree jobs.) If you find that your time and billing needs are more extensive than those provided by Peachtree, you might consider Timeslips, which links with Peachtree. See the appendix for details on Timeslips.

Time and billing functions are available only in Peachtree Complete Accounting, not in Peachtree First Accounting or Peachtree Accounting.

Creating Time and Expense Items

If you plan to use the time and expense features in Peachtree, you need at least two (but probably more) inventory items (yeah, we know that sounds weird, but it's true). You use one inventory item to enter time activities and the other item to enter expense activities. To create inventory items to use on time activities, follow these steps:

1. **Choose Maintain⇨Inventory Items to display the Maintain Inventory Items window (see Figure 10-1).**

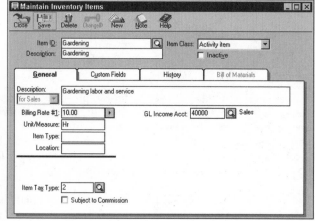

Figure 10-1:
Set up at least one Activity item and one Charge item.

2. **Type an Item ID.**

3. **For the Item Class, choose either Activity item for a time activity or Charge item for an expense activity.**

4. **Supply a Description in the box below the Item ID; this description appears on reports but *not* on invoices to your customers.**

5. **In the longer Description text box, fill in the description that you want to appear on customer invoices for time spent on this activity.**

   The description in the longer description box appears on the customer's bill unless you choose to display the description from the Time Ticket; for details on the Time Ticket's description block, see the next section.

6. **Enter up to five billing rates for the activity.**

7. **Use the lookup list to select a GL Income Account for the activity.**

   Unit/Measure, Item Type, and Location are all optional fields.

8. **Click Save.**

Entering Time Tickets

Peachtree's Time Tickets feature eliminates the need for timecards and old-fashioned push-in, punch-out tracking of employee hours. You can use Peachtree's Time Tickets to

✔ Record time spent by employees or vendors to bill to a customer or job.

✔ Provide employees with a method to track time so that you can pay them based on time spent.

Chapter 9 provides information about one of Peachtree's pay methods, Hourly – Time Ticket Hours, which you can use to pay your employees based on the hours they work. If you pay an employee based on time worked, you also need a way to account for employee time that you don't intend to charge to a customer or job — like overhead time spent doing marketing or book-keeping. Although you won't be billing the time to a customer, you need to include overhead hours on the employee's paycheck.

So, Peachtree allows you to enter overhead Time Tickets. Peachtree marks any overhead time you record as unbillable. And, as you might logically expect, you aren't able to bill any customer for that time.

If you don't pay your employees based on time worked, you don't need to assign time to overhead activities.

Follow these steps to enter a Time Ticket:

1. **Choose Tasks⇨Time/Expense⇨Time Tickets to display the Time Tickets window (see Figure 10-2).**

2. **Select either Employee or Vendor from the first list box and then select an employee or vendor.**

3. **Enter the Ticket Date, which should be the date you perform the work.**

4. **Select an Activity Item using the lookup list button.**

5. **From the list box below the Activity Item box, choose Customer, Job, or Administrative.**

   If you choose Customer or Job, you can include the Time Ticket on a bill; if you choose Administrative, Peachtree considers the Time Ticket unbillable. If you choose Customer or Job, select the appropriate customer or job using the lookup list button.

6. **In the Ticket Description for Invoicing box, you can enter up to 160 characters of text to use on the customer's invoice instead of the activity name.**

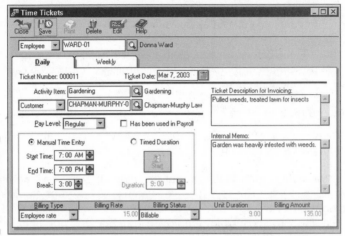

Figure 10-2:
Use this
window to
enter Time
Tickets.

7. **In the Internal Memo box, you can provide up to 2,000 characters of descriptive information.**

   You can't include the Internal Memo description on a customer's invoice, but Peachtree prints it on reports. Use it to provide details about the work performed.

   To start a new paragraph while typing in the Internal Memo box, press Ctrl+J.

8. **If you are entering a Time Ticket for an employee, choose a Pay Level.**

   Don't mess with the Has Been Used In Payroll check box. If it is checked, then you've paid the employee for the Time Ticket; unchecked means that you haven't included the Time Ticket on a paycheck yet.

9. **Choose Manual Time Entry or Timed Duration.**

   For manual entry, you supply a start and stop time as well as a break time, if appropriate. For Timed Duration, click Start, and Peachtree runs a timer (the Start button then becomes the Stop button). Regardless of your choice, Peachtree calculates the duration of the Time Ticket.

   You can't save a Time Ticket or close the Time Ticket window while the timer is running.

10. **Choose a Billing Type.**

    All billing types are available for employees, but only some are available for vendors.

    • **Employee Rate:** Uses the rate you enter on the Pay Info tab when you set up the employee in the Maintain Employees/Sales Reps window

    • **Activity Rate:** Uses the rate you enter when you set up the activity in the Maintain Inventory Items window

- **Override Rate:** Ignores both the employee and activity rates and allows you to enter any rate you want

- **Flat Fee:** Ignores the duration (and value) of the Time Ticket and allows you to establish an amount for the slip

11. **Choose a Billing Rate.**

The available rates depend on the choice you make for Billing Type. For example, you can establish only one employee rate, so if you choose Employee as the Billing Type, you can't change the billing rate. However, you can establish up to five rates for an activity, so you can choose a billing rate if you select Activity as the Billing Type. For either Override Rate or Flat Fee, you must enter a Billing Rate.

12. **Choose a Billing Status: Billable, Non-Billable, Hold, or No Charge.**

Billable and Non-Billable are self-explanatory. If you select Hold, you can't bill the ticket to a customer until you change the ticket's status. If you select No Charge, Peachtree changes the ticket's value to $0, so you can show your customer on the invoice that you performed work but didn't charge for it.

13. **If you choose Flat Fee or Override rate as the Billing Type, enter a Billing Amount.**

For all other Billing Types, Peachtree calculates the Billing Amount.

14. **Click Save.**

Whew! This process seems like a lot of steps to enter a ticket, but actually, when you do it, it goes quickly. The daily Time Tickets window appears in Figure 10-2, but Peachtree also provides a weekly view (see Figure 10-3). You can enter Time Tickets in the weekly view, and you can print the weekly timesheet by clicking the Print button in the window.

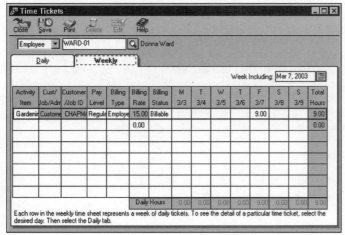

Figure 10-3:
The weekly view of the Time Tickets window.

The columns on the Weekly view aren't terribly wide, and most contain list box selectors. As you enter information for a particular column, the list boxes extend to cover up columns to the right of the current column. The visual effect may make you think that columns have disappeared — but they haven't.

Entering Expense Tickets

Okay, good news here. Almost everything we tell you about Time Tickets applies to Expense Tickets. For example, both employees and vendors can enter Expense Tickets. And, you can assign an Expense Ticket to a customer or job so that you can recover the expense. Or, you can assign an Expense Ticket to overhead, making it unbillable. If you assign an Expense Ticket to an employee, you also can place a check in the Reimbursable to Employee box; Peachtree prints reimbursable Expense Tickets on the Reimbursable Employee Expense report, making it easy for you to repay employees the expenses.

You have the same 160-character limit for the Ticket Description for Invoicing, which can print on the customer's invoice, and the same 2000-character limit for the Internal Memo description.

Unit Price is tied to the Charge Item you select — you may see up to five available unit prices. And you've got the same four Billing Status options for Expense Tickets that you have for Time Tickets: Billable, Non-Billable, No Charge, and Hold.

Paying Employees

Suppose that you pay employees for the hours they work. You've required that they enter Time Tickets. To pay them, you can use either of the payroll windows we describe in Chapter 9. Figure 10-4 shows the Payroll Entry window (choose Tasks ⇨ Payroll Entry). When you set the Pay Period End date, Peachtree automatically calculates the paycheck using Time Tickets from that pay period that are assigned to Customer or Administrative (in that unnamed list box we show you in "Entering Time Tickets," Step 5). If your employee assigned the Time Tickets to Job instead of Customer or Administrative, you need to click the Jobs button when you're paying the employee to see and select those Time Tickets.

Repaying employees for reimbursable expenses

Peachtree doesn't try to repay your employees automatically for Expense Tickets they enter. You must print the Reimbursable Employee Expense report (shown in the figure) for the specified pay period to identify expenses for reimbursement.

Then, you can repay the employee in one of two ways:

✔ Use the Write Checks window (Tasks ⇨ Write Checks) or the Payments window (Tasks ⇨ Payments) to write a separate expense reimbursement check to the employee.

✔ Include the reimbursement in the employee's paycheck by setting up a payroll field as an addition. See Chapter 9 for more details on setting up additions. You need to assign the reimbursement to a general ledger account but probably *not* to your wage expense account. And, because reimbursements aren't usually subject to payroll taxes, you need to click the Adjust button for each payroll tax and make sure that you're not including the reimbursement item. When you pay the employee, type a positive amount for the reimbursement to add it to the paycheck.

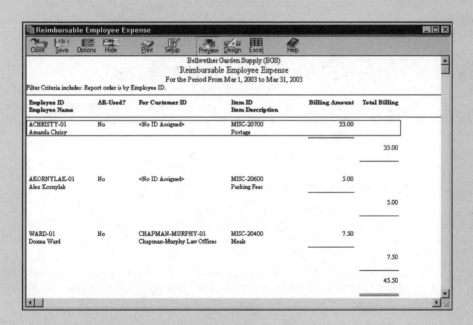

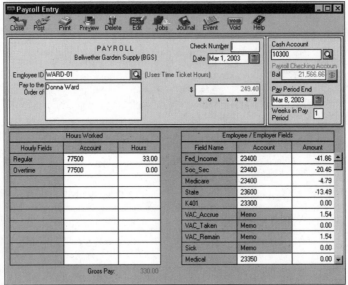

Figure 10-4:
Paying an
employee
for time
worked.

Using Tickets to Bill Customers

If your employees or vendors assign Time or Expense Tickets to customers or jobs, you can bill the customers for those costs. Follow these steps to bill customers using tickets:

1. **Choose Tasks⇨Sales/Invoicing to display the Sales/Invoicing window.**

2. **Complete most of your invoice as usual.**

   Select a customer using the lookup list indicator next to the Customer ID box and assign shipping information, terms, and line item information if this invoice includes more than reimbursable Time and Expense Tickets. For details on entering invoices, see Chapter 7.

3. **Click the Apply Tickets/Reimbursable Expenses button in the lower left corner of the window to display the Apply Tickets/Reimbursable Expenses window (see Figure 10-5).**

   You can view available Time Tickets on the Time Tickets tab and Expense Tickets on the Expense Tickets tab. To find out more about the Reimbursable Expenses tab, see Chapter 12.

4. **To include a ticket on the invoice, highlight the ticket on the appropriate tab and click the Use check box.**

5. **Verify or change the figure in the Invoice Amount column.**

To build some profit into a ticket or reimbursable expense, you change the amount in the Invoice Amount column. To mark up costs or reduce a group of tickets or reimbursable expenses, click the WriteUp icon to display the Select Tickets to Write Up/Down dialog box. You can adjust tickets up or down by a dollar amount or a percentage. To mark up, supply a positive number; to mark down, supply a negative number.

6. **Click OK to redisplay the Apply Tickets/Reimbursable Expenses window.**

WriteUp button

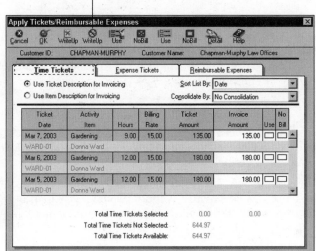

Figure 10-5:
Use the tabs in this window to select Time and Expense Tickets to include on a customer's invoice.

If you change your mind after you click OK and you *don't* want to mark tickets up or down, click the Remove WriteUp button in the Apply Tickets/Reimbursable Expenses window.

7. **Choose an option button to select a description for the ticket on the invoice.**

The first option tells Peachtree to use the description supplied on the Time Ticket; the second option tells Peachtree to use the description supplied when you set up the item in inventory.

If you leave the Consolidate By list box setting at No Consolidation, Peachtree creates separate lines on the invoice for each ticket you choose to bill. You can use other entries in the list to consolidate each type of ticket you use and reduce the number of lines on the invoice.

8. **Click OK. The reimbursable expenses appear on the customer's invoice.**

9. **Supply G/L accounts, Print, and post the invoice as usual.**

When you print tickets as separate lines on the invoice, Peachtree prints the description you supply on the expense when you create it. You see either ticket descriptions or item descriptions on the customer's invoice depending on the selection you make in the Apply Tickets/Reimbursable Expenses window. When you consolidate expenses on the bill, Peachtree does not supply a description. Instead, Peachtree prints the name of the G/L account you choose as the description on the invoice and then the total of all the tickets. If you want, you can type a description on the line for the consolidated tickets in the Sales/Invoicing window, and Peachtree uses that description instead of the G/L account name.

Keep the following notes in mind whenever you work with tickets:

✔ You can delete tickets from the Apply Tickets/Reimbursable Expenses window if you decide not to bill the client for them. Place a check in the No Bill box to the right of the expense. Deleting the ticket does *not* delete the transaction that created the ticket; instead, deleting in the Apply Tickets/Reimbursable Expenses window disconnects the ticket and the customer.

You can't undo deleting when you delete from the Apply Tickets/ Reimbursable Expenses window. As soon as you delete a ticket, the connection between the ticket and the customer is *permanently* broken unless you erase the ticket and reenter it completely.

✔ Be aware that *using* or applying a ticket makes it disappear from the Apply Tickets/Reimbursable Expenses window. If you subsequently delete the line from the invoice, the reimbursable expense *does not* reappear in the window. If you mistakenly use the ticket and post the invoice, delete the invoice and reenter it.

✔ You can edit a ticket you intend to bill to a customer by editing the ticket that assigns the expense to a customer. You can find the transaction by opening the Time Tickets window or the Expense Tickets window and clicking the Edit button.

Tracking Ticket Traffic

The Reimbursable Employee Expense report is one example of the reports Peachtree offers to help you keep track of the tickets that keep track of your time. Table 10-1, provides you with a description of the various other reports that pertain to time and expenses. See Chapter 15 for more details on printing reports.

Table 10-1	Other Reports Related to Time and Billing
Report Name	**Description**
Aged Tickets	Shows unbilled tickets and how old they are based on the aging brackets you set up in Customer defaults.
Employee Time	Lists, by employee, tickets and billing status.
Expense Ticket Register	Lists, by ticket number, detailed information about Expense Tickets.
Tickets Recorded By	Lists the tickets entered for each employee or vendor.
Tickets Used in Invoicing	Lists tickets that were included on customer invoices.
Tickets by Item ID	Shows tickets organized by Item ID so that you can see which activities are being used the most.
Time Ticket Register	Lists, by ticket number, detailed information about Time Tickets.
Ticket Listing by Customer	Lists each ticket assigned to the customer in the specified time period.
Payroll Time Sheet	Shows you the tickets entered by employee for the specified time period.

Chapter 11

Counting Your Stuff

*T*his chapter is about stuff. Many businesses sell stuff you can touch while others sell stuff you *can't* touch. Some stuff is made up of pieces of other stuff. Peachtree lets you sell all of these kinds of stuff. Enough stuff.

Of course, we're talking about inventory. And not just the goods you place on your shelves but other kinds of items such as services, labor, activities, and items you charge to your customer's bill.

We'll just warn you up front. The material in this chapter is rather dry, and you probably won't consider it too funny. Inventory management is, however, a crucial part of keeping your books. Peachtree makes handling inventory a lot easier than trying to track it all by hand.

Creating Inventory Items

When you create inventory items, you set up the goods and services you sell. You set a price (actually you can set up to five prices) at which you want to sell your product and the account you want Peachtree to adjust when you sell this item or service. But, before you can set up selling prices, you need to supply basic information about the item.

To create your virtual inventory, follow these steps:

1. **Click Maintain⇨Inventory Items.**

   Peachtree displays the Maintain Inventory Items window, with three tabs for each item in the header. The header information consists of the item ID, description, and class.

2. **In the header, type an item ID.**

   Keep in mind that the item the ID identifies appears in lookup lists for sales transactions and so on. Peachtree allows item IDs up to 20 characters.

   IDs are case sensitive and cannot contain the asterisk (*), question mark (?), or the plus symbol (+).

3. **Enter a description up to 30 characters.**

   This description appears in the item lookup lists. In the next section, you'll see how to type in descriptions that you can use for sales or purchase transactions. For example, in the lookup description you might refer to a specific birdbath as "Con BB w/birds," but when you sell this item, you'll want to be a little more descriptive, such as "Concrete bird bath with 2 bluebirds on pedestal base."

4. **Choose an Item Class to identify the type of inventory item.**

   Selecting the right classes for your inventory items helps ensure that Peachtree meets your business needs. Chapter 4 provides more information on the different Peachtree inventory classes, but these are the basics:

   - **Stock:** Inventory items you want to track for quantities, average costs, vendors, low stock points, and so on.

   - **Nonstock:** Items such as service contracts that you sell but do not put into your inventory.

   - **Assembly:** Items that consist of components that must be built or dismantled.

   - **Service:** Services provided by your employees.

   - **Labor:** Charges you bill to a customer for subcontracted labor on that customer's projects.

   - **Activity:** Records of how time is spent when performing services. Activity items appear only in Peachtree Complete Accounting.

   - **Charge:** On-the-job expenses of an employee or vendor. Charge items appear only in Peachtree Complete Accounting.

   - **Description only:** Timesaver when you track nothing but the description.

If you save an item as a stock item, an assembly item, an activity item, or a charge item, you cannot change its item class. Although you probably wouldn't want to, Peachtree does allow you to interchange the item class between nonstock, description, labor, and service items. Chapter 10 gives you more information on setting up Activity and Charge items.

General options

Enter basic item information such as descriptions, account numbers, sales prices, pricing methods, and other fields on the General tab.

Why does Peachtree list two different description lines? Well, the first description, the one you entered in the header information (Figure 11-1) appears when you open the inventory item lookup list.

Peachtree also provides a For Sales description and the For Purchases description. The description (up to 160 characters) you enter For Sales appears on quotes, sales orders, sales invoicing, and receipts, but the For Purchases description appears on purchase orders, purchases/receive inventory, and payments.

Sales/Purchase selection box

Sales/Purchase description box

Lookup description box

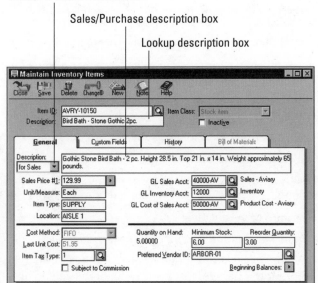

Figure 11-1:
Sales or
Purchase
descriptions
can be up
to 160
characters
in length.

Follow these steps to enter global inventory information:

1. **Click the arrow under description to select the description you want to enter.**

2. **Enter a description as you want it to appear on transactions.**

   If you need additional lines for description information, press Ctrl+Enter to start the next line.

   Entering information in the For Sales and For Purchases boxes is optional. If you do not specify a sales description, Peachtree uses the lookup description when you enter a quote, sales order, invoice, or receipt. If you don't specify a purchase description, Peachtree uses the For Sales description when generating purchase orders, purchases, or payments. If a sales description doesn't exist, Peachtree uses the lookup description.

3. **Type the price you want to charge.**

   Peachtree refers to the amounts that appear on your quotes, sales orders, and invoices as *sales prices*. The sales pricing levels correspond with those you assign your customers in the Maintain Customers/ Prospects window (see Chapter 7).

   If you charge only one price for this item, no matter which customer, enter only the Sales Price #1. To enter additional sales prices, click the arrow. The Multiple Pricing Levels dialog box as shown in Figure 11-2 appears. When you're finished, click OK to close the dialog box. In Peachtree 2002, you can store up to ten sales prices for each item and base the sales prices upon a calculation. See the appendix for details.

   Chapter 7 shows you how to customize customer information like pricing.

   Be consistent when entering item sales price levels (for example, from lowest to highest or highest to lowest).

4. **Enter a unit of measure (optional).**

   You may sell your products on an individual basis (each), a pair basis, per dozen, a per-pound or kilogram basis, or a per-ounce basis.

5. **Enter an item type (optional).**

   You'll really appreciate this when you're generating reports. Grouping items is much easier when they're marked "supplies" or "raw materials."

   Item types are case sensitive.

6. **Enter a storage location for the unit (optional).**

   Someday you may need to know where the unit is located, like Bin 17 or Shelf B3 or Mom's Garage, and it's very helpful when doing a physical inventory.

7. **If necessary, change the GL accounts for the item.**

   You can review setting up the default GL accounts in Chapter 4.

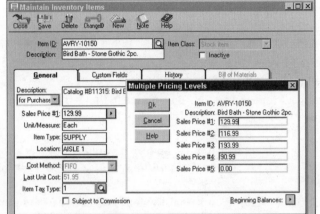

Figure 11-2:
Set up to
five sales
prices for
each item.

8. **If necessary, select a different Cost Method.**

    This is a *very important* field — the costing method. You cannot change a costing method once an inventory item is saved.

    Costing methods apply only to stock items and assemblies. Peachtree supports three different types of costing methods: Average Cost, LIFO (last in, first out), and FIFO (first in, first out). The sidebar "How do the costing methods work?" gives you more information on what these methods mean. Typically, you set all inventory items to use the same costing method so you probably determined a default method when you set up default Inventory Items information. If you're not sure, check with your accountant for advice about different costing methods.

9. **Enter, in the Last Unit Cost field, the last price you paid for this item (optional).**

    After you enter transactions against the inventory item, the Last Unit Cost field becomes unavailable. Peachtree automatically updates the Last Unit Cost as you enter purchases, payments, adjustments, or beginning balances, calculating the amount based on the costing method you select in Step 8.

10. **Choose an Item Tax Type.**

    The tax type you select applies when you enter the inventory item on quotes, sales orders, invoices, or receipts; however, the sales tax code you assign to each customer takes precedence over the inventory tax code. For example, if you set the item to be taxable, but the customer is tax exempt, Peachtree doesn't tax the item.

11. **In the Minimum Stock box, enter the quantity at which you want Peachtree to remind you it's time to reorder the item.**

    When the quantity on hand reaches the Minimum stock quantity, Peachtree prints the item on the Inventory Reorder Worksheet. Entering a minimum stock point is optional.

12. **Enter a Reorder Quantity.**

    Reorder Quantity is the quantity you generally purchase when you order the inventory item. Entering a reorder quantity point is also optional.

13. **Tell Peachtree where you prefer to buy this item by selecting the vendor ID in the Preferred Vendor field lookup box.**

    Selecting a Preferred Vendor doesn't mean that's the *only* vendor from which you can purchase the item. It just means that this vendor is your *favorite* vendor.

14. **Check the Subject to Commission box if you want to track the sales of the item and have it reported on the Accounts Receivable Sales Rep report.**

15. **If you're not creating an assembly item and are ready to move on, click Save to save the inventory item.**

    With assemblies, Peachtree requires you to generate the bill of materials before you can save the item. If your item is an assembly, jump ahead to the Setting Up Assemblies section in this chapter.

Whew! That's a *lot* of stuff to enter for one item! Fortunately, the rest of the Maintain Inventory Item window is easy and doesn't involve too many tough decisions.

How do the costing methods work?

If you're not sure which option to choose in the Last Unit Cost box, you may want to know how Peachtree handles these options. Peachtree supports three different costing methods: average, FIFO (first-in, first-out), and LIFO (last-in, first-out). (Those terms kinda remind us of Jack and the Beanstalk — Fee Fie Foe Fum. . . .) Here's how Peachtree calculates inventory costs based on the different methods:

If you use the averaging costing method, Peachtree calculates average cost by taking the total remaining value of the item (from the Valuation Report or the Item Costing Report) divided by the quantity on hand. Remember Peachtree calculates costs on a daily basis.

The only report that will give you quantity and remaining value for a particular day is the Item Costing Report.

If you use the FIFO costing method, Peachtree calculates costs at the *earliest* purchase price, inventory increase adjustment, build, sales return, or assembly unbuild (for the component item) for a particular item. FIFO produces the lowest possible net income in periods of falling costs because the cost of the most recently purchased item most closely approximates the replacement of the item.

If you use the LIFO costing method, Peachtree calculates costs at the most recent *(last)* purchase price, inventory increase adjustment, build, sales return, or assembly unbuild (for the component item) for a particular item. LIFO produces the lowest possible net income in periods of constantly rising costs because the cost of the most recently purchased item most closely approximates the replacement of the item.

Custom fields

If you're using other Peachtree modules, such as A/R, A/P, P/R, or Job Cost, you've seen custom fields before. Use custom fields to store miscellaneous pieces of information about the inventory item that just don't seem to fit anywhere else in the Maintain Inventory Items window. Examples might be the item shipping weight, average shelf life, or information about an alternate vendor for the product. One of our clients uses a custom field to store the chemical makeup of their product.

History

The History tab displays a summary of inventory transactions for stock and assembly items for past periods. Peachtree shows units sold and received as well as sales and costs by accounting period.

Nonstock, service, and the remaining class items do not retain history.

When you discontinue an inventory item, you can mark it inactive; redisplay the item in the Maintain Inventory window and check the Inactive box.

In the Beginning (Balance, That Is) . . .

Chances are, you've been in business for some time and have a current stock of inventory goods. If so, you need to enter beginning balances for the items you have on hand.

To enter inventory item beginning balances, follow these steps:

1. **Click Maintain⇨Inventory Items.**

   The Maintain Inventory Items window appears.

2. **From the General tab, click the Beginning Balances button (in the lower-right corner of the window).**

   The Inventory Beginning Balances dialog box, shown in Figure 11-3, appears.

3. **Click the inventory item in the list box, and the item appears at the top.**

4. **Enter a Quantity and the Unit Cost, which is the price you paid for the units.**

   The unit cost is very important! Not entering a cost can throw off your entire inventory valuation. Peachtree multiplies the quantity times the cost and gives the result in the Total Cost box.

Figure 11-3:
Only stock
items and
assemblies
appear
in the
Inventory
Beginning
Balance
dialog box.

Inventory Beginning Balances

Cancel   OK   Find   Next   Help

Item ID	Description	Quantity	Unit Cost	Total Cost
AVRY-10150	Bird Bath - Stone Gothic 2pc.	12.00	51.95	623.40

Item ID	Description	Quantity	Unit Cost	Total Cost
AVRY-10100	Bird House Kit	0.00	0.00	0.00
AVRY-10110	Bird House-Pole 14 Ft.	24.00	19.95	478.80
AVRY-10120	Bird House-Red 12-Room Unit	36.00	35.95	1,294.20
AVRY-10130	Bird Feeder-Plastic Hanging	18.00	7.95	143.10
AVRY-10140	Thistle Bird Seed Mix-6 lb.	18.00	7.95	143.10
AVRY-10150	Bird Bath - Stone Gothic 2pc.	12.00	51.95	623.40
BOOK-11000	BGS Floral Reference Guide	12.00	11.95	143.40
BOOK-11010	BGS Gardening Handbook	11.00	5.20	57.20
BOOK-11020	BGS Landscaping Techniques	12.00	11.95	143.40

Total Beginning Balances: 18,598.19

If you bought the items at a lot (bulk) price and don't know the cost of
each one, skip the Unit Cost and enter the Total Cost you paid for the
goods. Peachtree divides the Total Cost by the Quantity and displays the
result in the Unit Cost box.

5. **Repeat Steps 2 and 3 for each inventory item in which you have stock.**

6. **Click OK to update the inventory balance.**

Puttin' 'Em Together, Takin' 'Em Apart

Some stuff is made up of pieces of other stuff. Peachtree calls the pieces *"components"* and complete items *"assemblies."* Maybe your company sells bird
feeders as a standalone product or as part of a package deal that includes a
post, a hook, and birdseed. The package deal is an assembly. Or, maybe you
sell a "doobob" (Elaine, that one's for you!).This doobob is made up of several
"thingamajigs" and a couple of "whatchamacallits." You don't actually sell
thingamajigs or whatchamacallits to your customers, but you still need to
keep track of their quantities so you know how many doobobs you can make.
Peachtree also calls the doobob an *assembly.* In either situation, you create
the assembled items by building them out of a list of component parts, both in
your physical inventory and in your virtual store.

Creating a Bill of Materials

The Bill of Materials is a list of the individual parts that make up assemblies.
Before you can create an assembly item, you need to make sure each component part is set up already in Peachtree.

After an assembly has been used in a transaction, you can't add or remove component items from the Bill of Materials. If you need to change component parts, you need to create a new assembly item.

Create a Bill of Materials by following these steps:

1. **Click Maintain⇨Inventory Items to display the Maintain Inventory Items window.**

2. **Create the inventory item ID, description, and other information.**

   Make sure that you choose Assembly as the Item Class.

3. **Click the Bill of Materials tab to display a screen like the one in Figure 11-4.**

   Because assemblies are made up of other components, you need to use the Bill of Materials screen to list the component items. Assemblies must have at least one item listed in the Bill of Materials.

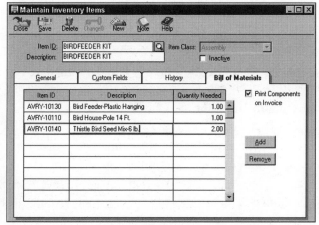

Figure 11-4:
Assemblies must have at least one item listed in the Bill of Materials.

4. **Choose or enter the first item to be included in the assembly.**

   Peachtree automatically fills in the description, but you can change the description.

5. **Enter a Quantity Needed for the assembly.**

6. **Repeat Steps 4 and 5 for each component item.**

   If you run out of lines on the Bill of Materials list and have additional components, click the Add button. Peachtree inserts a blank line above the current item.

7. **Check the Print Components on Invoice box if you want Peachtree to print the list of the individual components on the invoice.**

8. **Click Save to save the assembly item.**

Building assemblies

When you build an assembly item, Peachtree takes the individual components and reduces their quantity on hand. Peachtree does not allow negative component quantities when building assemblies; therefore you need enough component parts in stock to build the requested number of assemblies.

When building an assembly, Peachtree generates a *debit* entry for the *assembly's* inventory GL account and *credits* the *component's* inventory GL account for the cost of the assembly items.

Follow these steps to build assemblies:

1. **Select the assembly item ID from the ID lookup box.**

2. **In the Reference box, enter a reference number or any piece of information to identify this transaction, perhaps your initials.**

3. **Choose the transaction Date, which is typically the date the changes in your inventory occurred.**

4. **Type the Quantity to Build.**

   If you want to "unbuild" an assembly, if, for example, you need to sell the individual components, enter a negative number.

5. **Enter a reason to Build the assemblies.**

   You don't *have* to enter a reason. No doubt, you know exactly right now why you're building them, but will you remember six months from now?

6. **Click Post or Save to record the transaction.**

Making Inventory Adjustments

Let's face it, inventory counts get out of whack sometimes. Items get damaged, lost, or stolen. Sometimes, for reasons unknown, you might find several products that you didn't know you had, stashed away in a corner. So, periodically, you'll need to adjust your inventory.

Whether you take a physical inventory count of all your goods, or just need to adjust the quantity on hand of a single product, you'll use Peachtree's Inventory Adjustment feature.

Follow these steps to make adjustments to your inventory:

1. **Click Tasks➪Inventory Adjustments to display the Inventory Adjustments window you see in Figure 11-5.**

2. **Enter a Reference number, or any piece of information to identify this transaction, perhaps your initials.**

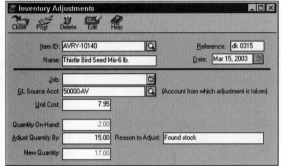

Figure 11-5: To reduce quantity on hand, enter a negative quantity.

Peachtree doesn't require reference numbers, but making sure that every transaction you enter into Peachtree has some type of a reference number is a good idea.

3. **Select a Date for the inventory adjustment.**

4. **If you use Peachtree's job costing, select the job (and optionally, phase or cost code) to which you want to charge the adjustment.**

   Chapter 12 shows you all about job costing.

5. **Choose the GL Source Account you want to charge for the adjustment cost.**

If you decrease the item quantity, Peachtree debits the GL Source Account and credits the item's Inventory Account. If you increase the item quantity, Peachtree credits the GL Source Account and debits the item's Inventory Account.

6. **Enter a Unit Cost.**

   The Unit cost defaults to the last purchase price you entered in the system. If you use the Inventory Adjustment transaction to *increase* your inventory count, you can change the unit cost. If, however, you are *reducing* the quantity on hand, the unit cost field becomes disabled. Peachtree costs the adjustment based on the item's costing method at the time of the sale.

The unit cost is very important! Not putting in a cost can throw off your entire inventory valuation.

7. **Type a quantity to adjust in the Adjust Quantity By box.**

   You enter the quantity as a negative number if you need to decrease your quantity on hand. Peachtree displays the new quantity on hand.

8. **Optionally, in the Reason to Adjust box, type an explanation why you're creating the transaction, for example, damaged or annual inventory.**

   You may know quite well why you're creating this adjustment, but will you remember later?

9. **Click Post or Save to save the transaction.**

Adjusting Prices

One day you suddenly realize you haven't raised the prices on your products for a long time. Your costs have gone up and you know you have to pass some of that increase on to your customers. We know this is not a step you take lightly; after all you still want to be competitive, but you *are* in the business to make money, *not lose it.* So, you make the decision, you're going to increase your prices.

Originally, you entered the sales prices when you created the inventory item in the Maintain Inventory Items window. You *could* go back to the Maintain Inventory Items window and pull each item up individually, change the sales prices, then save the inventory item again.

Oh no, you say! I've got too many inventory items to change the prices individually. Isn't there a faster way? Yes. Peachtree provides an easy way to update prices on all of your inventory items, a range of items, or a single item. For example, you can mark up sales prices for all your stock items by 10 percent. You can even adjust the prices for only the products you purchase from a specific vendor. Peachtree allows you to adjust the item sales prices up or down.

Make a backup before you change item prices.

To adjust sales prices, follow these steps:

1. **Click Maintain⇨Item Prices to display the Maintain Item Prices – Filter Selection dialog box you see in Figure 11-6.**

2. **Enter any desired filter information.**

   The Filter Selection box gives you lots of different ways to select the products that need a price increase. If you don't choose any settings from the filter box, Peachtree assumes you want to change the price on all of your products. You can however, select just the stock items. Or maybe the stock items you purchase from vendor JONES-01. Or how about only the products that cost more than $10.00 but less than $50.00. You can select any of these combinations from the Filter Selection box. Figure 11-7 shows what you see if electing to change the price on only our books, so select the IDs that begin with BOOK in the Item ID From and To boxes.

3. **Click OK to display the Maintain Item Prices dialog box, shown in Figure 11-7.**

   Now you have to make some decisions. First, you have the option of adjusting the sales prices based on the Current Price or by Last Cost. Some companies mark up their products by a flat percentage, say 25 percent over cost. In that case, they'd select the Last Cost option. If you want to increase the current sales price, say an item sold for a dollar and now you want to sell it for $1.15, you'd choose the Current Price option.

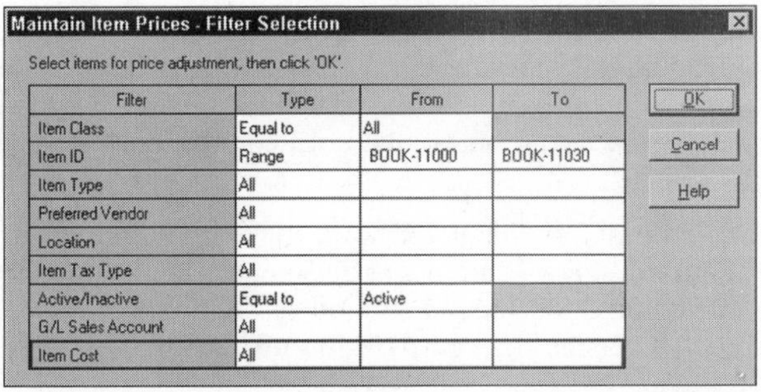

Figure 11-6: Adjust inventory sales prices for all or part of your items.

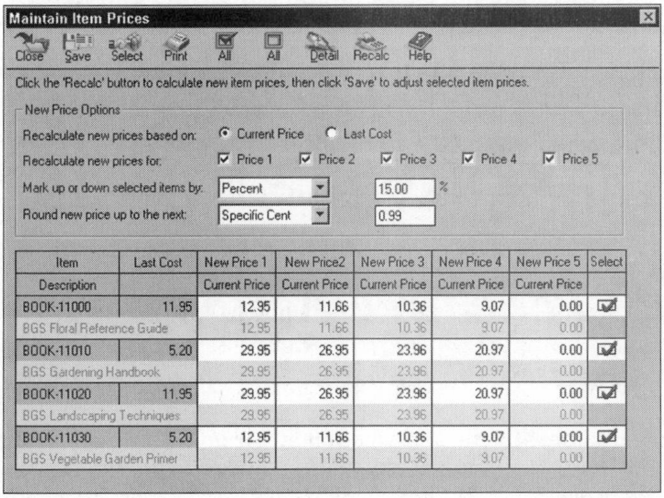

Figure 11-7: Peachtree displays items based on your filter selection.

4. **Choose an adjustment method: Current Price or Last Cost.**

5. **Because Peachtree assumes that you want to change all five pricing levels, you have to remove the check next to each price level that you do not want to change.**

6. **Choose a markup method and enter an amount or percentage to mark up the item.**

   Peachtree allows you to change prices on the selected items by an amount or a percentage. If you choose Amount, enter the amount as a positive or negative dollar amount. If you choose Percent, enter the amount as a positive or negative percentage (for example, enter 6 for a 6 percent markup).

   Enter a negative number if you want to mark down the current price.

7. **Select a method for rounding the new prices.**

   - **Dollar:** If you choose Dollar, Peachtree rounds the item prices up to the nearest dollar amount. For example, you increased the price of a product you previously sold for $11.60 by 15 percent. The calculated price would be $13.34, but Peachtree rounds the new price up to $14.00.

   - **Specific Cent:** Use this if you want to round all prices up to a specified cent level. For example, at a 95-cent price level your products would sell for 5.95, 7.95, 11.95, and so on. If you choose Specific Cent, then specify the cents (95 in our example), in the amount box.

   - **Do Not Round:** Select this if you don't want the prices rounded at all.

8. **Click the Recalculate toolbar button to see the new item prices or you can manually change individual prices.**

   Click the Detail button to display additional information about an item or click the Print button to print a report of your proposed price adjustments.

9. **Click Save to record the new prices.**

10. **Click Close to close the Maintain Item Prices dialog box.**

When Does Peachtree Assign a Cost to Items?

We'll be very honest here. This section is Boring with a capital 'B'. You certainly don't have to read this information, but our experience shows that many clients want to know how Peachtree's inventory system works — not just the mechanics of entering items or transactions, but what's happening behind the scenes. We don't give you any steps or tasks to accomplish — just some plain old facts about inventory.

This whole inventory state of affairs can be confusing. You've probably already noticed that Peachtree's inventory module is perfect for a buy/sell situation where you purchase a product then resell it, but it doesn't work very well for tracking raw materials used in production, especially if scrap is involved. Add that factor to all the different item transactions that can affect the cost, and sometimes the entire picture becomes a little blurred.

Peachtree calculates the value of inventory items on a daily basis. To ensure that increases to inventory are posted before decreases to inventory, Peachtree posts transactions in the following order:

1. Purchases

2. Payments

3. Increase adjustments

4. Assembly builds (for an assembly item)

5. Sales returns

6. Receipts return

7. Assembly unbuilds (for a component item)

8. Purchase returns

9. Payment returns

10. Assembly unbuilds (for an assembly item)

11. Sales

12. Receipts

13. Decrease adjustments

14. Assembly builds (for a component item)

Peachtree creates three types of system-generated adjustments: the purchase return adjustment, the assembly unbuild adjustment, and the system cost adjustment. You cannot erase these types of adjustments. These adjustments appear in the Inventory Adjustment journal and on the Item Costing report. The reference for a System cost adjustment is SysCost, the reference for a Purchase return adjustment is the reference number of the purchase transaction (usually the invoice number), and the reference for the assembly unbuild adjustment is the reference number of the assembly unbuild transaction.

Figure 11-8 shows an inventory adjustment journal with a system generated cost (SysCost) adjustment.

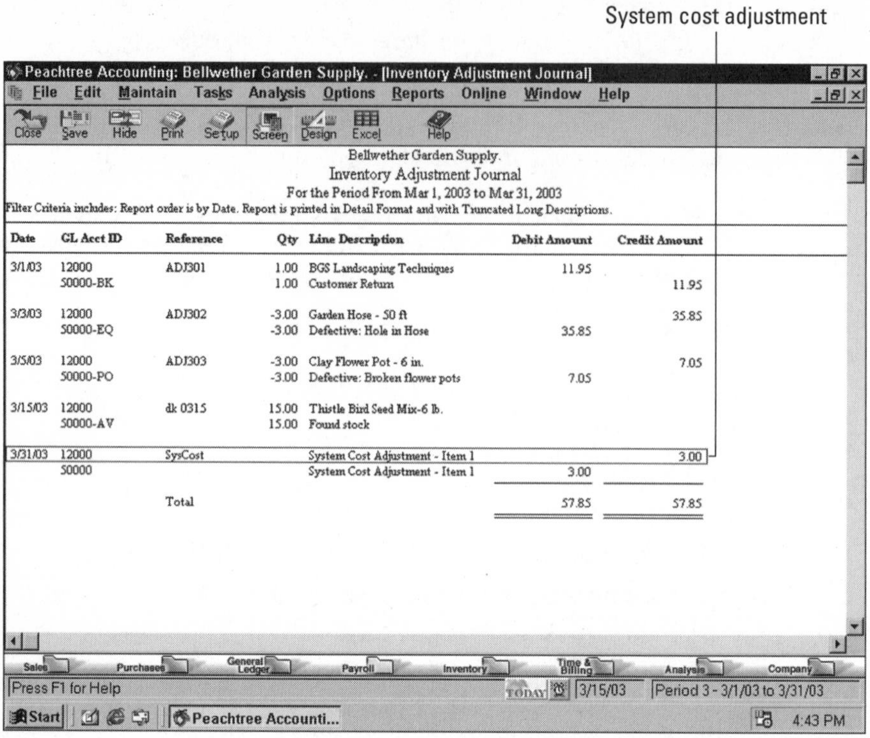

System cost adjustment

Date	GL Acct ID	Reference	Qty	Line Description	Debit Amount	Credit Amount
3/1/03	12000	ADJ301	1.00	BGS Landscaping Techniques	11.95	
	50000-BK		1.00	Customer Return		11.95
3/3/03	12000	ADJ302	-3.00	Garden Hose - 50 ft		35.85
	50000-EQ		-3.00	Defective: Hole in Hose	35.85	
3/5/03	12000	ADJ303	-3.00	Clay Flower Pot - 6 in.		7.05
	50000-PO		-3.00	Defective: Broken flower pots	7.05	
3/15/03	12000	dk 0315	15.00	Thistle Bird Seed Mix-6 lb.		
	50000-AV		15.00	Found stock		
3/31/03	12000	SysCost		System Cost Adjustment - Item 1		3.00
	50000			System Cost Adjustment - Item 1	3.00	
		Total			57.85	57.85

Bellwether Garden Supply.
Inventory Adjustment Journal
For the Period From Mar 1, 2003 to Mar 31, 2003
Filter Criteria includes: Report order is by Date. Report is printed in Detail Format and with Truncated Long Descriptions.

Figure 11-8:
See system generated adjustments in the Inventory Adjustment Journal.

Reporting

Here comes the spiel you may have seen in many other chapters. . . . While it would be nice to print a sample of every report Peachtree offers, (especially in this chapter because Peachtree has a number of valuable inventory reports), there simply isn't space in this book to do so. So, in Table 11-2, we provide you with a description of the reports that pertain to maintaining your inventory. (Chapter 15 describes how to print and customize reports.)

One report you should definitely know is the Inventory Valuation report that shows the quantity on hand, value, average cost, and percent of inventory value for all in-stock items. To arrive at the percent of inventory value number, Peachtree takes the value of the item divided by the total value of items that have a positive item value. The example in Table 11-1 shows you how the percent-to-total value works.

Table 11-1		Sample Inventory Valuation	
Transaction #	*Quantity*	*Total Item Value*	*% of Inventory*
1	4.00	10.00	33.33
2	1.00	−5.00	
3	2.00	20.00	66.67
Total		25.00	

In Table 11-1, Peachtree calculates the % of Inventory on the percent of the positive item values (Items 1 and 3), which equal $10.00 + $20.00, or 30.

Many inventory reports only include stock and assembly item information (see Table 11-2).

Table 11-2	Reports Related to Inventory
Report Name	*Description*
Assemblies adjustment journal	Shows built and unbuilt assembly transactions in journal format.
Assembly list	Lists each assembly with the components that make up the assembly.
Cost of Goods sold journal	Shows cost of goods sold in journal format.
Inventory adjustment journal	Lists inventory adjustments in journal format.
Inventory profitability report	Lists each item with units sold, cost, gross profit, adjustments, and percent of total.
Inventory reorder worksheet	Displays reorder amounts for inventory items when they fall below the specified Minimum Stock amount.
Inventory stock status report	Lists items, quantity on hand, and reorder quantity.
Inventory unit activity report	Lists items' beginning quantity, units sold, purchased, adjusted, and assembled and an ending quantity on hand.
Inventory valuation report	Shows the quantity on hand, value, average cost, and percent of inventory value for all in-stock items.

(continued)

Table 11-2 *(continued)*

Report Name	Description
Item costing report	Lists each inventory item with costing information for quantities received and sold.
Item list	Lists each item, item description, class, type, and quantity on hand.
Item master list	Lists items with detail information as entered in maintain items.
Item price list	Lists each item with quantity on hand and each available sales price.
Physical inventory list	A worksheet you can use to check the actual quantity of items on hand versus what the system reports on hand.

Chapter 12

Tracking Project Costs

Some businesses lend themselves well to organizing work by project, and for the purposes of this discussion, *project* is synonymous with *job*. In particular, these companies perform the same general type of work for each customer — that is, all their projects are similar to each other. Companies who use *Job Costing* (assigning costs to jobs) in their business want to track expenses and revenues for each job so that they can determine the net profit from the job. These companies often bid for the services they sell by providing an estimate. Then, if they get the work, they want to compare the estimated costs to the actual costs so that they can improve their estimating skills for future jobs and increase revenues.

In this chapter, we describe the Job Costing features available in Peachtree Complete for Windows. In Peachtree for Windows, you can create Jobs, but not Phases or Cost Codes. Peachtree First Accounting doesn't support Job Costing.

Understanding Job Costing

What kinds of companies use Job Costing? Well, Job Costing is widely used in the construction industry, but it also can be used by a variety of other businesses, such as convention planners, party planners, landscapers, cleaning services, and printers (the people who produce things like letterhead).

Do you need to use Job Costing? If the jobs you perform tend to stretch out over time, you're more likely to use Job Costing. If, however, you complete a job in a short period of time — a week or less — you probably don't need to use Peachtree's Job Costing because the time you'd spend entering Job information would exceed the value you'd receive from the information.

We offer a cautionary note to potential Peachtree Job Cost users. It is very difficult to purge jobs — we explain why in the section on purging later in the chapter. The difficulty with purging Jobs becomes an issue if you create lots of jobs. Your data files become very large, and you won't be able to reduce their size. We recommend that you carefully consider the number of jobs you're going to create before you start using Job Costing in Peachtree. You may need a different software package to fill your Job Costing needs. But don't let that deter you from using Peachtree, because you can still use Peachtree for all other aspects of your business.

You can purchase a special Contractor's Tool Kit from Peachtree Software — see the appendix for details.

Creating custom fields for jobs

In Chapter 4, we set up defaults for other areas of Peachtree; for jobs, you only can establish custom fields because this feature has no other preferences to set. Choose Maintain⇨Default Information⇨Jobs to display the Job Defaults dialog box. Place a check mark next to any of the five field labels to enable the custom field. Then, type a description for the custom field. Click OK when you finish.

Reviewing Job examples

Before you dive in and start creating things, we think you'd benefit by examining a few examples. We think that you might understand the order in which we choose to create things better after you read these examples.

Jobs are a method of organizing accounting information. Through this chapter, we're going to use one example to explain the various facets of Jobs: a company that builds swimming pools. Consider each swimming pool the company builds to be a separate job.

Phases

You can use *Phases* to further break down the costs of a project. Phases are optional; use them only if you want to organize your project in some way and look at costs and revenues at a more detailed level. In the case of our swimming pool builder, we might use five Phases:

- ✔ Design
- ✔ Permits
- ✔ Site preparation

✔ Installation

✔ Finishing/landscaping

Peachtree allows you to assign each Phase to a cost type: Labor, Materials, Subcontract Labor, Equipment Rental, and Other.

Cost codes

If you need a further breakdown of any of these cost types for a particular Phase — for example, you need to track the costs of specific materials like concrete and tile — you can create *Cost Codes*. If you choose to create Cost Codes for a Phase, you won't assign a cost type to the Phase. Instead, you can assign a cost type to each Cost Code: Labor, Materials, Subcontract Labor, Equipment Rental, and Other.

Cost Codes, like Phases, are optional. You may find that you need Cost Codes for only one cost type, perhaps Labor. You can set up specific Cost Codes for Labor and then assign those Cost Codes as needed to Phases. For Phases that don't need the Cost Codes, you can simply use the Phase — and its cost type.

If you use Cost Codes, we recommend that you try to use the same Cost Codes for every project. That way, you can set up one set of Cost Codes and assign them, as needed, to a Phase of a project. You may also be able to use the same Phases (or a subset of Phases) for each project.

Consider one more example. Suppose that you manage an apartment complex, and you want to monitor the costs associated with each building on the property. You could set up each building as a job. Then, as you make purchases for a particular building, you can assign the purchases to the building. Your job reports show you the costs of each building in the complex. Note that we haven't suggested using Phases or Cost Codes because they are optional.

Suppose, however, that you want to track costs for the complex at a more detailed level — by apartment. In that case, you could set up the apartments in each building as Phases and assign expenses to particular apartments.

"So, what's your point? Why are you telling me all this now?" you ask. Well, in Peachtree, you must decide when setting up a job, whether it uses Phases. Similarly, you must decide when setting up a Phase, whether it uses Cost Codes. So, you need to understand what each entity is before you can start creating things.

Creating Jobs and Estimates

To set up a job, follow these steps:

1. **Choose <u>M</u>aintain⇨<u>J</u>ob Costs⇨<u>J</u>obs to display the Maintain Jobs window (see Figure 12-1).**

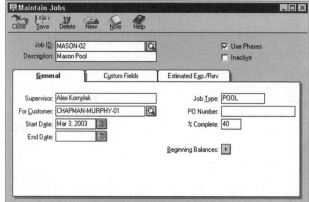

Figure 12-1:
Set up a
Job in this
window.

2. **Provide the Job I<u>D</u>.**

    You can use up to 20 alphanumeric characters, excluding the asterisk (*), the question mark (?), and the plus sign (+). IDs are case sensitive, so POOL-1 is different from pool-1.

3. **In the Descri<u>p</u>tion box, provide a description for the job.**

4. **If the job uses Phases, place a check mark in the Use Phases check box.**

5. **On the General tab, fill in any pertinent information, all of which is optional.**

    Peachtree doesn't limit the number of jobs you can assign to customers, but you don't *need* to assign jobs to customers. Remember, if you don't need jobs for any reason other than charging customers for expenses, you can use time and expense slips. See Chapter 10 for details.

6. **If you work on the job before you enter it in Peachtree and you have historical revenues and expenses for the job, click the Beginning Balances button to display the Job Beginning Balances window.**

    Use the Job Entries For tab to enter beginning balances. From the Job Balances tab, you can view the beginning balances of all jobs in the system.

You may want to read the next two sections before entering beginning balances. If you choose to use Phases and Cost Codes with your job, you can enter beginning balances by Phase and Cost Code.

7. **Enter a Date for the balance you intend to enter and a beginning balance amount in *either* the Expenses column *or* the Revenues column.**

Make sure that you enter the difference between revenues and expenses. If you subtract expenses from revenues and the number is positive, enter it in the Revenues column; if the difference is negative, enter the amount in the Expenses column.

You can enter balances for more than one date.

8. **When you finish entering beginning balances, click Save to redisplay the Maintain Jobs window.**

9. **Click the Custom Fields tab of the Maintain Jobs window to supply information for enabled custom fields.**

10. **Click the Estimated Exp./Rev. tab and use the list box selectors to enter estimated expenses and revenues.**

These estimates are optional. In Figure 12-2, you see the Estimated Exp./Rev. tab for a job that uses Phases. If you don't use Phases with your job, you see only two boxes: one for total estimated expenses and one for total estimated revenues.

11. **Click Save to store the job's information.**

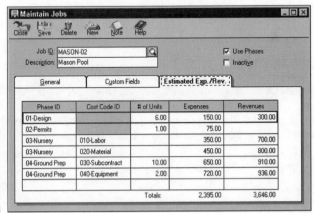

Figure 12-2: Enter estimated expenses and revenues for the job.

Phase ID	Cost Code ID	# of Units	Expenses	Revenues
01-Design		6.00	150.00	300.00
02-Permits		1.00	75.00	
03-Nursery	010-Labor		350.00	700.00
03-Nursery	020-Material		450.00	800.00
04-Ground Prep	030-Subcontract	10.00	650.00	910.00
04-Ground Prep	040-Equipment	2.00	720.00	936.00
		Totals:	2,395.00	3,646.00

When you complete a job, you can mark it inactive; redisplay the job in the Maintain Jobs window and check the Inactive box.

Establishing Phases

To create a Phase, follow these steps:

1. **Choose Maintain⇨Job Costs⇨Phases to display the Maintain Phases window (see Figure 12-3).**

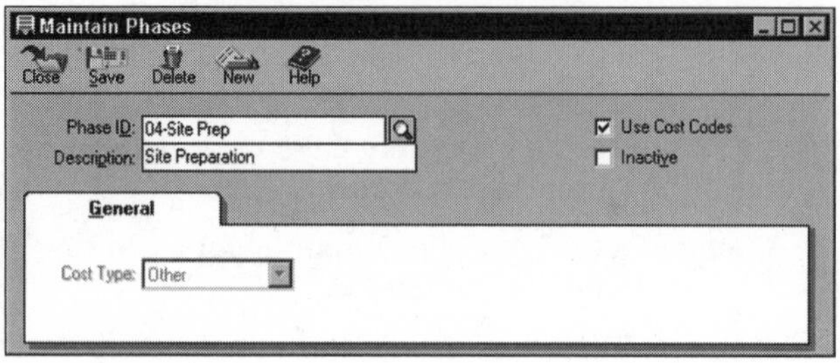

Figure 12-3:
Creating a
Phase that
uses Cost
Codes.

2. **In the Phase ID box, type an ID (up to 20 alphanumeric characters).**

3. **In the Description box, type a description for the Phase.**

4. **If you plan to use Cost Codes for the Phase, place a check mark in the Use Cost Codes box.**

   Peachtree disables the ability to choose a Cost Type.

5. **If you don't plan to use Cost Codes, choose a cost type for the Phase to categorize it in a general way: Labor, Materials, Equipment Rental, Subcontractors, or Other.**

6. **Click the Save button.**

Repeat these steps to set up other Phases you need for your job.

If you no longer need a Phase, you can mark it inactive; redisplay the Phase in the Maintain Phases window and check the Inactive box.

Coding Costs

You create a cost code exactly the same way you create a phase (see the previous section) with two exceptions:

✔ You use the Maintain Cost Codes window (choose Maintain⇨Job Costs⇨ Cost Codes).

✔ You won't find a Use Cost Codes check box to check (obviously!), so you'll be able to select a Cost Type. The Cost Types are the same for Phases and Cost Codes: Labor, Materials, Equipment Rental, Subcontractors, or Other.

If you no longer need a cost code, you can mark it inactive; redisplay the cost code in the Maintain Cost Codes window and check the Inactive box.

Assigning Jobs to Transactions

Okay, you've set up jobs (and maybe phases and cost codes, too). Now, you can use them.

Purchasing

Suppose that you're buying something to use on a job. You want to assign the expense to the job. You can assign the expense to the job from the Purchases/Receive Inventory window, the Write Checks window, or the Payments window, and the method is the same, regardless of the window you choose. In the following steps, we show you the process in the Purchases/Receive Inventory window:

1. **Choose Tasks➪Purchases/Receive Inventory to display the Purchases/Receive Inventory window (see Figure 12-4).**

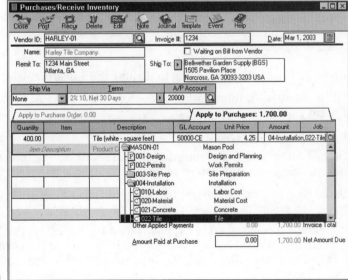

Figure 12-4:
Assign a Job to a purchase of anything but stock inventory items.

2. **Fill in the purchase information at the top of the window as you would for any purchase.**

   As you can see in Figure 12-4, when you open the Job list, the box overlays the Amount box, making it look like the amount disappears. It doesn't. (For details on filling in a purchase, see Chapter 5.)

3. **In the bottom portion of the window, enter the information for the item that you're purchasing.**

   In the Job column, use the lookup list indicator (this time it looks like a file folder) to assign the line to a job. If the job uses phases or cost codes, you see a folder in the list representing the job. You need to double-click the folder to open it and select the appropriate phase or cost code.

   You cannot purchase a stock inventory item to use on a job. If you already own a stock item that you want to use on a job, you can enter an inventory adjustment (see Chapter 11), or you can place the item on the customer's invoice. If you invoice the customer, you don't need to make the inventory adjustment.

4. **Continue entering lines as needed; you can include lines that you assign to jobs and lines that you don't assign to Jobs on the same purchase.**

5. **Click the Post button to save the purchase.**

Invoicing

By default, Peachtree sets up purchases you assign to jobs as reimbursable expenses that you can include on a bill to a customer. You also can choose not to include these reimbursable expenses on customer bills. Follow these steps to work with reimbursable expenses generated by assigning jobs to purchases or payments:

1. **Choose Tasks⇨Sales/Invoicing to display the Sales/Invoicing window.**

2. **Fill in the invoice information at the top of the window as you would for any purchase.**

   For details on filling in an invoice, see Chapter 7.

3. **In the bottom portion of the window, enter one line of information for each of the items that you're selling.**

   In the Job column, use the list box selector (this time it looks like a file folder) to assign the lines to a job, as appropriate.

4. **To include a reimbursable expense on an invoice, click the Apply Tickets/Reimbursable Expenses button in the lower left corner of the window to display the Apply Tickets/Reimbursable Expenses window (see Figure 12-5).**

5. **Click the Reimbursable Expenses tab to see expenses you entered in the Purchases/Inventory window, the Payments window, or the Write Checks window and assigned to a job.**

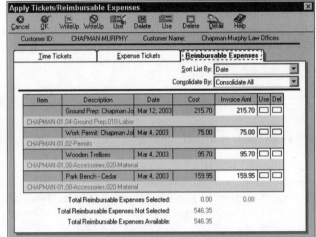

Figure 12-5:
You can bill the selected customer for any or all of these reimbursable expenses.

6. **To include a reimbursable expense on the invoice, highlight the reimbursable expense and click the Use check box.**

7. **To build some profit into a reimbursable expense, change the amount in the Invoice Amount column.**

   To mark up or down a group of reimbursable expenses, click the WriteUp toolbar button to display the Select Reimbursables To Write Up/Down dialog box.

When you use reimbursable expenses, keep these points in mind:

✔ You can delete reimbursable expenses from the Apply Tickets/ Reimbursable Expenses window if you decide not to bill the client for them. Place a check in the No Bill box to the right of the expense. Deleting the reimbursable expense does *not* delete the transaction that created the reimbursable expense; instead, deleting in the Apply Tickets/Reimbursable Expenses window breaks the tie between the reimbursable expense and the customer.

   You can't undo deleting here. After you delete a reimbursable expense, the connection between the reimbursable expense and the customer is *permanently* broken unless you erase the purchase or payment that created the reimbursable expense and reenter it completely.

✔ Be aware that using a reimbursable expense makes it disappear from the Apply Tickets/Reimbursable Expenses window. If you subsequently delete the line from the invoice, the reimbursable expense *does not* reappear in the window. If you mistakenly use a reimbursable expense and post the invoice, delete the invoice and reenter it.

✔ You can edit a reimbursable expense you intend to bill to a customer by editing the purchase or payment that assigns the expense to a job. You can find the transaction by opening the Purchases/Receive Inventory window, the Payments window, or the Write Checks window and clicking the Edit button.

Adding Overhead to a Job

To run your business, you incur certain expenses that accountants call *overhead* — expenses like telephone, postage, and electricity. You can think of overhead expenses as expenses you incur even if you don't sell anything (of course, you wouldn't incur overhead for long if you didn't sell anything, because you'd go out of business, but you get our drift).

If your company uses Job Costing, you need to divide your overhead and assign it to jobs. And, there's no standard method to do this in Peachtree. But, you *can* do it. The method we're going to describe assumes that you know the amount of overhead to add to each job. It could be a percentage of the expenses you incur, or it could be an hourly rate; if you *don't* know, you need to talk to your accountant, who figures out the overhead burden rate for you.

After you've gotten the rate from your accountant, you need to know your expenses by job, so that you can apply the overhead burden rate to each Job.

We suggest that you customize the Job Ledger report (choose Reports⇨Jobs and select the Job Ledger report). On the Fields tab, include the following fields: Job ID, Job Description, Phase ID, Cost Code ID, Transaction Date, Description, Actual Expenses, and Hours with Totals. When you print the report, you have all the information you need to apply the burden rate to your expenses and then assign the overhead to various jobs. For more information on customizing reports, see Chapter 15.

Okay. Now you know how to get the overhead amount. Enter the amount into Peachtree using a journal entry.

For this task, you need a Suspense account. We use a Suspense account to handle amounts that are temporary in nature. You can set up a Suspense account as any kind of account: Asset, Liability, Income, or Expense. But we suggest that you make it an account you're likely to notice if it appears on reports, because ultimately, your suspense account shouldn't have a balance. For help creating an account, see Chapter 3.

To assign overhead to a job, you make a journal entry (don't worry — it's easy). For more details on entering journal entries, see Chapter 18. Follow these steps:

1. **Choose Tasks⇨General Journal Entry to display the General Journal Entry window (see Figure 12-6).**

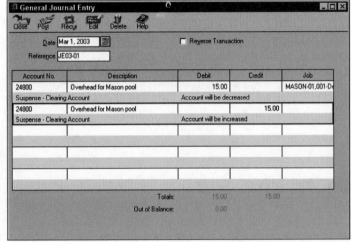

Figure 12-6:
Creating the journal entry to assign overhead to Jobs.

2. **Supply a Date and a Reference number for the journal entry, and ignore the Reverse Transaction check box.**

3. **Supply two lines for every overhead amount you want to assign, choosing the Suspense account on both lines.**

4. **On the Debit line, assign the job, but on the Credit line, don't assign the job.**

5. **Click Post to save the entry.**

This journal entry debits and credits the same account, which makes it have no affect on your books. However, assigning the job to the debit side of the transaction allocates the overhead expense to the job.

Purging and Jobs

When you perform year-end functions (see Chapter 18), you're given the opportunity to purge Jobs. Peachtree purges only those jobs that are not tied to any active transactions in the system. Suppose that you complete a job for a customer and mark the job as Inactive in the Maintain Jobs window. Further suppose that, while doing the job, you purchase items from a vendor and assign the items to the job. If the vendor or customer's bills remain unpaid, the job won't purge. See Chapter 18 for more information on purging.

Early in the chapter, we told you that you might not want to use Peachtree's Job Costing feature if you have a large number of jobs. Because you won't be able to purge jobs easily, your data files grow. As they grow, the response time of the system slows down.

You don't need to use jobs if your only purpose is creating reimbursable expenses. You can, instead, use Time and Expense tickets that you can bill back to a customer. You won't run into the same purging problems.

There is no good work around for this problem; you just need to be aware of it. If you choose to use Job Costing and the system slows down to an unacceptable level, you need to recreate your company. You can save list information (customers, vendors, employees, Chart of Accounts, and so on), but you lose historical information when you recreate.

Reporting on the Job

If you refer to Figure 12-5, you can see a modified version of the Job Ledger report. The default version shows all transactions that you've assigned to each job. Table 12-1 shows a list of the other reports that relate to Job Costing. See Chapter 15 to find out how to print reports.

Table 12-1	Other Reports Related to Job Costing
Report Name	*Description*
Cost Code List	Lists all defined cost codes, along with their description and cost type.
Estimated Job Expenses	Shows estimated and actual expenses and the difference by job and, if appropriate, by phase and cost code.
Estimated Job Revenue	Shows estimated and actual revenues and the difference by job and, if appropriate, by phase and cost code.
Job Costs by Type	Shows estimated and actual expenses by cost type for jobs that have phases.
Job Estimates	For each job (and, if appropriate, phase and cost code), lists estimated units and expenses.

Report Name	Description
Job List	Lists each job's ID, description, the starting and ending dates for the job, the customer to whom you assign the job, and the percentage complete.
Job Master File List	Lists all the details you entered in the Maintain Jobs window for each job.
Job Register	Shows an overview of job transaction dollars as of a certain date.
Phase List	Lists all defined phases, along with their description, cost type, and, if appropriate, cost codes.
Job Profitability Report	Shows the actual expenses and revenues for each job — and phase and cost code, if appropriate.
Unbilled Job Expense	Helps you identify existing reimbursable expenses that you can, if you want to, bill to a customer.

Part III
The Fancy Stuff

The 5th Wave — By Rich Tennant

"OUR GOAL IS TO MAXIMIZE YOUR UPSIDE AND MINIMIZE YOUR DOWNSIDE WHILE WE PROTECT OUR OWN BACKSIDE."

In this part . . .

*I*n this part, we cover many of the tasks you *don't* do every day. First, we show you how to customize Peachtree to make it work your way. Then we show you how to customize forms and produce and modify reports — after all, you put information *into* Peachtree, so you should be able to get it out and see the effects of your business habits. Then we cover reconciling the bank statement and the stuff you do monthly, quarterly, or annually. We also provide some real-life situations encountered by people just like you and ways you might handle similar situations.

Last, we show you how to easily keep your accounting information safe — a *very* important chapter. Why? Because you spend so much time putting stuff into Peachtree that it would be criminal to lose it just because your hard drive crashes or your office is robbed.

Chapter 13

Doing Things Your Way

. . . .

. . . .

*I*f old Blue Eyes (that's Frank Sinatra for all of you who are too young to remember) could do it "his way," so can you. Peachtree allows customization of how the program reacts to different things you do.

In this chapter, you discover how to change things such as how numbers display when you type them in, the colors that display, and what fields you see on your screen during data entry.

Setting Global Options

You can use the Global Options feature to set the way Peachtree functions as well as to select the color of your Peachtree windows. After all, you do want to make sure that it matches your office decor don't you? The options contain various "personality" types that control the behavior, look, and feel of the program. If you operate on a network, each workstation can apply its own options.

To set the global options, choose Options➪Global. The Maintain Global Options dialog box appears with the Accounting tab in the front.

The Accounting Screen tab

The first section of the Accounting Screen tab determines how Peachtree inserts decimal points and how many decimal points to use. You have a choice between allowing the Peachtree Accounting program to place a decimal point in figures or entering the decimal point yourself.

Choosing the Automatic setting causes Peachtree to insert the decimal point before the last two digits of the number. For example, if you type 10, Peachtree enters it as 0.10; however, if you set the decimal point entry to Manual, Peachtree enters 10 as 10.00.

Most people prefer to set the decimal point entry to Manual. This option affects any field that requires numbers, whether a Quantity field or a Price field.

Use the second section on the Accounting Screen tab to optionally hide the general ledger account number fields in certain task windows. Transactions created with the GL account number hidden, automatically use the default general ledger accounts that you have set up. (You can find out how to set default general ledger accounts in Chapter 4.)

You can hide general ledger accounts in the following task areas:

- ✔ **Accounts Receivable:** Select this option to hide G/L accounts in the Quotes, Sales Orders, Sales Invoicing, and Receipts windows.

- ✔ **Accounts Payable:** Select this option to hide G/L accounts in the Purchase Orders, Purchases/Receive Inventory, and Payments windows.

- ✔ **Payroll:** Select this option to hide G/L accounts in the Payroll Entry window.

For example, selecting the Accounts Receivable option changes the look of the Sales/Invoicing window. The Accounts Receivable account and the G/L account field of each line item are hidden. When you enter a sales invoice, Peachtree uses the sales default G/L account set up for the customer in Maintain Customers/Prospects. If you select an inventory item, Peachtree uses the default G/L accounts set up in Maintain Inventory Items for this item.

Should you hide these accounts? Well, look at it this way. If your chart of accounts has one G/L sales account and one accounts receivable account that you use most of the time, then these numbers would never change, so you may as well hide them. You can then generate your invoice faster because you won't have to press the Tab key at these fields when you create an invoice. If, however, the G/L sales account number changes depending on the product or service provided, you should leave the account numbers displayed so that you can change them as necessary.

If you have chosen the Hide General Ledger Accounts option, you can access the transaction's G/L accounts by selecting the Journal button in various task windows.

Other options on the Accounting tab include

✓ **Warn If A Record Was Changed But Not Saved:** When you select this option, Peachtree displays a warning if you try to exit a new or modified record without saving it. If you turn off this option, you won't see the warning. We strongly recommend that you select this option.

✓ **Warn If Inventory Item Is Out Of Stock:** When you select this option, Peachtree warns you if you try to sell an inventory item with a zero or negative balance on hand. This feature doesn't prevent such a transaction; you are only choosing to be informed of out-of-stock situations.

✓ **Hide Inactive Records:** When you select this option, Peachtree doesn't display inactive records in the lookup lists. (Lookup lists are the ones with the magnifying glass.)

✓ **Recalculate Cash Balance Automatically In Receipts And Payments:** When you select this option, Peachtree automatically updates the Cash Balance fields in the Receipts, Payments, and Payroll Entry windows as you post or save transactions. The balance displays as of the date that appears in the task window.

✓ **Use Timeslips Accounting Link:** If you also use the Timeslip program, you can electronically transfer revenue information from Timeslips' general ledger to Peachtree's. (You can discover more about Timeslips in the appendix.)

Click the check box next to any desired feature. A check mark appears next to the selected items.

The General tab

The General tab includes features that affect Peachtree's performance as well as the visual color schemes. If you change a color scheme preference, you must exit and restart Peachtree Accounting before the color changes take effect.

The first two options affect how Peachtree performs:

✓ **Do Not Print Total Page Length Of Reports In Report Headers:** When you select this option, Peachtree calculates the total number of pages in a report before printing the report. Selecting this option allows reports to print faster, skipping the initial calculation of total number of pages prior to printing. Instead of displaying "page 1 of 12" or "page 2 of 12" in the report header, your reports will display "page 1" or "page 2."

Quite honestly, we think the time saved is minimal and having the total number of pages is very useful, so we suggest that you do not activate this feature.

✔ **Do Not Show Quantity On Hand In Inventory Item Lookups:** Selecting this option speeds up the display of inventory item lookup lists because it skips the process of calculating each item's current quantity on hand every time you display the inventory item lookup list. We recommend that you select this option if you have a large number of inventory items.

Depending on the configuration of your computer, you may or may not see a noticeable improvement when selecting these performance options.

The Line Item Entry Display setting allows you to determine whether one or two lines will display per line item in the various task windows. Two-line entry displays the name of the sales account and description of the product, while single-line entry allows display of more items on the screen.

The Smart Data Entry options enable lookup lists to display instantly and anticipate what you want to enter. They make data entry faster in most cases. Unless you have a very slow computer, you'll probably want both of these features activated:

✔ **Automatic Field Completion:** Anticipates what you're typing by filling in the field with the nearest match to the characters you enter as you enter them. With it, you can avoid having to enter all characters.

✔ **Drop-Down List Displays Automatically:** Allows Peachtree to automatically display a list of choices when you place the insertion point in a lookup field and type at least one character.

The last part of the General window affects the colors of the Peachtree windows and dialog boxes. When you select a color scheme, this default affects all Peachtree companies you open at this computer.

These color schemes only apply to windows and dialog boxes within the Peachtree Accounting program, not other Windows applications or the Windows desktop.

Click the check box next to any desired feature and then click OK.

Customizing Data Entry Windows

Over the years, our clients have commented that they want to be able to enter their data quickly and go on to the next project. To aid in this goal, Peachtree allows you to modify several of the Peachtree windows to display certain portions of the window while hiding others. For example, if your business doesn't use job costing, why not hide the job box in the Sales/Invoicing or Purchases/Receive Inventory windows? By hiding a portion of the window, the person entering the data skips the hidden areas, which allows for faster data entry.

You can also set up different formats, known as *templates,* for entering and reviewing data in several of the task windows. You can modify the following windows: Quotes, Sales Orders, Sales/Invoicing, Purchase Orders, and Purchases/Receive Inventory.

Modifying a template doesn't change the way a form prints.

For example, you can remove the Jobs and Ship To information from the Sales/Invoicing window. To customize the data entry window:

1. **Choose Tasks⇨Sales/Invoicing to display the Sales/Invoicing window.**

2. **Create a customized window by clicking the Template button on the Sales/Invoicing toolbar.**

   A listing of available templates appears, with a check mark next to the template currently in use.

   You can't edit or delete predefined templates. To customize a template, you must first create a new, customized template.

3. **From the list of templates, click Customize Templates.**

   The Maintain Sales/Invoicing Templates window appears.

4. **Before you can modify the template, you need to enter a name and description, so click in the Template ID box and type a unique name for the template.**

   An example may be to use your company name.

5. **Press the Tab key and enter a description of the template.**

   Now you can determine which fields you want to be hidden during data entry. Some fields are required and cannot be hidden.

6. **To hide certain data entry fields, click the word <Show> next to the field to be hidden.**

   The word <Show> changes to <Hide>, which indicates that you want to hide the field.

   In Figure 13-1, we've chosen to hide the Ship To: and the Job fields.

   Select the Set Template As Default check box if you want to use this template each time you open the task window.

7. **When you finish choosing the fields that you do not want to display, click the Save button and then click Close.**

To see the changes, you need to close the current window and then reopen it.

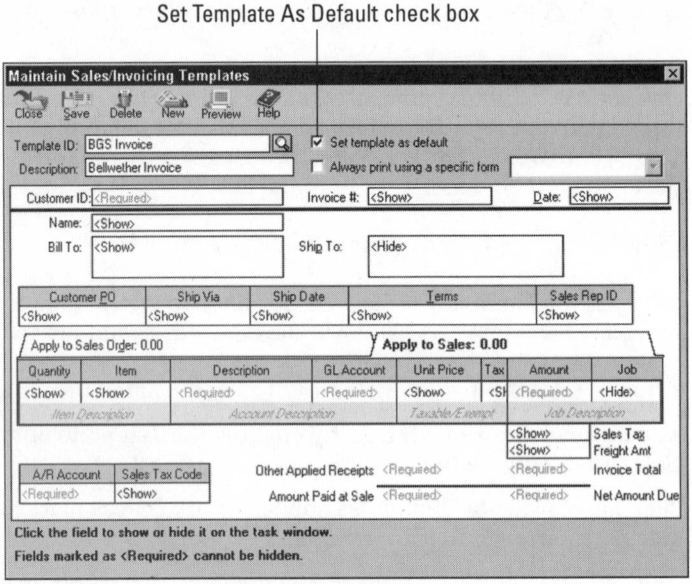

Set Template As Default check box

Figure 13-1:
Fields marked
cannot be hidden.

Memorizing Transactions

Peachtree has a feature called Memorized Transactions that can save you a great deal of time in repetitive data entry tasks. Because they're different from recurring transactions, you can use memorized transactions repeatedly and at whatever time interval you choose. You can enter memorized transactions for General Journal entries, Quotes, Sales Invoices, Purchase Orders, and Payments.

With memorized transactions, you can enter the G/L accounts and general information without knowing an exact amount. They are great for transactions that occur irregularly because they do not automatically post and you can use them as needed.

Creating memorized transactions

Suppose that you sell a product line in which a customer will probably need several parts at once, instead of just one part. By creating a memorized Sales Invoice, each time one of these units is sold you won't need to look up or enter the invoice information. In our sample company, we sell bird feeders. When a customer orders two bird feeders and poles, we give them the birdseed at no charge. To create a memorized transaction to store the invoice information, follow these steps:

1. **Choose Maintain⇨Memorized Transactions to list available memorized transactions types.**

   In Peachtree 2002, you can save memorized transactions from a Task window. See the appendix for details.

2. **Choose the type of transaction, which, in this case, is Sales Invoices.**

   The Maintain Memorized Sales Invoices window appears.

3. **Enter an ID and description that defines the transaction.**

   IDs can be up to 20 alphanumeric characters, whereas the description can be up to 30 characters in length.

4. **If you're designing this invoice for a specific customer, enter the customer ID; otherwise, leave the customer ID blank so that you can use it for any of your customers.**

5. **Enter the transaction information and then click the Save button.**

Did you notice that this transaction does not have an invoice number or date? That's because not all transaction fields are maintained in memorized transactions. The date and invoice number fields will display when you actually use this memorized transaction.

Using memorized transactions

You can use a memorized transaction at any time. To see how to use the invoice we create in the preceding section, follow these steps:

1. **Choose Task⇨Sales/Invoicing (or whatever type of transaction you want to use) to display a task window.**

   In Peachtree 2002, you can enter memorized transactions from a Task window. See the appendix for details.

2. **Choose Edit⇨Select Memorized Transactions.**

   A window appears, displaying all the Sales/Invoicing memorized transactions.

3. **Click the transaction you want to use and then click OK.**

Violà! The invoice information appears. You only need to enter the header information such as customer name, invoice number, date, and so forth. You can edit the transaction lines as needed. We told you this could save you time!

You can find out how to enter invoices in Chapter 7.

You can enter and save existing transactions as memorized transactions for later use. After entering the transaction, choose Edit⇨Save as Memorized Transaction. Enter an ID and description for the transaction.

A Strange Turn of Events

Are you a Post-It note fanatic? Is your desk littered with lots of little notes with no clear place to put them yet you know they are important? If these notes pertain to customers, vendors, or employees, you may want to take a look at Peachtree's Event feature.

Turning off the automatic events

We all know that too much of a good thing is not good. So it is with the event log. By default, Peachtree keeps a log file of every type of transaction you make for customers, vendors, and employees. Now, we're not talking about the journals where the actual transactions are stored. No, we're talking about a second place to store a list of transactions. It's a nice enough feature, but . . . if you decide to use Peachtree's default event log settings, eventually, you can plan on going to lunch when you try to store a transaction or print a report. We recommend that you turn off the event log's automatic features and only create events when you want them.

To turn off the automatic events:

1. **Choose Options⇨Action Items/Event Log Options to display the Action Items and Event Log Options screen.**

2. **Click the Transactions tab.**

3. **Remove all the check marks from the Create Event column and then click OK.**

   Peachtree no longer automatically lists transactions into the Event Log file. Peachtree 2002 automatically turns on event tracking, even if you previously turned it off. See the appendix for details on how to turn it off.

Creating your own events

Suppose that you've contacted a delinquent customer and would like to make a note of the conversation, or perhaps an employee received a favorable comment from a customer or a reprimand for being late. Maybe your favorite vendor sales representative has promised you a special discount on your next order. For notes like these, you can effectively use Peachtree's event log. Throw those Post-It notes away!

You can create events from the Maintain Customers, Vendor, or Employees windows; from most task windows involving customers, vendors, or employees; or even from the Action Items window (also available under the Tasks menu).

For this example, create an event note tracking a telephone call we received about one of our employees, Melvin Foster.

1. **Choose Maintain⇨Employees/Sales Reps to display the Maintain Employees/Sales Rep window.**

2. **Click the Event button to reveal the Create Event window, as shown in Figure 13-2.**

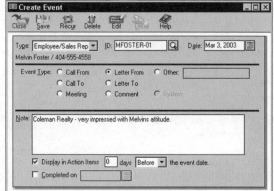

Figure 13-2:
Click the
Edit button
to modify an
existing
event.

3. **Choose the Employee ID from the ID lookup list.**

4. **Optionally, change the date of the "event."**

   You can type the event date or select a date from the calendar icon.

5. **Choose an Event Type.**

   If you select the Other category, you can write your own event description.

6. **Type a note describing the telephone conversation in the Note field.**

   You can enter up to 255 characters in the note. To start a new paragraph, simply press Ctrl + Enter.

7. **Click Save and then close the Event window.**

Looking at the event log

You can see or print all the events pertaining to a customer, vendor, or employee.

You can access the event log through the Maintain Customers, Vendors, or Employees screens. Take a look at a list of events that have been created for our employee Melvin Foster.

1. **Choose Maintain⇨Employees/Sales Reps to display the Maintain Employees/Sales Rep window.**

2. **Enter the Employee ID or choose it from the lookup list.**

3. **Click the Log button and Peachtree displays the log file.**

We do have a complaint about this feature, though. You can click Print if you want to print the event log, but it only prints the portion of the note that fits on one line of the printed page (approximately what's displayed on the screen). If your note is longer — sorry — you can't print any more of it. If you would like to see this feature enhanced, let Peachtree know by contacting them at www.peachtree.com. You've heard the saying, "The squeaky wheel gets the grease." Who knows . . . maybe future versions of Peachtree will allow for better printing of the event log.

Making a To-Do List

While numerous uses exist for the Event Log and Action Items features, this book can contain only a specific number of pages. Because of that, we can't show you every possible feature, or even all the things you can do with some of the features, but we focus on one of the more useful features — creating a "to do" list in the Action Items window.

Keeping track of the things you need to do with the Action Items feature is like having your own little Personal Information Manger (PIM) stored right in Peachtree.

To use the Action Items feature:

1. **Choose Tasks⇨Action Items to display the Action Items window.**

2. **Click the To Do tab to bring the To Do list to the front.**

   Use the To Do tab to set up a list of tasks that you need to complete. These tasks are ones not associated with a vendor, customer, or employee.

3. **Enter a date for the first To Do item.**

   Peachtree assumes that you want to accomplish this task as of the current date.

4. **Click the Notes section of the first line and type your first task.**

After you complete a task, select the Complete check box at the beginning of the line. To hide completed items, click the arrow next to the drop-down list at the top of the dialog box and choose Uncompleted Events. Peachtree then hides the completed events.

Although you see only eight lines for To Do items, when you reach the last line, press the Tab key from the Notes field and Peachtree will create a new line and add a scroll bar.

Other useful buttons are the Delete button to delete a selected task, and the Print button to print a copy of your To Do list.

Finding Transactions

Looking for specific transactions can be time consuming. In many cases, the Customer and Vendor ledger reports give a lot of information, but what about employees? What if you're looking for inventory information that could be affecting a customer and a vendor? Fortunately for us, Peachtree includes a new feature in Version 8 called Find Transactions. Thank you, thank you, thank you, Peachtree! (Sorry, we get carried away sometimes.)

The Find Transaction feature is new to Peachtree Version 8.

You can activate the Find Transaction feature at any time or from any window in Peachtree. To search for transactions:

1. **Choose Edit⇨Find Transaction or press Ctrl + F.**

   The Find Transactions window opens, showing a number of conditions by which to search. You can use any option by itself, or in combination with another option. If you combine two options, Peachtree searches for a transaction that matches *both* criteria. Here are the conditions you can use to search:

   • **Date:** Find transactions based on To and From dates.

   • **Transaction Type:** Find transactions based on the type of transaction such as Invoice, Purchase, or Inventory Adjustment.

   • **Reference Number:** Find transactions based on the transaction reference number. You entered this number when you created the transactions. For payments or checks, the reference number usually refers to the check number.

   • **Customer, Vendor, or Employee ID:** Find transactions for a specific or range of customers, vendors, or employees.

   • **Job ID:** Find transactions related to a specified job.

   • **Item ID:** Find transactions related to a specified inventory item.

   • **Transaction Amount:** Find transactions equal to, greater than, less than, or in a specified dollar range.

   • **General Ledger Account:** Find transactions that affect specified G/L accounts.

Figure 13-3 shows an example. We want to see any transactions created this year for one of our customers, Coleman Realty. We'll let the Find Transactions feature do the detective work for us.

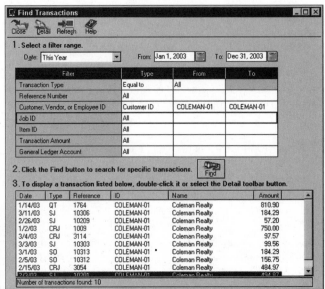

Figure 13-3:
Enter the criteria to search.

2. **Click the date drop-down arrow and choose This Year.**

3. **Click the drop-down list next to Customer, Vendor, or Employee ID and choose Customer ID.**

4. **In the From and To boxes, enter the customer ID you want Peachtree to find.**

   For this example, enter COLEMAN-01.

5. **Click the Find button.**

   Peachtree searches all journals for any transactions referring to customer COLEMAN-01. The results display at the bottom of the Find Transactions window.

The window lists each transaction with the date, type, reference, ID, name, and amount. The Type field indicates the source of the transaction. Table 13-1 shows the possible transaction types as well as the name of their respective journals and the source of the reference.

Table 13-1	Transaction Types and Sources	
Type	*Name*	*Source*
ASBY	Assemblies Adjustment Journal	Build/Unbuild Assemblies
CDJ	Cash Disbursement Journal	Payments
CRJ	Cash Receipts Journal	Receipts
ET	Expense Ticket	Time/Expense
GENJ	General Journal	General Journal Entry
INAJ	Inventory Adjustments Journal	Inventory Adjustments
PJ	Purchase Journal	Purchase/Receive Inventory
PO	Purchase Order Journal	Purchase Orders
PRJ	Payroll Journal	Payroll
QT	Quote	Quotes
SJ	Sales Journal	Sales/Invoicing
SO	Sales Order Journal	Sales Order
TT	Time Ticket	Time/Expense

Click any column heading to sort the transactions in descending order by the selected column. Click the column heading again to sort the transactions in ascending order.

Double-click any transaction line to view or edit the actual transaction.

After you finish viewing the transactions, click the Close button to close the Find Transactions window.

Chapter 14

Working with Forms

*P*eachtree defines a *form* as a document you exchange with your customers, vendors, or employees. Usually, you print these documents on preprinted forms, but you can design a form and print it on blank paper.

If you want to use preprinted forms, you can purchase your forms from your local printer, or you can use the offers you receive in your Peachtree software box. Chapter 23 lists Web contact information on a couple of sources for forms: Deluxe Forms or Peachtree Forms. If you contact Deluxe Forms at 1-800-328-0304 and reference this book and discount code R03578, you'll receive 20 percent off your first order.

Printing Forms

You use essentially the same steps for printing any forms whether you're printing a quote, a purchase order, a check, or a customer invoice. Peachtree can print your forms one at a time or together in a batch. Peachtree also includes other forms for printing customer, vendor, or employee labels as well as collection letters, 1099s, and various payroll forms such as W2s or 941 reports.

A variety of forms are available, but you can customize any form.

Previewing forms in the document window

Because Peachtree has several forms, you may want to see what your quote, purchase order, check, or invoice would look like in each form. You can use the new Preview feature to examine the transaction.

New to Peachtree Version 8, you now have the ability to preview forms prior to printing.

1. **Display the transaction you want to preview on the screen.**

   If necessary, click the Edit button and choose from a previously posted transaction.

2. **Click the Preview button.**

   The Preview Forms dialog box appears, listing the available forms (see Figure 14-1). The forms listed vary depending on the transaction type.

Preview button

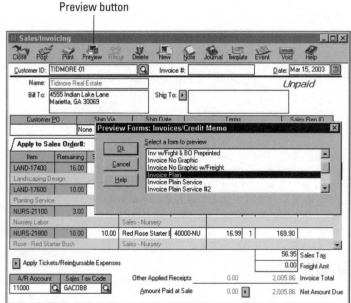

Figure 14-1: Choose the form that best suits your needs.

3. **Choose the form you want to print and then click OK.**

   The About to Preview dialog box appears, in which you verify (or change, if necessary) the first form to view.

   The dialog box, which prompts you for a number, does not display when you preview a Sales Order because Peachtree assigned a number when you created the Sales Order.

4. **Click OK to display the form in the Print Preview window.**

   Don't strain your eyes! Notice the mouse pointer turns into a magnifying glass. Use the mouse to zoom in or out on the form.

5. **Click anywhere on the form to enlarge the view; click a second time to enlarge the view even more (see Figure 14-2).**

Print button   Magnifying glass

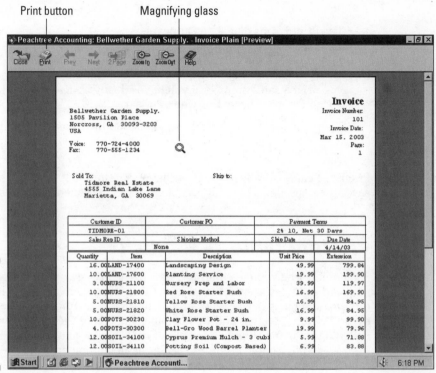

Figure 14-2:
Click the
document to
enlarge or
reduce the
view.

Click the Close button if you need to make changes to the form.
Peachtree returns to the form window.

6. **After you preview the form, click Print to print the transaction on the
   selected form.**

Printing from the document window

In the previous section, you discover how to preview and then print a document from the preview window. If, however, you don't want to preview the
document, you can print directly from the data entry window.

To print a form, follow these steps:

1. **Click the Print button (or press Ctrl+P).**

   You'll see the Preview Forms dialog box like the one shown previously in
   Figure 14-1. The form names listed vary depending on the type of
   transaction.

2. **Select the form to print and click OK.**

    The Print Forms dialog box appears.

3. **Click Real. (Meaning you want to *really* print the document.)**

    When you print most forms, the About to Print dialog box appears. If you print a sales order, or if you have already assigned a number to the document, this dialog box won't appear.

4. **Verify the number Peachtree will assign to the transaction and click OK.**

    Peachtree prints the document.

Peachtree automatically posts a transaction after printing. Posting a transaction saves the transaction and, if applicable, updates the general ledger as well.

Printing forms in a batch

Sometimes, when you're entering data such as invoices, you don't want to stop and go through the steps to print the invoice each and every time. In this case, you may like Peachtree's batch printing feature. If you want to print several of your invoices at the same time, you create each invoice without assigning an invoice number and click Post. Then, whenever you're ready to print your transaction, Peachtree can print all unnumbered invoices at the same time. You also can batch-print statements, quotes, sales orders, purchase orders, and both A/P and P/R checks.

If you read Chapter 1, you may remember the Peachtree Navigation Aid. If so, you've probably noticed by now that we haven't been using it much. We've found using the Peachtree menus the quickest and most straightforward way to accomplish most tasks. However, you can print forms in a batch much quicker by using the Navigation Aid at the bottom of your screen.

1. **Click the applicable Navigation Aid (see Figure 14-3).**

    For statements, quotes, sales orders, or invoices, click the Sales Navigation Aid. For purchase orders or A/P checks, click the Purchases Navigation Aid. For PR checks, click the Payroll Navigation Aid.

2. **Click the form you want to print.**

    Peachtree displays the Print Forms dialog box, which shows forms you can use to print on either plain paper or preprinted forms.

3. **Click the form you want to use and then click OK.**

4. **Click Real.**

    Peachtree prompts you for a beginning number.

5. **Verify the beginning number and then click OK.**

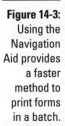

Figure 14-3:
Using the
Navigation
Aid provides
a faster
method to
print forms
in a batch.

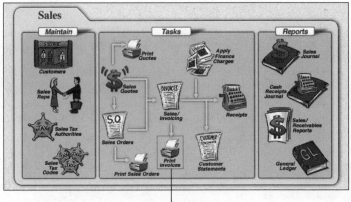

Print Invoices

Peachtree immediately prints forms for all unnumbered transactions and displays a dialog box asking whether the forms printed properly. If you click Yes, Peachtree assigns the numbers to the forms. If you click No, the forms remain unnumbered, and you need to reprint them.

Modifying Forms

You can customize any form to better meet your needs. You can move, add, or delete fields, change fonts, or even add your company logo.

Exploring the Form Designer

The Form Design window enables you to create new, customized forms or edit existing forms to match your business's needs. If you've used an earlier version of Peachtree, you'll notice changes to the Version 8 Form Designer. To use the Form Designer, follow these steps:

1. **Choose Reports⇨Accounts Receivable (or whichever report area) for the form you want to modify.**

   You can find forms in three Report Areas: Accounts Receivable, Accounts Payable, or Payroll.

2. **From the report list, locate and click the folder containing the form you want to modify.**

   Because Peachtree lists forms after reports, you may need to scroll down the Report List a bit (see Figure 14-4).

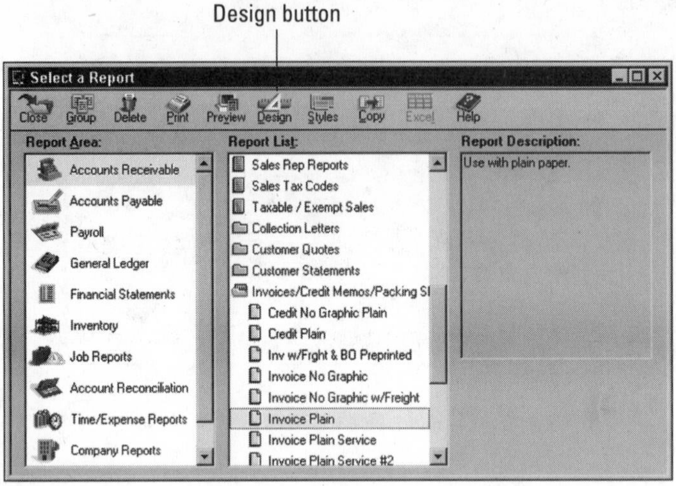

Design button

Figure 14-4:
Peachtree
displays a
list of
available
forms.

If you're using Peachtree Version 7 or earlier, double-click the form
folder to display the forms.

3. **Click *once* on the form you want to modify, then click the Design button.**

The selected report appears in Design view (see Figure 14-5).

Maximize the design window for optimal viewing.

The design window has two main parts: the design area that displays
Peachtree data fields and other objects such as rectangles or pictures, and the
toolbars. Five different toolbars display on the design window. Each toolbar
has a specific function:

✔ **Alignment toolbar:** Use this toolbar to line up two or more objects
together.

✔ **Cursor Position toolbar:** Use this toolbar to determine the location of
selected objects.

✔ **Main toolbar:** Use this toolbar to accomplish many common steps,
including Save and Close.

✔ **Object toolbar:** Use this toolbar to add new objects to the window.

The Selection tool is the first tool on the Object toolbar. Use this tool to
select objects you want to move, modify, or delete.

✔ **Properties toolbar:** Use this toolbar to determine an object's content,
size, order, position, and appearance.

Object toolbar Main toolbar Cursor Position toolbar Alignment toolbar

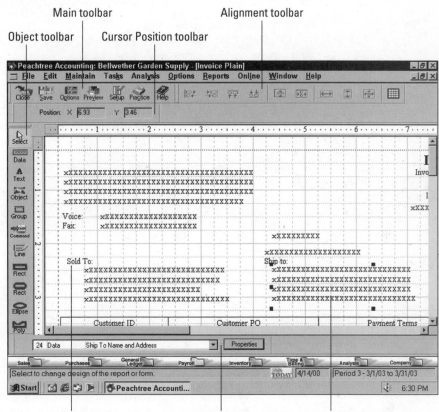

Text object Properties toolbar Selected data field object

Figure 14-5:
A customer
invoice in
Design
view.

Everything on a form is a type of object. You can find data field objects, text field objects, text objects, shaped objects, or even grouped objects. Take a look at the first of two main object types you find on a form. A data field object is the most common object you see on a form. Peachtree obtains information, either from the Maintain window or from the Tasks window, and places it in data fields. Peachtree indicates data field objects with XXX's for words or NNN's for numbers.

The second most common object on a form is a text object. Peachtree calls those objects that show a specific piece of text such as "Sold to" or "Thank you for your business" text fields. You can easily identify text objects because you just read them on the screen.

To modify any type of object, you first need to select the object. "Okay," you say, "but how do I know which object to modify?" Well, you click any object to select it. The object has eight small black box "handles" around it, and the Properties toolbar indicates the content of the selected object.

Make sure that you maximize your window to view the Properties toolbar.

Moving objects

Moving objects is easy. If an object isn't located where you want it, you move it by selecting it. Then, hold down the left mouse button and drag the object to a new location. After you move the object to the correct position, release the mouse button.

Optionally, move an object by selecting it and using your arrow keys to move it to a new position.

Deleting objects

Deleting objects is easy, too. If you want to get rid of something on a form, click the object to select it, and then press the Delete key. Poof . . . it's gone!

If you delete the wrong object, immediately choose Edit⇨Undo to reverse the last step you took.

Adding data field objects

If you want to add additional data field objects to a form, you need to tell Peachtree where you want to place the field and which field you want to add. To do so:

1. **Click the Data button on the Object toolbar.**

   As you move your mouse over the form design area, the mouse pointer turns into a thin, black cross.

2. **Click the mouse at the approximate location you want to place the new data field object.**

   The Data Object Properties dialog box, like the one you see in Figure 14-6, appears.

3. **Click the Data Field Name drop-down list and click the field you want to add.**

   You see only fields applicable to the current form.

   We show you in a little while how to modify the appearance of any field.

4. **Click OK to close the Data Object Properties dialog box and add the object to your form.**

Data tool   Data Field Name selection list

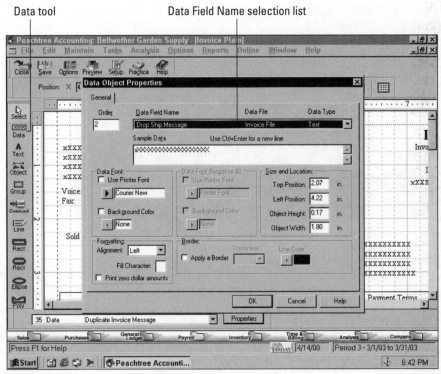

Figure 14-6:
Choose a
data field to
add to your
form.

Adding Text objects

Data field objects contain variable information, in that they will vary from one page of the invoice to the next, while text field objects are static. Static means the information won't change; the same words appear on each and every page of the form.

You add a text object in a similar method to adding data fields, but instead of Peachtree specifying the object size, you determine the size yourself.

1. **Click the Text button on the Object toolbar.**

   As you move your mouse over the design area, the mouse pointer turns into a thin, black cross.

2. **Click the mouse at the approximate location you want to place the new text object, hold down the mouse button, and drag the mouse to the right and slightly downward to draw the approximate size of the text object you want to add. Then release the mouse button.**

   The Text Object Properties dialog box, shown in Figure 14-7, appears.

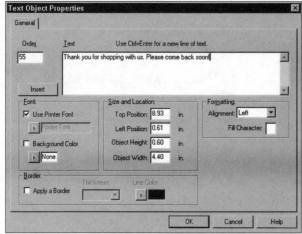

Figure 14-7:
Enter text
information
here.

3. **Enter the text you want to appear on the form. If you need a second line, press Ctrl+Enter to move the insertion point to the next line.**

4. **Click OK to add the next text object to your form.**

Resizing an object

If an object is too long, too short, too narrow, or too wide, resize it with your mouse.

1. **Select the object you want to resize, then position the mouse over one of the object "handles."**

   As you do so, the mouse pointer turns into a double-headed black arrow.

2. **Drag the handle in the direction you want to resize the object, then release the mouse button.**

   Peachtree resizes the object.

Formatting field properties

With all those XXX's and NNN's on the screen, how do you know what a data field looks like? Well, you examine the field properties. The properties tell you what each field represents as well as its size and appearance. You can determine properties for both data fields and text objects.

To view or modify object properties, follow these steps:

1. **Click to select the object you want to modify.**

   To make all objects the same font, press Ctrl+A to select all objects, then right-click and choose Font. From the Font dialog box, select the font you want for the entire form and then click OK.

2. **On the Properties toolbar, click the Properties button.**

   An Object Properties dialog box appears.

Using the Object Properties dialog box, you can choose a specific font, size, and color for each object, or you can change how you want numbers to print when designing forms. We talk about numbers first.

Peachtree designates numbers that appear before the decimal point with a capital N, and designates numbers that appear after the decimal point with a lowercase n. Suppose you wanted normal decimal points and commas. You might use NNN,NNN.nn as your template. Using this template, one thousand would print as 1,000.00 and ten thousand would print as 10,000.00.

In Table 14-1, we show the values 1234.56 and –1234.56 using various formats.

Table 14-1	Number Samples	
Format	*Positive*	*Negative*
NNN,NNN.nn	1,234.56	–1,234.56
NNN,NNN.nn–	1,234.56	1,234.56–
(NNN,NNN.nn)	1,234.56	(1,234.56)

To change the number format for the selected field, modify the template to match the appearance you want.

To change the font for the selected object, follow these steps:

1. **If you see a check mark in the Use Printer Font box, remove it by clicking the box and then click the font selection arrow.**

   The Font dialog box appears, allowing you to select a font, style, size, color, and special effects.

2. **Click OK after making your font selection.**

3. **When you finish using the Data Object Properties box, click OK to close it.**

Aligning objects

When you select multiple objects in the Forms Design window, Peachtree can align those objects in relation to each other. You can align their top, bottom, left, or right edges together, or you can choose to align the centers vertically or horizontally. To align multiple objects:

1. **Click the Selection tool and then select the objects you want to align.**

   To select multiple objects, use Windows selection techniques and hold the Shift or Ctrl keys and click each object you want to modify as a group.

2. **Click a tool from the Alignment toolbar.**

   The objects align based on your choice.

When you've selected multiple objects to align them, how does Peachtree determine which of the selected objects' edges to use when aligning fields? If you pay close attention, you'll notice that all the selected objects have gray handles, except the object you selected last, which has black handles. Peachtree aligns the objects to the one with the black handles — we call it the "foundation" object. Rule to remember: Select the "foundation" object last.

Grouping fields

When you have a series of rows of data, such as lines on an invoice, a customer statement, or a purchase order, instead of creating each field individually, use the Group command to list data fields displayed in columns and rows.

To create a group object follow these steps:

1. **Click the Group button on the Object toolbar.**

2. **Click the mouse at the approximate location you want to place the new group object, hold down the mouse button, and drag the mouse to the right and slightly downward to specify the approximate size of the group object you want to add. Release the mouse button.**

   The Group Object Properties dialog box, shown in Figure 14-8, appears.

   The Group Object Properties dialog box has several columns, most importantly to define which fields you want included in the group table. The list of fields varies depending on the type of form:

   • **Show Field:** Check this box to include the data field in the group table.

   • **Column Number:** This option specifies the order in which the data fields appear in the group table. You cannot change order directly here; use the Move Field up and down-arrow buttons to change the column number.

- **Field Name:** This option identifies the fields included in the group table.

- **Number Format:** In numeric data fields, a number (#) button appears here. Clicking the # displays the Number Formatting window. (See "Formatting field properties" earlier in this chapter.)

- **Field Title:** Peachtree calls the heading that prints out for the column a field title. You can change this option for any of the data fields or leave it blank.

- **Column Width:** You can enter a column width to three decimal places.

- **Title Alignment:** This aligns the title within the column.

You can set other options for your grouped object, including the font for the data or headings, whether to define a border to print around the grouped object, and row spacing.

Row spacing is new to Peachtree Version 8.

By checking the Row Spacing box, you can define the spacing between rows of data fields in the Group object. The value you enter determines additional space between data rows. You can enter any amount from –10 to 100. For example, if you use a 10-point font for data and you want the data rows double-spaced, enter a 10 in the Row Spacing box.

3. **Make your group object selections and then click OK.**

   Peachtree places the grouped object on your page.

Move Field button

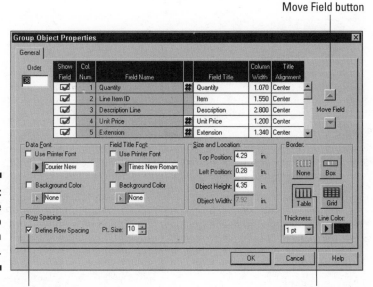

Figure 14-8:
Choose fields to include in a data group.

Define Row Spacing check box

Border selections

Saving forms

After you've modified a form, you'll want to save it. In fact, we recommend you save it *as* you're modifying it. Then resave it again every few steps or so. To save a form:

1. **Click the Save button to display the Save As dialog box.**

2. **Enter a name for the form.**

   You cannot use the exact name of one of Peachtree's standard forms. You must give your form a unique name.

   When printing forms, the list of available forms appears in alphabetical order. To make your customized form appear at the top of the forms selection box, make the first character of the form a number. For example, "1My Invoice" appears before "My Invoice."

3. **Optionally, type a description of the form in the Description box.**

4. **Click Save to save the form for future use.**

Peachtree identifies custom forms by a red flag on the form icon.

Delete any customized form by highlighting the form name in the Select a Report window and clicking the Delete button.

We would have loved to consider including Shapes, Commands, Field Order, and Graphic objects. Unfortunately, these items are beyond the scope of this book, but you can find information about them in your Peachtree Users Guide.

Chapter 15

Making Reports Work for You

In This Chapter

▶ Viewing reports

▶ Modifying reports

▶ Choosing report styles

▶ Sending reports to Excel

▶ Making report groups

*P*eachtree Accounting includes more than 125 standard reports, ranging from a list of your chart of accounts to a check register to a job profitability report. In each chapter of Part II of this book, you find a list of the standard reports Peachtree supplies. In this chapter, we show you how to print those reports to your screen, your printer, or an Excel workbook. We also show you how to modify and optionally save any report.

Both Peachtree 8 and Peachtree 2002 now work with Crystal Reports. See the appendix for details.

Viewing Standard Reports

Save a tree! Instead of printing on paper, print your Peachtree reports directly to your computer screen. To preview reports on your screen, follow these steps:

1. **To print reports, choose <u>R</u>eports and then select the module you need, such as Accounts Payable.**

   The Select a Report window (see Figure 15-1) appears with a listing of available reports.

2. **Click the report to view.**

   A small red triangle to the left of the report icon indicates a customized report.

   New to Peachtree Version 8, Peachtree lists forms in alphabetical order with customized forms appearing before standard forms.

Customized Report icon

Print to Screen button ─┐ ┌─Standard Report icon

Print to Paper button   Send a Report to Excel button

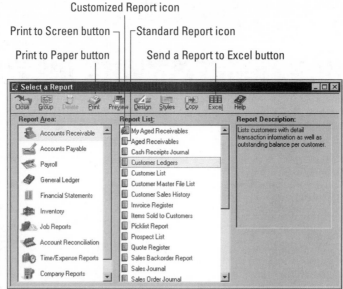

Figure 15-1:
Selecting
reports to
print.

3. Click either the Preview, Print, or Excel button.

If you click Preview, Peachtree prints the report to your monitor. If you click Print, Peachtree prints the report to your printer. If you click Excel, Peachtree sends the report to an Excel workbook. (You can find out more about sending the report to an Excel workbook later in this chapter.)

To print a report to your screen using the report's default settings, double-click the report.

Peachtree displays a dialog box that allows you to set up the report to limit the information that appears on the report. In most cases, the dialog box contains three tabs: Filter, Fields, and Format. The next couple of sections show you how to use this dialog box to customize a report.

4. To print a report with the standard settings, click the OK button.

While previewing the report on-screen, click the Setup button to display the Page Setup dialog box. From this dialog box, you can change paper size, source, orientation, and margins.

In most cases, when you print a report to the screen, you can "drill down" to view the details of the transaction. As you move the mouse pointer over the transaction, it changes to the shape of a magnifying glass that contains a Z (for Zoom). Double-click, and Peachtree displays the transaction in the window where you entered it. You can make changes to the transaction and when you save it, in most cases, Peachtree automatically updates the report to reflect the changes. If the report doesn't automatically update, you need to click the Options button in the report window on-screen and then click OK to "reprint" the report.

Customizing Reports

Sometimes, the standard reports just don't contain enough information to meet your needs, or perhaps they contain too much information — more than what you're looking for. Maybe you want to see the information only for a particular customer or vendor and over a different time frame than is specified in the report. You can modify any report to allow changes to the date range, field information, font, or page layout.

Using filters

Filtering is the process of restricting the report data to a different set of specifications than Peachtree shows in standard reports. Suppose that you take a standard report — for example, the Customer Ledger — and view it a little differently.

In Figure 15-2, you see the Filter tab of the Customer Ledger report. By default, the standard Customer Ledger report shows all activity for all your customers for the current month, but what if you want to see the transactions (both sales and receipts) for the entire year for customer Coleman Realty? By using filtering, you can have Peachtree display that information.

To use a filter, follow these steps:

1. **Double-click the report you want to filter; in this example, the Customer Ledger report under Accounts Receivable.**

   The report displays on-screen with the default options.

2. **Click the Options button to display the Customer Ledgers options dialog box.**

   The first thing to change is the time frame. By default, this report displays for the current month. We want to see the transactions for the entire year.

3. **Click the drop-down arrow next to the Date box and change the date from This Period to This Year.**

   Optionally, you can enter a more specific date range by entering the beginning and ending dates in the From and To boxes.

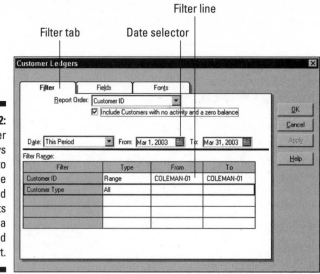

Figure 15-2:
The Filter
tab allows
you to
decide time
frame and
other limits
for a
selected
report.

4. **Click in the From box on the Customer ID filter line and type in or look up and select the first Customer ID you want to view.**

   In this example, we use COLEMAN-01.

5. **Click in the To box on the Customer ID filter line and type in or look up and select the last Customer ID you want to view.**

   If you're only looking for one specific customer, enter the same ID in both the From and To boxes.

   If you want to see a list of IDs from a certain point on down through the list, only enter the From ID and leave the To ID blank. For example, if you want to see every customer from SHARP-01 through WILLIAMSON-01, who is the last customer on the list, only enter SHARP-01 in the From box and leave the To box empty.

6. **Click OK to display the report on-screen.**

   Peachtree displays transactions for the entire year for only the specified customer.

7. **Click Close when you've finished reviewing the report.**

Adding, deleting, and moving report fields

The reports in Peachtree consist of data fields. Those data fields come from the various modules in Peachtree. For example, an Aged Receivable report comes from the Customer and Sales fields, while the payroll register displays information from the Employee and Payroll entry fields. You have the option of including or excluding any applicable fields to create a customized report.

For an example, add the current balance to the Chart of Accounts. Also remove the field Active/Inactive. To customize a report, follow these steps:

1. **Locate and double-click the report you want to modify, which in this example is the Chart of Accounts report.**

   (Here's a hint: Choose Reports⇨General Ledger.)

   Take a look at the standard report. A standard Chart of Accounts displays these fields:

   - Column one shows the account ID.

   - Column two displays the account description.

   - Column three indicates whether the account is active or inactive.

   - Column four shows the account type.

2. **To add an account balance column, click Options.**

   The Chart of Accounts options box appears.

   If you want to modify a report that's not currently displayed on-screen, highlight a report in the Select a Report window and click the Screen button. The Options dialog box then appears.

3. **Click the Fields tab, which is where Peachtree determines which fields to display.**

   You can display any field in the dialog box on the selected report. You'll find some fields grayed out, unavailable for change. As you remove checks from certain columns on the Options tab or as you change settings on the Filter tab, the grayed (unavailable) columns may become available. The fields currently being displayed have a red check mark in the first column (the Show column).

4. **Select the check box of the field you want to add.**

   For this example, check the box next to the Current Balance field. (See Figure 15-3.)

5. **Click the check box of the field you want to remove — in this example, the Active/Inactive field.**

   Removing the check mark removes the field so that it no longer appears on the report.

   When you remove a field from a report, the columns previously displayed to the right of the removed field move to the left. In this example, when you added the Current Balance column, it became the fifth column, but when you removed the Active column, Current Balance became the fourth column.

Fields tab   Column Break

Show box   Column #

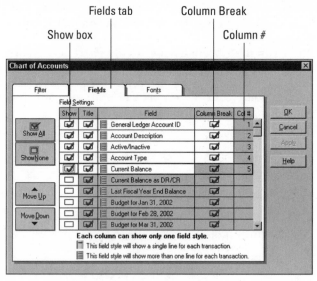

Figure 15-3:
Adding the
Current
Balance
makes the
report have
five
columns.

Now, suppose that you would really like the Current Balance to appear next to the Account Description. No problem! Just use the Peachtree Report Designer's Move Up command to change its location.

6. Click the field name you want to move.

Use caution not to click the Show column, or you'll turn off the display of the field. When you select a field, a red border appears around the entire selected line.

7. Click the Move Up or Move Down button to move the field up or down one column at a time. Continue clicking the Move Up or Move Down button until the field appears in the location you want.

Click the check box in the Column Break section to make the selected field appear on a new line on the report. If you want to place more than one field in a column, first make sure that you check the Show check box and then remove the check from the Break check box. Doing so means that Peachtree doesn't place a break (column) between the fields.

8. Click OK, and the report redisplays with the changes you selected.

Changing report column width

Adding too many columns may cause some to fall off the edge of a page. Well, they don't really fall off, but it does cause the report to print two or more pages in width. You have several choices at this point: You can let the report print multiple pages in width; you can remove some of the report columns; or — and this is probably the best choice — you can change the column widths:

1. Preview the report on-screen and then click the Underline{D}esign button.

Short blue column marker lines appear to the right of each column. (See Figure 15-4.) If you see a long vertical dashed line, your report prints multiple page width.

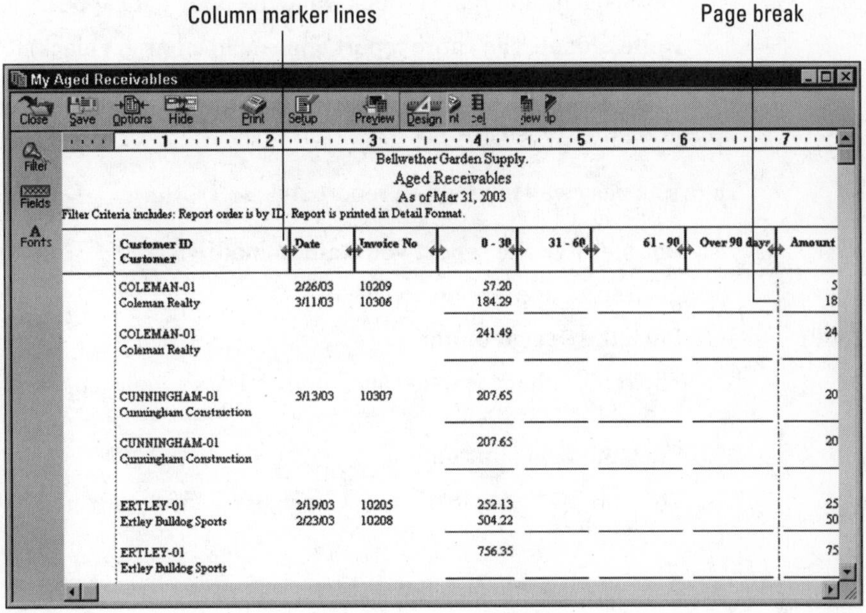

Column marker lines   Page break

Figure 15-4:
Drag the
column
markers to
change
column
width.

2. Drag the short blue column markers to the left to make a column narrower or to the right to widen a column.

You'll know the report fits on one page when the long blue dashed line disappears.

Keeping in style

Report styles are new to Peachtree Version 8.

What's your style — Classic, Elegant, Contemporary, or Professional? By default, Peachtree uses the Classic style, which simply means all reports print in a Times New Roman font. You can display any or all of your reports in any of the aforementioned styles. Here's a list of Peachtree's furnished styles and their descriptions:

✔ **Classic:** The entire report uses a Times New Roman (black) font.

✔ **Contemporary:** The report heading appears as an Ariel (red) font, the data uses a Times New Roman (black) font, and the report totals appear in Times New Roman (red) font.

✔ **Elegant:** The entire report uses a Garamond font; however, black is used for headings and report totals while the body data appears in navy blue.

✔ **Professional:** The entire report appears in an Ariel (black) font.

If you have a color printer, the reports also print using the same colors as appear on the screen.

Here's an easy way to modify a report style:

1. **Double-click the report you want to modify.**

   The report appears on-screen.

2. **Click the Design button.**

   The report changes to design mode and three icons appear on the left side of the screen.

3. **Click the Fonts button.**

   The options dialog box you see in Figure 15-5 appears.

Style Selection list

Fonts button   Design button

Figure 15-5:
Click the
Filter or
Fields
button to
change
displayed
fields or
filter
specific
information.

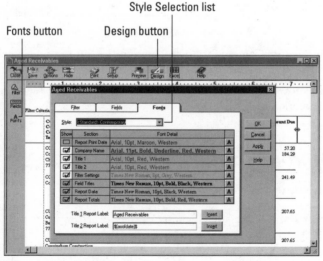

4. **Click the down arrow to the right of the Style box to display a list of available styles.**

5. **Click the style you want for this report and then click OK.**

The report redisplays on the screen with the new style.

You also have the ability to create and save your own styles, choosing the font, color, and sizes you prefer; however, we simply don't have the room in this book to show you how. Hummmm, you say, I wonder if they could put that in an IDG Peachtree Bible? You've seen our commercials before. . . .

Saving a customized report

Sometimes you customize reports for a one-time use, while other reports you use frequently. To save yourself the trouble of recreating the customized report each time you want to display it, save the report with a name that you'll recognize.

To save a customized report, follow these steps:

1. **Display the report on the screen.**

2. **Click the Save button.**

A Save As dialog box appears.

3. **Enter a name for the report.**

You cannot use the exact name of one of the Peachtree predefined standard reports. You must give it a unique name. For the customized Chart of Accounts report, call it "My COA."

Optionally, type a description of the report in the Description box.

4. **Click Save.**

The report is saved for future use.

You can identify custom reports by the red flag Peachtree places on the report icon.

5. **Click Close to close the report window.**

Delete any customized report by highlighting the report name and clicking the Delete button.

Excel with Peachtree

If you have Microsoft Excel 97 or higher, you can send any report you show on your screen, including financial statements, to an Excel workbook.

Why would you want to send a report to Microsoft Excel? Well, perhaps you would like to sort the report in a different manner than Peachtree sorts, or maybe you would like to add an additional column based on a calculation, or how about creating a chart based on the data? We like to use this function to copy customer sales information that can be sorted and ranked in Excel. Those are just a few things you can do by copying a report to Excel.

Follow these steps to copy report data to Excel:

1. **Either display the Peachtree report on your screen or highlight the report name from the Select a Report window.**

2. **Click the Excel button to display the Copy Report To Excel dialog box.**

   You have two ways you can copy the report. You can choose Create a New Microsoft Excel Workbook, or you can choose Add a New Worksheet to an Existing Microsoft Workbook. The latter option appends the report to an existing Excel file. Click the Browse button to select an existing file.

3. **Select the desired option and then click OK to copy the report to Excel.**

Peachtree copies only values, not formulas, to Excel.

Stay in a Group Now . . .

If you have a number of reports you need at the same time, you can create a report group to print them all at once. Report groups print directly to the printer or Microsoft Excel and cannot be previewed on the screen.

In Chapter 18, we suggest reports that you should print at the end of the month — placing them in a report group will make the report printing process much easier.

Follow these steps to create a Report Group:

1. **From anywhere in the Select a Report window, click the Group button.**

   The Report Groups window, shown in Figure 15-6, appears.

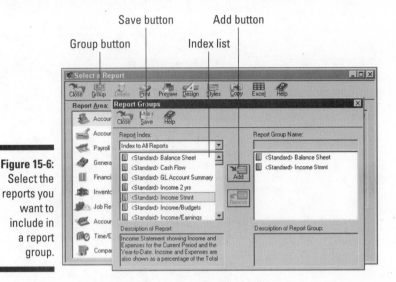

Figure 15-6:
Select the
reports you
want to
include in
a report
group.

All standard and custom reports appear in the index list.

2. **To build a report group, select the first report from the index list and click the Add button.**

   Added reports appear on the right side of the window.

3. **Add any additional reports to the group.**

   You can mix and match report categories. For example, you may want to print an Aged Payables and Aged Receivables report.

4. **Click the Save button when you finish adding reports to the group to display the Save As dialog box.**

5. **Enter a name for the group, such as Monthly Reports, and an optional description of the reports.**

6. **Click Save to save the report group.**

7. **Click Close to close the Report Groups window.**

When you're ready to print the report group, click Report Groups from the Select a Report window, then click the name of the report group to print.

Click Print to print the reports to the printer with no further action on your part or click the Excel button to send the reports to Microsoft Excel.

Chapter 16

Reviewing the Financial Picture

● ●

In This Chapter

▶ Printing financial reports

▶ Printing financial statements

▶ Creating a departmentalized income statement

▶ Copying reports and statements

● ●

*B*efore you change the Peachtree accounting period, you'll probably want to print a series of reports for your records and possibly for your accountant. Reports you may find useful include your General Ledger, Trial Balance, Balance Sheet, and Income Statement. Peachtree provides lots of other reports you may want, but these are the most common ones. You'll probably want to include them in a report group. (See Chapter 15 for creating a report group and Chapter 18 for instructions to change the accounting period.)

The preceding reports fall into two categories: General Ledger reports and Financial Statements. We begin by taking a look at the General Ledger reports.

Reviewing Standard General Ledger Reports

Two of the standard reports you'll use frequently include the General Ledger and the Trial Balance. Peachtree lists both of these reports in the General Ledger report area of the Select a Report window. (You can find out how to display, filter, and customize reports in Chapter 15.)

The General Ledger report is the mother of all accounting reports. This report lists all transactions you enter into Peachtree *that affect the general ledger*. Figure 16-1 shows a sample General Ledger report. Notice the column titled Jrnl. The reference in this column represents the source of the transaction. Table 16-1 lists the different Jrnl codes and their source.

Some transactions do not affect the general ledger, including purchase orders, quotes, and sales orders.

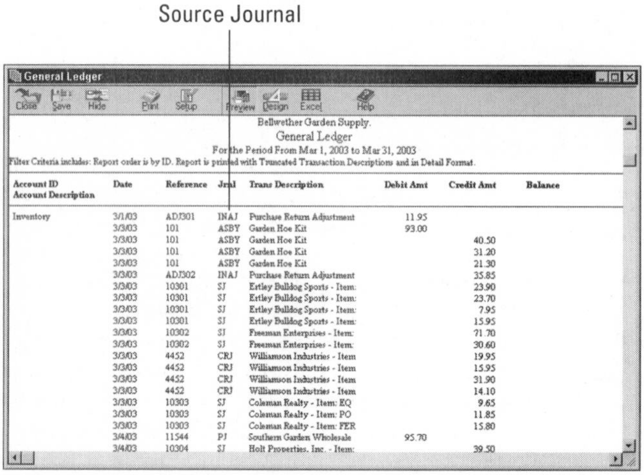

Source Journal

Figure 16-1: See all transactions affecting the general ledger in the General Ledger report.

Table 16-1	General Ledger Source Codes	
Jrnl Code	*Description*	*Source*
SJ	Sales Journal	Sales/Invoicing
CRJ	Cash Receipts Journal	Receipts
PJ	Purchase Journal	Purchases/Receive Inventory
CDJ	Cash Disbursements Journal	Payments and Write Checks
PRJ	Payroll Journal	Payroll Entry
INAJ	Inventory Adjustment Journal	Inventory Adjustments
ASBY	Assemblies Adjustment Journal	Assemblies
GENJ	General Journal	General Journal Entry

Peachtree actually provides two different Trial Balance reports. The first report, called the General Ledger Trial Balance, shows each account and its balance as of the last day of the current period. The report displays the account ID and description as well as the debit or credit balance.

Peachtree calls the other Trial Balance report the Working Trial Balance. Actually, the Working Trial Balance report provides a worksheet where you can list adjusting entries. Each account includes the current balance and a series of lines where you can write down any necessary adjusting amount. Referring to your handwritten trial balance entries speeds up data entry when you need to make adjusting entries.

Using Masking in Reporting

If you set up your Chart of Accounts so that it utilizes department masking, you can print departmental reports. You use the mask by using a "wildcard" character, the asterisk (*), to represent all the other digits of the account number *except* the mask. For example, Bellwether Garden Supply references two departments as Aviary and Landscape Services — and represents them as AV and LS in the Chart of Accounts. In Bellwether Garden Supplies, 40000-AV is the account number for the Aviary sales account, and 40000-LS is the account number for the Landscape Services sales account. So a mask for the Aviary sales would look like *****-AV. On many of the standard Peachtree reports, you can use the mask when you set the report options.

For review on designing your Chart of Accounts for masking, see Chapter 3.

To use a mask, follow these steps:

1. **From the Select a Report window, click General Ledger from the Report Area and then choose the report you want to print.**

2. **Click Preview to preview the report on the screen.**

3. **From the resulting options box, you'll specify the mask in two steps:**

    • **In the Department Mask Type box, choose Mask.**

    • **In the Department Mask From box, enter the masking information.**

   Figure 16-2 shows that when you print the General Ledger Trial Balance report, you see only those accounts for the Aviary department.

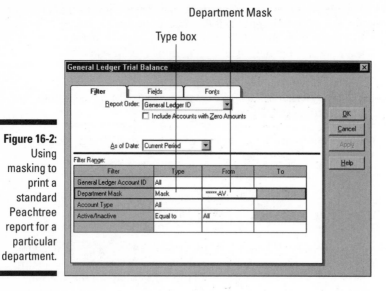

Department Mask

Type box

Figure 16-2:
Using
masking to
print a
standard
Peachtree
report for a
particular
department.

Producing Financial Statements

You display or print financial statements through the Select a Report window
in the same manner as reports. Peachtree provides nine predefined financial
statements, including a balance sheet and income statement. Financial statements are similar to other reports, because you can preview them, print
them to the printer, or send them to an Excel workbook. Table 16-2 provides a
list of all the standard financial statements. If any of these statements don't fit
your needs, look in the next section to find out how to customize them.

All statements and reports appear for the current period unless you select
otherwise.

Table 16-2	Furnished Financial Statements
Report Name	**Description**
<Standard> Balance Sheet	Lists your company assets, liabilities, and capital.
<Standard> Cash Flow	Shows the cash receipts, cash payments, and change in cash in a business.
<Standard> GL Account Summary	Shows account number and description, beginning balance, activity, and ending balance for each account.
<Standard> Income 2 yrs	Compares revenue and expenses for the current month totals to the same month last year, and the current year's totals to last year's totals.

Report Name	Description
\<Standard\> Income Stmnt	Sometimes referred to as a P&L (Profit and Loss) statement. Shows income and expenses and the difference between them.
\<Standard\> Income/Budgets	Compares income and expenses to the amounts budgeted for.
\<Standard\> Income/Earnings	Shows income and expense activity as well as retained earnings information.
\<Standard\> Retained Earnings	Shows beginning and ending retained earnings amounts, adjustments to retained earnings within the period, and the detail for all Equity-gets closed accounts.
\<Standard\> Stmnt Changes	Describes changes in a company's overall financial position.

As we mentioned earlier, the two most frequently used financial statements include the Balance Sheet (Figure 16-3) and the Income Statement (Figure 16-4).

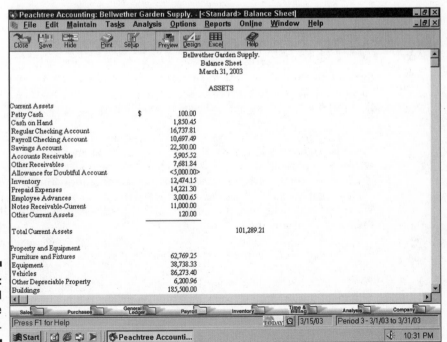

Figure 16-3: A typical balance sheet.

Peachtree Accounting: Bellwether Garden Supply. - [<Standard> Income Stmnt]

File   Edit   Maintain   Tasks   Analysis   Options   Reports   Online   Window   Help

Close   Save   Hide   Print   Setup   Preview   Design   Excel   Help

Bellwether Garden Supply.
Income Statement
For the Three Months Ending March 31, 2003

		Current Month			Year to Date	
Revenues						
Sales	$	4,000.00	14.06	$	4,000.00	9.92
Sales - Aviary		3,508.41	12.33		4,608.19	11.43
Sales - Books		89.85	0.32		3,594.70	8.91
Sales - Equipment		2,249.78	7.91		7,011.40	17.39
Sales - Food/Fert		349.62	1.23		679.26	1.68
Sales - Furniture		15,000.00	52.71		15,000.00	37.20
Sales - Hand Tools		199.92	0.70		801.64	1.99
Sales - Landscape Services		1,179.72	4.15		1,899.58	4.71
Sales - Nursery		782.58	2.75		1,020.44	2.53
Sales - Pots		504.59	1.77		574.54	1.42
Sales - Seeds		229.11	0.81		772.18	1.91
Sales - Soil		371.46	1.31		385.44	0.96
Sales Discounts		<5.80>	<0.02>		<19.52>	<0.05>
Total Revenues		28,459.24	100.00		40,327.85	100.00
Cost of Sales						
Product Cost - Aviary		1,407.90	4.95		1,846.80	4.58
Product Cost - Books		3.65	0.01		1,404.75	3.48
Product Cost - Equipment		1,027.05	3.61		3,090.25	7.66
Product Cost - Food/Fert		138.70	0.49		271.10	0.67
Product Cost - Hand Tools		76.40	0.27		316.45	0.78

Sales   Purchases   General Ledger   Payroll   Inventory   Time & Billing   Analysis   Company

Press F1 for Help   TODAY 3/15/03   Period 3 - 3/1/03 to 3/31/03

Start   Peachtree Accounti...   10:31 PM

Figure 16-4:
A typical income statement.

Modifying Financial Statements

Chapter 14 shows you how to customize Peachtree's reports, while Chapter 15 shows you how to customize Peachtree's forms. Now we take a look at Peachtree's third designer — the Financial Statement designer.

Peachtree provides two ways to create customized financial reports: using the Financial Statement Wizard or the conventional method of customizing a statement yourself through the Financial Statement Design window. The Financial Statement Design window gives you more individual control over each aspect of the financial design process, but the Financial Statement Wizard provides a grasp of the basic elements of a statement and how to put them together effectively.

New to Peachtree 8 is the Financial Statement Wizard.

The Financial Statement Wizard can assist you with great detail in creating a financial statement. At every point in the process, the wizard makes your choices clear so you know what effect each choice has on the finished statement.

Using the Financial Statement Wizard

From the Select a Report window, click the Financial Statement Wizard button located in the lower right corner of the Select a Report window. An introduction screen appears, as shown in Figure 16-5, showing you the processes you can specify by using the wizard.

Click Next to display the Financial Statement Name screen to name the statement you're creating and choose an existing financial statement design to use as the model for your new statement. Click Next to continue to the Financial Statement Wizard design screens.

Each screen of the Financial Statement Wizard defines a specific area of your financial statement:

- **Headers and Footers:** Enter the text of each header and footer you want to include.

- **Dates and General Ledger Account Masking:** Choose the range of dates you want the statement to cover and, if you have set up your general ledger accounts for department masking, you can enter an account mask that limits reporting to just one of your departments. In the next section, we show you how to create a departmental income statement using the Financial Statement Design window.

- **Column Properties:** Select the type and properties of data that appears in each of up to 30 columns.

- **Column Options:** For each type of column you set up in your statement, you can determine secondary titles, width, and alignment for the column.

- **Fonts:** You can choose the fonts that Peachtree uses to display or print each of the sections of your statement.

- **Formatting and Default Printer:** You can tell Peachtree which printer you want to use, whether you want to print page numbers, show zero dollar amounts, center the report on the page, and so forth.

- **Congratulations:** Decide whether you want to display the newly created statement, modify the new statement in the designer window, or create another financial statement using the Financial Statement Wizard.

Using masking in financial reporting

Suppose that you want to compare the current period with the year-to-date information for only one department. The standard income statement compares current period information to year-to-date information for your whole company. The upcoming steps outline how to create a departmental version of the standard income statement, using the department mask.

Creating a new financial statement by using an existing financial statement as a model is always easiest. To avoid accidentally damaging the model, make a copy by saving it under a new name in the Design window. Then, modify the properties of the column heading to include a department mask.

For review on designing your Chart of Accounts for masking, see Chapter 3.

1. **Choose Reports⇨Financial Statements.**

   Peachtree displays the available financial statement report formats in the Select a Report window.

2. **Select the <Standard> Income Statement report and then click the Design button.**

   Peachtree's Financial Statement Designer window for the Income Statement appears (see Figure 16-6).

3. **First things first — save the report under a different name by clicking the Save button to display the Save As dialog box.**

Financial Statement Wizard button

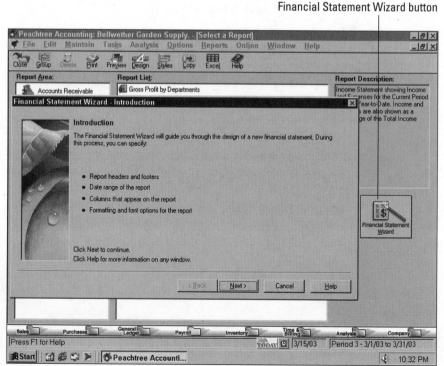

Figure 16-5:
The
Financial
Statement
Wizard
opening
screen.

Property button

Save button

Column Desc.

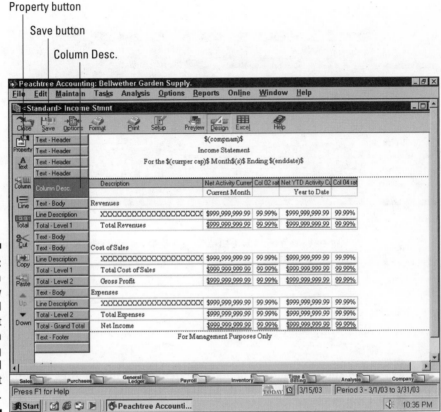

Figure 16-6:
Create a new financial statement by using an existing financial statement as a model.

4. **In the Name box, type a new name for the report; for example, Income Statement–Aviary.**

5. **Optionally, enter a Description and click OK.**

   Peachtree changes the report title in the title bar.

6. **Click the column marked Column Desc. and then click the Property button.**

   The Column Description dialog box appears, as shown in Figure 16-7.

7. **Click the row for Column 2 Activity to select it and activate the Dept. Mask field.**

   Just like in the earlier section, "Using Masking in Reporting," you create the mask by using a "wildcard" character, the asterisk (*), to represent all the other digits of the account number *except* the mask.

8. **Add an appropriate mask. To mask just the Aviary department, enter *****-AV.**

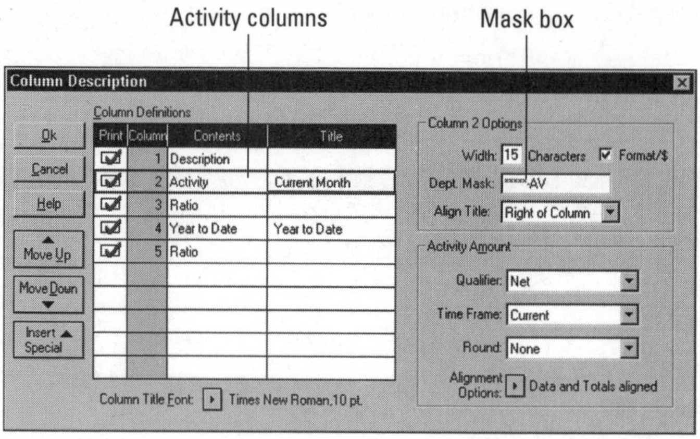

Activity columns   Mask box

Figure 16-7:
Add a
department
mask to
print this
report for
only one
department.

		Column Definitions				
	Print	Column	Contents	Title		
Ok	☑	1	Description			
Cancel	☑	2	Activity	Current Month		
Help	☑	3	Ratio			
	☑	4	Year to Date	Year to Date		
Move Up	☑	5	Ratio			

Column 2 Options
Width: 15 Characters ☑ Format/$
Dept. Mask: *****AV
Align Title: Right of Column ▼

Activity Amount
Qualifier: Net ▼
Time Frame: Current ▼
Round: None ▼

Alignment Options: ▶ Data and Totals aligned

Column Title Font: ▶ Times New Roman,10 pt.

9. **Repeat the row for Column 4 Y-T-D Activity to select it and activate the Dept. Mask field.**

10. **Again, enter the mask.**

11. **Click OK to redisplay the report design, then save the report again.**

When you print the report, it includes information only for the department you specified.

Delete any customized financial statement by highlighting the financial statement name and clicking the Delete button.

Copying Reports and Financial Statements

You'll find customized reports and financial statements available only in the company you created them in. However, you can copy reports and financial reports you create in one company to another company. This feature comes in particularly handy if you create a second company and would like to use a customized report or financial statement that you created in the first company.

Peachtree has long had the ability to copy financial statements between companies but the ability to copy reports is new to Peachtree 8.

To copy reports or financial statements between companies, follow these steps:

1. **Open the company that does *not* have the necessary report.**

2. **In the Select a Report window, click the Copy button on the toolbar.**

   The Copy Reports and Financial Statements dialog box shown in Figure 16-8 appears.

3. **In the Select a Company to Copy from list box, select the company containing the report you want to copy — in Figure 16-8, we selected Pavilion Design Group.**

4. **In the Report or Financial Statement to Copy list, click the report you want to copy.**

5. **Optionally, click in the New Name box and type a new name for the report.**

6. **Click Copy.**

   Peachtree copies the report from the company that you selected to your company. Peachtree copies only the design, not any data.

7. **Repeat Steps 3 through 6 for each report you want to copy and then click the Close button.**

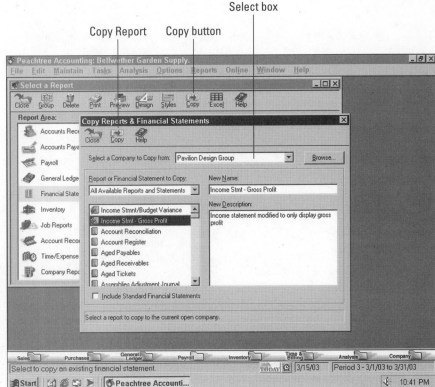

Figure 16-8: Use this box to copy custom reports and financial statements.

Chapter 17

When the Bank Statement Arrives . . .

*E*ach month, the mailman delivers to you an envelope full of checks. Don't get too excited; unfortunately, they aren't checks written to you. They are checks or copies of checks you've written to others.

So why is the bank sending you this information? Well, the bank is obligated to tell you each month how much money you have in your account. "Uh . . . okay, so what?" you ask.

Well, if you're smart, you'll want to make sure that the bank thinks you have the same amount of money *you* think you have. After all, banks make mistakes and you wouldn't want to "give your money away" to the bank just because you didn't take the time to check their accounting and find their error. The process of comparing the bank's balance to yours is called *reconciling*.

Face it; accounting is not exactly a barrel of laughs. And, reconciling your bank statement probably wins the award for the "least fun thing" you can do when working with your company's books. Unfortunately, reconciling is an important function because it's the only way to confirm that you and the bank agree on the amount of money you have in your account.

Anyone who has ever tried to reconcile a bank account knows that the process can be, at best, tedious, and, at worst, a nightmare when you just can't make the bank's numbers match yours. When you reconcile your bank statement using paper and pencil, you add "time-consuming" to the list of negative adjectives.

So, let Peachtree help you. At least when you reconcile your bank statement *electronically,* you finish more quickly. This chapter shows you how to use Peachtree's Account Reconciliation feature — and how to track down problems when things don't balance on the first try.

Understanding the Concept of Balancing

Along with the checks in that envelope, you'll find a statement that summarizes the transactions the bank has processed for you during the month. These "transactions" include checks you've written, deposits you've made, and actions the bank has taken, such as charging your account for checks you ordered or adding interest to your account.

You need to use the statement to compare the balance that the bank says you have with the balance you think you have. In the best of all worlds, they should match. If they don't match, you need to figure out *why* they don't match and then take some action (we talk later in this chapter about "what" action) to make them match — that's the part that most people think isn't fun.

After you record the transactions the bank has taken (the check order charge and the interest), the difference between your account balance and the bank statement's balance should be the total of the *uncleared transactions.* Uncleared transactions include any checks you've written or deposits you've made since the cutoff date on the bank statement. You can think of uncleared transactions as transactions that the bank, according to the statement, doesn't know about. To reconcile your account, you need to add to the bank statement balance any deposits you've made since the bank prepared the statement. Similarly, you need to subtract from the bank statement balance any checks you've written since the bank prepared the bank statement.

Typically, the bank's cutoff date for a business checking account is the last day of the month — which coincides with the end of an accounting period for most businesses. So, when you reconcile your bank statement, you effectively determine your actual cash balance as of the last day of the accounting period. Your accountant needs to know your cash balance on the last day of the accounting period to prepare accurate financial statements, so reconciling your bank statement helps your accountant prepare financial statements.

When you reconcile using paper and pencil, you list and total all checks you've written that don't appear on the bank statement and all deposits you made that don't appear on the bank statement. This part of the process alone can be time-consuming. Peachtree shortens the process by doing the arithmetic for you.

Starting Reconciliation

For deposits, some bank statements list individual items rather than the deposit ticket total. Other banks, however, list deposit ticket totals rather than individual items. If your bank lists deposit ticket totals, print the Bank Deposit Report, shown in Figure 17-1. Peachtree lists, in the Account Reconciliation window, each individual item rather than the deposit ticket total. The Bank Deposit Report helps you tie back the individual items to a particular deposit. To print the report, follow these steps:

1. **Choose Reports⇨Account Reconciliation.**

   The Select a Report window appears, showing available Account Reconciliation reports.

2. **On the right side of the window, highlight the Bank Deposit Report.**

3. **Click the Print button.**

When you receive your statement from the bank, make sure you're working in the accounting period covered by the bank statement. Check the lower-right corner of your screen to determine the current accounting period.

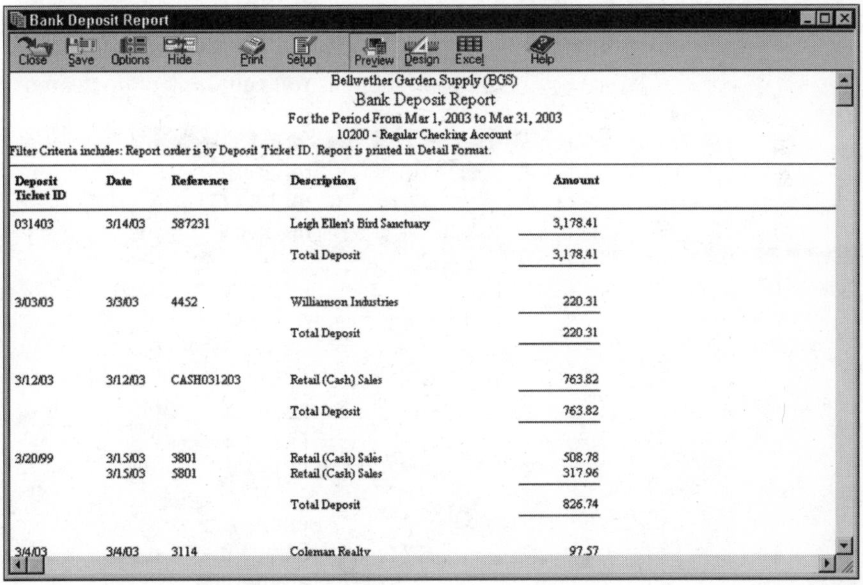

Figure 17-1:
The Bank
Deposit
Report
lists the
individual
items
that were
included on
each bank
deposit
ticket.

If you need to change the accounting period, choose Tasks➪System➪ Change Accounting Period. In the Change Accounting Period dialog box that appears, click the arrow on the drop-down list box. Select the period you want to reconcile, and click OK. For details on changing the accounting period, see Chapter 18.

To start the reconciliation process, follow these steps:

1. **Choose Tasks➪Account Reconciliation.**

   Peachtree displays the Account Reconciliation window.

2. **Click the list box selector next to the Account to Reconcile box to display the list of your accounts.**

3. **Select the account you want to reconcile.**

4. **Click OK.**

In Peachtree, you can balance *any* account, not just a checking account. You can also balance savings accounts, petty cash accounts, and credit card accounts.

After you select an account, Peachtree shows you all the transactions available for reconciliation for the period (see Figure 17-2).

List box selector

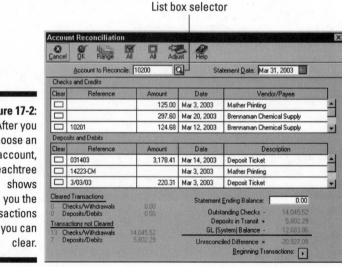

Figure 17-2:
After you
choose an
account,
Peachtree
shows
you the
transactions
you can
clear.

Reconciling for the first time

If you're reconciling for the first time in Peachtree, you will, undoubtedly, find checks and deposits on your bank statement that you haven't entered in Peachtree because the transactions occurred *before* you started using Peachtree. To make your life easier when balancing your first bank statement, you need to enter the outstanding transactions in Account Reconciliation *before* you begin the reconciliation process. Start by making sure that you're working in Peachtree in the accounting period that you want to reconcile. Open the Account Reconciliation window (choose Tasks➪Account Reconciliation) and then click the Beginning Transactions button. Peachtree displays the Beginning Transactions window as shown in the following figure. In this window, enter transactions that appear on your bank statement but which occurred before you started using Peachtree.

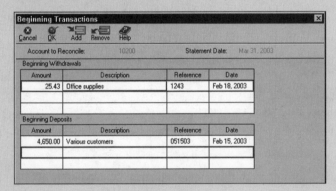

Enter outstanding checks in the top portion of the window; enter outstanding deposits in the lower portion of the window. For checks, assign the check number as the Reference number. Click OK when you finish. The transactions you entered will appear in the Account Reconciliation window so that you can mark them as cleared and reconcile your bank statement.

Marking Checks and Deposits

The bank statement shows you checks and deposits that have cleared the bank.

Cleared means that the bank has processed the transaction.

You need to identify the cleared transactions to Peachtree. Checks that you've written appear in the top portion of the window, and deposits you've made appear in the bottom portion of the window. The reference number for the check is the check number you assigned to the check, and the reference number for the deposit is the Deposit Ticket ID number you entered for the receipt.

Using the Deposit Ticket ID effectively

Peachtree lumps together all receipts with the same Deposit Ticket ID. If you read Chapter 8, you may remember that, when you start to record a receipt in the Receipts window, Peachtree automatically fills in the Deposit Ticket ID field with today's date — making it look like all deposits for the day are lumped together.

Why does Peachtree work this way? Because most banks consider all items on one deposit ticket as one "deposit" and list the sum of the items as the amount of the deposit. And, most people make up one deposit ticket for "today's" receipts. Under these conditions, the deposits on your bank statement would match, one to one, the deposits in the Bank Reconciliation window.

Suppose, however, that you make up separate deposit tickets for checks, credit card deposits, and cash — all for the same day. You may have some other way of organizing your receipts for deposit, but we'll operate on this assumption to make the following example clear. In Peachtree, change the Deposit Ticket ID in the Receipts window so that each item on a particular deposit you plan to make to the bank has the same Deposit Ticket ID number. You might code your Peachtree receipts with today's date and an abbreviation that represents cash, checks, and credit cards. For example, you might use something like 03/02-C for a cash deposit on 03/2, 03/02-Ch for a check deposit on 03/2, and 03/02-CC for a credit card deposit on 3/2. Then, you should find that your bank statement deposits match your deposits in the Account Reconciliation window.

If you're having trouble matching deposits on your bank statement to deposits in the Account Reconciliation window, try editing receipts in the Receipts window and assigning the same deposit ticket ID to all items you deposited in the bank on the same deposit ticket.

If you read Chapter 8, you may recall that the Receipt window contains two fields: one called Reference and one called Deposit Ticket ID. We realize that it's confusing, but, in the Account Reconciliation window, Peachtree displays the Deposit Ticket ID, not the Reference, from the Receipt window.

Follow these steps to continue the reconciliation process:

1. **At the bottom of the window, enter the ending balance that appears on the bank statement you received in the Statement Ending Balance box.**

2. **Click in the Clear box at the left edge of a Checks and Credits entry if the entry appears on the bank statement.**

   Peachtree places a check in the box, indicating that the bank has processed the item.

3. **Click in the Clear box at the left edge of a Deposits and Debits entry if the entry appears on the bank statement.**

4. **Repeat Steps 2 and 3 until you have accounted for each transaction that appears on the bank statement.**

Instead of clicking one transaction at a time, you can mark groups of transactions. If a consecutive range of check numbers cleared, you can click the Range button and enter the range of numbers for Peachtree to mark. As a shortcut, if most of the transactions in the window cleared the bank, click the All Checked button and then remove the checks from the ones that *did not* clear the bank by clicking in the Clear box. Similarly, you can remove all marks by clicking the All Clear button.

Double-check the check numbers in the range both in Peachtree and on the bank statement. Occasionally, you'll write a check and forget to post it in Peachtree, and the check will clear the bank. When you mark a range, finding that transaction can be difficult.

Now check the Unreconciled Difference value — your goal is to make that value equal 0. If the Unreconciled Difference value equals 0 after you have checked all transactions that appear on the bank statement, you've reconciled and you're done (pat yourself on the back). Just click OK to save your work.

When the Account Doesn't Balance

But what do you do when you've marked everything and the Unreconciled Difference does not equal 0? Well, you do a little detective work. Go dig out your detective hat and magnifying glass out of the closet so you can prepare to snoop around. We'll wait. . . .

Items to review

The Unreconciled Difference may not equal 0 for several reasons.

- ✔ **The bank may have recorded a transaction that you have not recorded in Peachtree.** Look for bank charges such as check reorder charges, service charges, or if your account is interest-bearing, interest payments.

- ✔ **The bank may have recorded a transaction *for a different amount* than you recorded in Peachtree.** Compare the amounts of checks you've recorded in Peachtree to the amount the bank cleared for the check. Similarly, compare deposit amounts you recorded in Peachtree to deposit amounts on the bank statement.

Add the digits of the Unreconciled Difference and see whether they equal 9 or a multiple of 9. If so, the odds are good that you have transposed the digits on one or more checks or deposits. We don't know why this works, but it does.

✔ **You may have cleared a transaction that didn't clear the bank.** Review the transactions you have cleared.

✔ **You may have recorded the Statement Ending Balance incorrectly.** Make sure you typed the amount correctly.

If you determine that you need to correct an existing transaction or enter a check or receipt, you can click OK to leave reconciliation and edit or add the transaction in the appropriate window. That is, edit or enter a check in the Payments window and edit or enter a receipt in the Receipts window. Peachtree saves your reconciliation just the way it appears. After you add missing transactions, you can reopen the Account Reconciliation window to finish the process. If you determine that you need to record either a bank service charge or an interest payment, you can make an adjustment.

"Why do I need to close reconciliation to enter additional checks or receipts that I forgot to record?" you may ask. Checks and receipts are tied to vendors and customers. If you don't use the appropriate window to enter them, you'll adjust your cash balance, but you won't adjust the vendor's or customer's balance, and your Accounts Payable or Accounts Receivable will be inaccurate.

You can enter and leave Account Reconciliation as many times as you want during a single accounting period.

Making adjustments

You make adjustments under two circumstances:

✔ When you want to record a bank service charge or an interest payment

✔ When you can't find the problem and you decide to "write it off" as a lost cause

Accountants do not frown on adjusting to reconcile the account when the difference is small (less than $5). You need to weigh the trade-offs: Is it worth spending hours to find a nickel? Your time is worth more if you're doing something other than looking for a dime or a quarter. On the other hand, don't write off large unreconciled differences and don't make a practice of writing off unreconciled differences; eventually, they will come back to haunt you.

To record an adjustment, follow these steps:

1. **Click the Adjust button to open the Additional Transactions window (see Figure 17-3).**

Figure 17-3:
Record
deductions
from your
bank account
at the top
of the
window and
additions to
your bank
account at
the bottom
of the
window.

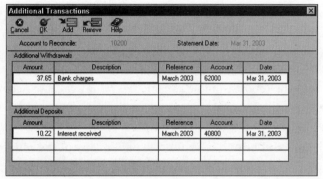

2. **Record additional withdrawals (bank service charges) at the top of the window and additional deposits (interest earned) at the bottom of the window.**

   What about when you're "off" by a small amount that you want to ignore? Remember this rule: If the Unreconciled Difference is negative, you need to record an Additional Withdrawal for the amount you're "off" to reduce the Unreconciled Difference to 0. If the Unreconciled Difference is positive, you need to record an Additional Deposit for the amount you're "off" to reduce the Unreconciled Difference to 0.

   We know it sounds weird, but it works.

3. **When you finish, click OK to redisplay the Account Reconciliation window.**

4. **Click the adjusting entries to mark them as Cleared and balance your account.**

5. **When the Unreconciled Difference equals 0, you can consider the account reconciled. Click OK to close the Account Reconciliation window.**

When you make an adjustment in Peachtree, you actually record a Journal Entry. If you find the source of the problem later and want to delete or change the adjustment, you must open the General Journal Entry window and click the Edit button. Double-click the adjustment to display it; then edit it or click the Delete button.

Printing the Reconciliation Summary

Now you want to print a record of the balanced reconciliation. Follow these steps:

1. **Choose Reports⇨Account Reconciliation.**

   The Select a Report window appears, showing available Account Reconciliation reports.

2. **From the list on the right, choose Account Reconciliation.**

3. **Click the Print button to produce a paper copy of the report.**

   Peachtree prints a report similar to the one you see in Figure 17-4, showing that the Unreconciled Difference is 0.

In transit refers to checks you've written or deposits you've made that have not yet cleared the bank.

You may have noticed other available reports when you printed the Account Reconciliation report. You don't really need the Deposits in Transit, Outstanding Checks, or Outstanding Other Items reports, because all of that information appears on the Account Reconciliation report. We've already discussed the Bank Deposit Report; the Account Register lists individual deposits and withdrawals in the selected account.

Figure 17-4:
The
Account
Reconcil-
iation report
shows the
matching
ending
balances as
well as
deposits
and checks
that have
not yet
cleared
the bank.

2/20/00 at 12:31:18.06			Page: 1

Bellwether Garden Supply (BGS)
Account Reconciliation
As of Mar 31, 2003
10200 - Regular Checking Account
Bank Statement Date: March 31, 2003

Filter Criteria includes: Report is printed in Detail Format.

Beginning GL Balance			20,927.09
Add: Cash Receipts			5,802.29
Less: Cash Disbursements			<4,045.52>
Add <Less> Other			<10,027.43>
Ending GL Balance			12,656.43
Ending Bank Balance			12,683.86
Add back deposits in transit			
	Mar 4, 2003 3/4/03	97.57	
Total deposits in transit			97.57
<Less> outstanding checks			
	Mar 3, 2003	<125.00>	
Total outstanding checks			<125.00>
Add <Less> Other			
Total other			
Unreconciled difference			0.00
Ending GL Balance			12,656.43

Chapter 18

When Accounting Cycles End . . . And Other Miscellaneous Stuff

. . . .

In This Chapter

▶ Changing accounting periods

▶ Making General Journal entries

▶ Preparing the payroll quarterly report

▶ Completing year-end tasks

. . . .

A lot of stuff happens at the end of an accounting period — a month, a quarter, a year. And, most of it deals with finishing the transactions that belong in the period that's ending. You'll need to start working in a new period before you finish working in the old period. Why? Because you don't have all the information you need to finish working in a period on the last day of the period. For example, you can't reconcile your bank statement on the last day of the period because you haven't received it from the bank yet.

In this chapter, we talk about the things you do at the end of each period — and some other topics that just don't fit well in any other chapter, like (and here come those words!) making journal entries.

Changing Accounting Periods

Each day, when you open Peachtree, you'll notice a date in the lower-right corner of the window — along with the current period. The date matches the system date on your computer, and Peachtree will use that date as the default date for every transaction you enter.

True, except when the accounting period changes. Look at an easy example: You use standard months in the calendar year for accounting periods, and your fiscal year is the same as the calendar year.

Fiscal year refers to the year your business uses. The fiscal year can be the same as the calendar year — and run from January 1 to December 31. Or, the fiscal year might run from April 1 to March 31 or from July 1 to June 30. You and your accountant establish your fiscal year with the IRS.

Your current accounting period is January. All through the month, Peachtree will default transaction dates to the current day of the month in January. On February 1, Peachtree will correctly report the date in the lower-left corner of the screen, but the default date for transactions will not be February 1 — because you haven't changed the accounting period. The default date on transactions will be January 1— and will remain January 1 for all subsequent days until you change the accounting period.

So, what's the big deal? Well, that means that you may be sitting around posting February transactions in the accounting period that runs from January 1 through January 31. That, of course, will misstate the financial condition of your business for both January and February. So, you need to change the accounting period on the first day of each new period.

"Is this a difficult thing?" you ask. Nope. "Don't you need to wait to change the accounting period until you've posted everything into the current period?" Nope; you can switch back to any open period at any time. "You mean that changing the accounting period doesn't close it?" Yes, that's what we mean. In fact, in Peachtree, you can't close a single accounting period; you can only close a fiscal year, which we talk about later in this chapter.

In Chapter 24, you find out that you can change back to an earlier period — we just don't recommend that you make changes to a prior period after giving your data to your accountant.

When you move forward to a new accounting period, Peachtree asks you whether you want to print invoices, checks, and reports before changing the period. If you haven't finished entering transactions for the period, obviously, you don't need to print anything. But we suggest that you simply answer no to these questions, even if you have completed entering transactions. Instead, when you've finished entering everything for a period, print all the reports for the period — the journals discussed at the end of the chapters in Part II and the financial reports discussed in Chapter 16.

To make the report printing process easier, create a report group that contains all the reports you want to print at the end of a period. Then, you won't need to select and set up each report. To learn how to make a report group, see Chapter 15.

So, why do we suggest that you print reports *before* you change the accounting period? Well, first, the window you see when you're selecting reports to print while changing the accounting period doesn't include a few reports that you might find useful, such as the Balance Sheet, Income Statement, Trial

Balance, and any other financial reports of interest to you. And, while you can print these reports at any time for any period, printing them for an accounting period while you're working in that accounting period is easiest.

Second, for reasons we don't understand, when you print reports while changing the period, Peachtree displays reports from prior periods as well as reports from the current period. You may think the reports appear because, somehow, you've changed a transaction in a prior period, but we can't prove that. So, we've found that printing reports using a report group is faster and easier.

Follow these steps to change the accounting period:

1. **Choose Tas<u>k</u>s⇨S<u>y</u>s<u>t</u>em⇨Change <u>A</u>ccounting Period to display the Change Accounting Period dialog box (see Figure 18-1).**

   In Peachtree 2002, you can double-click the interactive period button in the lower right corner of the screen. See the appendix for details.

Figure 18-1:
Use this dialog box to switch to a different period.

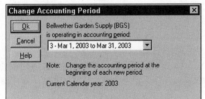

2. **Click the drop-down arrow, select the new period you want to use, and click OK.**

   Peachtree displays a dialog box asking whether you want to print checks or invoices.

   If you choose Yes, Peachtree prints any unnumbered checks or invoices that you didn't previously print.

3. **Choose Yes if you won't be returning to this period; choose No if you'll be returning to this period to enter additional transactions.**

   If you choose Yes, Peachtree simply redisplays the Change Accounting Period dialog box with the original period selected. You'll need to click Cancel and print invoices or checks. If you choose No, Peachtree displays a dialog box asking whether you want to print reports.

4. **Choose No.**

   Peachtree changes the accounting period; you'll see the new period reflected in the lower-right corner of the screen.

If you choose Yes to print reports while changing the accounting period, Peachtree displays the window shown in Figure 18-2. You would need to remove checks from the reports you don't want to print and click OK. Our suggested technique — using a report group to print before changing the accounting period — is faster and easier.

Figure 18-2:
The window
you see if
you choose
to print
reports
while
changing
the
accounting
period.

Print Reports

The following reports should be printed before the Accounting Period is closed.

Report Name	Reporting Period	Print?
General Journal	1 - Jan 1, 2003 to Jan 31, 2003	☑
General Journal	2 - Feb 1, 2003 to Feb 28, 2003	☑
General Journal	3 - Mar 1, 2003 to Mar 31, 2003	☑
Cash Receipts Journal	1 - Jan 1, 2003 to Jan 31, 2003	☑
Cash Receipts Journal	2 - Feb 1, 2003 to Feb 28, 2003	☑
Cash Receipts Journal	3 - Mar 1, 2003 to Mar 31, 2003	☑
Cash Disbursements Journal	3 - Mar 1, 2003 to Mar 31, 2003	☑
Sales Journal	1 - Jan 1, 2003 to Jan 31, 2003	☑
Sales Journal	2 - Feb 1, 2003 to Feb 28, 2003	☑

Ok   Cancel   Help

Making General Journal Entries

Okay, don't be freaked by the title. Journal entries are nothing more than another type of transaction to enter in Peachtree — you just won't use it as often as you do other types of transactions. In fact, here's a good rule to follow:

Don't enter journal entries unless

✔ Your accountant tells you to make the entry.

✔ You *really* know what you're doing.

You see, the truth is, you usually can find another way to enter the information — and if you can, you don't need to use the General Journal Entry window. For example, when you pay your telephone bill of $37.50, you spend money ($37.50) from your Cash account, and you identify what you spent the money on by making an entry in your Telephone account for $37.50. But this example demonstrates perfectly that you *don't* need to use the General Journal Entry window — because you'd write a check from either the Payments or the Write Checks window.

By the way, the example also demonstrates what "accounting types" mean when they talk about *double-entry bookkeeping*. The term simply means that each transaction conducted by your business causes you — and your accounting software — to make at least two entries. And here come those dreaded words: One entry is a *debit* and one entry is a *credit*. The most important thing to know about debits and credits is that they need to equal each other. Do you *need* to know this? No. Peachtree will do most of it for you. Can it *hurt* you to know this? No. Who knows . . . knowing may even help you.

So, when *would* you use the General Journal Entry window? Well, you'd use it to record the depreciation of assets. Most businesses let their accountants figure the amount of the depreciation — and then the accountant gives you the journal entry information so you can enter the transaction. Or, if you use job costing (see Chapter 12), you can add overhead to a job using a journal entry.

Okay, now that we've told you *not* to make journal entries unless you really need to make them, we'll show you how to make them.

If you're really interested in the "how and why" of debits and credits, read the sidebar "The Accounting Equation — and how it works."

1. **Choose Tas_k_s⇨_G_eneral Journal Entry to display the General Journal Entry window (see Figure 18-3).**

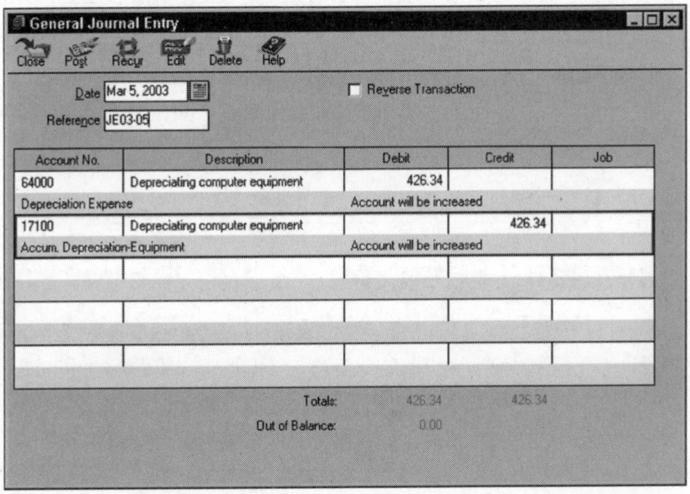

Figure 18-3:
To be able to record a journal entry, it must be in balance.

2. **If necessary, change the date.**

3. **Enter a reference number to identify the transaction. We use JE (for Journal Entry) and then the month and date (refer to Figure 18-3).**

4. **In the Account No. column, select the first account you want to change.**

Accountants like you to list debits first and then credits, but that's not a rule. Listing debits first and then credits will make you look more professional, though, — and we're going to assume that you want to look professional, so enter the debit first and then the credit.

5. **In the Description column, enter words that describe the reason for the transaction.**

   Peachtree copies these words to the next line for you, saving you typing.

6. **In the Debit column, enter the amount.**

7. **If necessary, assign a job to the entry.**

8. **Repeat Steps 4–7, but in Step 6, enter the amount in the Credit column.**

   When you finish, debits should equal credits. Peachtree shows you the amount you're out of balance if they don't.

9. **Click Post to save the journal entry.**

Peachtree won't let you post or save the entry if it's out of balance.

For some journal entries, you may need to enter multiple debits to offset one credit or multiple credits to offset one debit. That's fine. A journal entry consists of a set of debits and credits that equal each other. Also, your accountant may send you a list of entries to make before you close the fiscal year. You can make all the entries in one General Journal Entry transaction — maybe even with a description like "Adjustment per CPA." That is, you can keep entering lines in the General Journal Entry window using only one transaction number.

The Accounting Equation — and how it works

We're going to start with a little history — after all, debits and credits didn't just magically appear. And, with the history lesson, at least you'll know who to hate for inventing debits and credits. (We've always found that directing anger correctly is more productive than just being angry in general.)

You can trace double-entry bookkeeping back to Luca Pacioli's book, *Summa de Arithmetica, Geometria, Proportioni et Proportionalita* (Everything about Arithmetic, Geometry, and Proportion). Pacioli was a Franciscan friar in Venice, Italy, and wrote the Summa in 1494. One part of his book described a method of "keeping accounts" so that the trader could get, without delay, information about his assets and liabilities. Pacioli's interrelating system of accounts was based on two fundamental principles that are still the foundation of accounting today:

- The accounting equation (also called an *accounting model*): ASSETS = LIABILITIES + OWNER'S EQUITY

- Debits equal credits

Assets are those things of value, such as cash, receivables, inventory, equipment, deposits, and investments that your company owns. These "things of value" help you operate your business. *Liabilities* are the debts owed by the company, such as accounts payable, loans, taxes, and interest. *Owner's Equity* (also called Equity, Capital, and Paid-In Capital) is the owner's interest in the company.

To understand how the accounting equation works, we'll start a fictitious cash-based business with $1,000 of our own money, giving the company one asset of cash. To represent our investment into the business, we record the $1,000 as equity, as you can see from Line 1 in the following table of fictitious accounting transactions.

Line	Assets	=	Liabilities	+	Owner's Equity
1	$1,000	=			$1,000
2	$3,000	=	$3,000		
	$4,000	=	$3,000	+	$1,000
3	$2,000	=			$2,000
4	($1,200)	=			($1,200)
	$4,800	=	$3,000	+	$1,800

To run our business, we purchase a delivery truck by borrowing $3,000 from the bank (we'll buy a cheap truck), which we record as Line 2 in the table. Combining this entry with the original investment, we have $4,000 of assets (the initial cash and the truck), $3,000 of liabilities (the bank loan for the truck), and $1,000 of equity. Notice that the accounting equation balances. That is, assets equal liabilities plus owner's equity. And, the table is looking suspiciously like a Balance Sheet (now you understand why they call it a "Balance" sheet; see Chapter 16 for a sample of the Balance Sheet).

Okay, every business has sales (income) and expenses. Pacioli realized this, too. We're sure you would agree that what you earn belongs to you. At least, you should get to keep most of it. We handle income and expenses in the accounting equation by expanding the equation to include them in owner's equity:

```
EQUITY = ORIGINAL INVESTMENT + INCOME - EXPENSES
```

In our example, the original investment was $1,000. Suppose that we made $2,000 of cash sales and pay for $1,200 of expenses. What would happen to our accounting model? Line 3 in the table shows how $2,000 of cash sales increases our assets (cash) and the income portion of owner's equity. Line 4 shows that $1,200 of cash expenses decreases our assets (cash) and the expense portion of owner's equity.

Income minus expenses is net income, as you may remember on your Income Statement in Chapter 16 — and the business pays taxes on this amount. And, when you close the year,

Peachtree posts net income after taxes to the equity section of the Balance Sheet. You can gain numerous insights about your business by studying your Balance Sheet and Income Statement. Wish we had space to show you, but . . . think Peachtree Bible. . . .

Now consider Pacioli's second principle of accounting: debits = credits. Pacioli needed some mechanical device to make sure that the accounting equation was always in balance. He developed the following four rules — and we find them most helpful when preparing journal entries:

(continued)

(continued)

1. Debits increase Asset accounts and decrease Liability and Equity accounts.

2. Credits decrease Asset accounts and increase Liability and Equity accounts.

Expense and Income accounts behave like equity accounts, so

3. Debits increase Expense accounts and decrease Income accounts.

4. Credits decrease Expense accounts and increase Income accounts.

Return to our example to see how these work. In Line 1 of the table, we started our business by investing $1,000. We increased our assets and increased our equities. According to Rules 1 and 2, we debited assets and credited equity.

Line 2 shows how we handled the purchase of our truck. Because both an asset (purchase of truck) and a liability (borrowed money) increased, we debited assets and credited liabilities (again, Rules 1 and 2).

In our last transactions (Lines 3 and 4 of the table) we earned $2,000 of income and paid $1,200 of expenses. Note the following:

✔ The income increased our cash asset by $2,000 and also increased our income by the same amount. Therefore, Rules 1 and 4 say we should debit (increase) the cash asset and credit (increase) income.

✔ Expense transactions have the opposite effect; therefore, Rules 2 and 3 say we should credit (decrease) the cash asset and debit (increase) expenses.

✔ These debit/credit rules are necessary to make sure we always keep the accounting model in balance.

Accounting Behind the Scenes

If you chose the Hide General Ledger Accounts option for your company, then your transaction windows don't look like the ones we show throughout this book. In particular, you don't see any general ledger accounts in your transaction windows. See Chapter 13 for a comparison of what windows look like when you hide or show general ledger accounts.

In Chapter 5, we promised to tell you about a neat way to identify the accounts Peachtree updates as you enter transactions even if you don't display the general ledger accounts in your transaction window. Click the Journal button in the window, and Peachtree displays the Accounting Behind the Screens window you see in Figure 18-4.

And yes, you *can* make changes in this window to modify the accounts Peachtree updates for this transaction, but we don't recommend it. Notice that you can't change a debit to a credit or vice versa; if you change the accounts and you don't really know what you're doing, you'll really mess up your company's books.

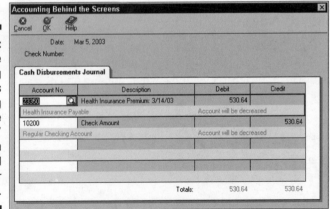

Figure 18-4:
The accounting Peachtree is doing "behind the screens" when you hide general ledger accounts.

Batch Posting

Don't read this section if you're using real-time posting. You'll just waste your time.

We've never really understood why some people really like batch posting, but they do. When you use batch posting in Peachtree, you save transactions as you enter them but they don't update your accounts until you post, which means that transactions won't appear on reports until you post. You choose batch or real-time posting in the Maintain Company window. See Chapter 2 for more information.

Okay, so you know you need to post to update your accounts. You also need to make sure you post all journals before you try to change the accounting period. To post, follow these steps:

1. **Choose Tasks⇨System⇨Post to display the Post dialog box you see in Figure 18-5.**

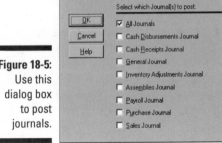

Figure 18-5:
Use this dialog box to post journals.

2. **Select the journal you want to post or leave the check in** <u>A</u>**ll Journals to post everything.**

3. **Click the OK button.**

   Peachtree displays a bar across the screen as it posts and then redisplays the main Peachtree window when posting finishes.

Preparing the Payroll Quarterly Report (941)

This one's easy. You're gonna love it. You just print a form. Actually, you need to print the form onto the IRS form you receive in the mail. (See Chapter 14 for information on aligning information on forms.) If you're afraid to mess up the form, print Peachtree's version to paper and transfer the numbers (be sure to put everything in the right box).

We recommend that you print the 941 Worksheet before you print the Federal Form 941 — the worksheet will show you the amount you were supposed to deposit each quarter — and we assume that you make your payroll tax deposits in a timely fashion, as required by law. You'll need the amount you deposited to print an accurate Federal Form 941. You can take advantage of the new Print Preview feature and display the 941 Worksheet on-screen to get the tax deposit amount.

1. **Choose** <u>R</u>**eports➪Payroll to display a list of Payroll reports.**

2. **From the Report List on the right, double-click the Federal Form 941 folder to display the available versions of the 941 and 941B report.**

3. **Highlight the version you want to print and click the** <u>P</u>**rint button.**

   Peachtree displays the options dialog box for the form (see Figure 18-6).

4. **Supply the total tax liability amount you paid for the current payroll quarter.**

5. **Make sure that you're printing the form for the correct quarter.**

6. **Click OK.**

7. **When Peachtree prompts you to select a printer, click OK again.**

   Peachtree prints the form.

If you need to complete form 941B — the second page of the payroll tax liability form — repeat these steps, choosing the correct form in Step 3.

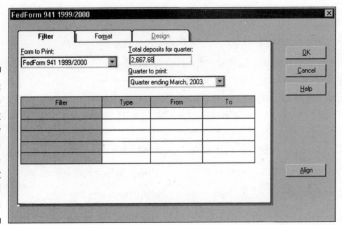

Figure 18-6:
Supply the
total tax
liability
amount you
paid for the
current
payroll
quarter.

Printing W-2s

Same concept here — W-2s are forms that you print. You'll need to purchase W-2 forms and load them into your printer.

You can purchase your forms from your local printer, or you can use the offers you receive in your Peachtree software box. Chapter 23 lists Web contact information on a couple of sources for forms. If you contact Deluxe Forms at 1-800-328-0304 and reference this book and discount code R03578, you'll receive 20% off your first order.

By default, Peachtree automatically includes all employees that you've paid during the current year when you print W-2s, even if you've marked an employee inactive.

You mark an employee inactive in the Maintain Employees/Sales Reps window when the employee no longer works for you. But, if the employee worked for you during any part of a calendar year, you must provide the employee with a W-2. Also, by marking the employee inactive, you make the employee a candidate for purging, which we talk about later in this chapter.

You must print W-2s before you close the Payroll year. If the federal government has changed the form, you'll need to modify the form (see Chapter 14). Or, you can subscribe to Peachtree's payroll tax table service; toward the end of December, the service will provide you with the latest update that will include any form modifications. (You find out more about updating payroll tax tables later in this chapter.)

To print W-2s, follow these steps:

1. **Choose Reports⇨Payroll to display a list of payroll reports.**

2. **From the Report List on the right, double-click the Federal Form W-2 folder.**

   Peachtree displays available versions of the W-2 — four per page, double wide, and standard. The form you select should match the form you purchased.

3. **Highlight the form you want to print and click the Print button.**

   Peachtree displays the options dialog box for the form.

4. **If necessary, make changes in the options dialog box.**

   You can (but shouldn't need to) change the form to print select employees by ID, or change the year for which you want to print W-2s to any open year.

5. **Click OK.**

6. **When Peachtree prompts you to select a printer, click OK.**

   Peachtree prints the W-2s.

Printing 1099s

I know it's beginning to sound like a mantra, but same concept here — 1099s are a form that you print. You'll need to purchase 1099 forms and load them into your printer.

You can purchase your forms from your local printer, or you can use the offers you receive in your Peachtree software box. Chapter 23 lists Web contact information on a couple of sources for forms. If you contact Deluxe Forms at 1-800-328-0304 and reference this book and discount code R03578 you'll receive 20% off your first order.

By default, Peachtree automatically includes all vendors who meet both of the following criteria:

- ✔ You've selected Independent Contractor or Interest in the 1099 Type field of the Maintain Vendors window.

- ✔ You've paid more than $600.00 during the calendar year.

Refer to Chapter 5 for information on setting up vendors and the 1099 Type field.

You must print 1099s before you close the Payroll year. If the federal government has changed the form, you'll need to modify the form (see Chapter 14). Or, you can subscribe to Peachtree's payroll tax table service; toward the end of December, the service will provide you with the latest update that will include any form modifications. (You find out more about updating payroll tax tables later in this chapter.)

You use the same steps to print 1099s that you use to print W-2s, except that you'll find the forms in the 1099 Forms folder under Accounts Payable in the Report list.

Peachtree supports producing 1099s for only two types of vendors: Interest and Independent Contractors. If you need to produce 1099s for more than two types of 1099 vendors, workarounds exist, but they are beyond the scope of this book. So, once again, if you *like* this book, contact Laura Moss at IDG Books Worldwide, Inc. and tell her that you want her to hire us to write a Peachtree Bible.

Updating Payroll Tax Tables

To calculate payroll accurately, Peachtree uses tax tables. Each tax table is associated with the current year. In fact, the name of the table ends with the last two digits of the current year, which means that as you begin a new calendar year, you must have new tax tables with names that include the last two digits of the new year. In addition, the calculations in the tax table may have changed, and you need to make sure that the tax tables will calculate correctly. So, how do you do this? We suggest that you subscribe to Peachtree Corporation's payroll tax table update service. Whenever the government makes changes to payroll tax tables or payroll forms, the service sends you a disk that you load to update your tax tables. For more information on the service and subscribing, call 1-800-336-1420 or visit www. peachtree.com/html/tax_pca.cfm to order tax tables online.

Starting with Version 8, Peachtree Corporation no longer supplies global tax tables when you purchase the product. Global tax tables include the tables that calculate Federal Income Tax, Social Security, and Medicare. To use payroll, you *must* have these tables.

You may need to know your global tax table version. Start the Payroll Setup Wizard (choose Maintain⇨Default Information⇨Payroll Setup Wizard), and the first screen will show you the version.

Closing Payroll and Fiscal Years

Closing the Payroll Year and the Fiscal Year are not difficult or time-consuming. The activities you should complete *before* closing can be time-consuming but usually aren't difficult. In this section, we examine year-end tasks in the various areas of Peachtree: Payroll, Accounts Payable, Inventory, Accounts Receivable, Jobs, Account Reconciliation, and General Ledger

Peachtree 2002 contains a new Year End wizard. See the appendix for details..

A few notes about closing

Closing in Peachtree automatically does the equivalent of manually preparing and posting closing entries to the general ledger. In addition, Peachtree resets all your vendors', customers', and employees' year-to-date totals to zero. That way, you can begin monitoring the new year's purchases with each vendor, sales with each customer, and wages, benefits, deductions, and taxes with each employee.

Why does Peachtree contain two closing commands? The Close Payroll Year command operates on a calendar year and closes Payroll and Accounts Payable information. The Close Fiscal Year command operates on a fiscal year and closes everything else in Peachtree, including the general ledger. If your fiscal year is the same as your calendar year, you still need to execute both commands to close everything in Peachtree. And, even if you don't use Payroll, you need to close the payroll year to zero out vendor balances.

Both commands automatically close the oldest open year. For example, if you currently have 1999 and 2000 open, Peachtree closes 1999.

Timing is everything when you talk about closing. Typically, no one is ready to close a year on December 31. But, because Peachtree allows you to have two years open simultaneously, you should have no trouble moving forward to 2001 while still leaving 2000 open. Therefore, closing should not become a pressing issue unless you failed to close 1999 prior to trying to move into 2001.

To identify the years you have open, choose Tasks⇨System⇨ Change Accounting Period. Scroll through the list box in the dialog box that appears to identify the available years. If you find 2000 and 1999 open, you need to close 1999 (both payroll and fiscal years) to open 2001. Closing 1999 will not affect your 2000 information.

One last note about closing: We strongly recommend that you *back up* before closing anything; then, close the Payroll Year first and then the Fiscal Year. After you start the closing process, you cannot cancel it, so restoring from a backup becomes the only way you can "undo." And you *never* know when you'll need to go back. Alternatively, you can create a prior year company; see Chapter 20 for more information on creating a prior year company.

Payroll

Before you close the 2000 Payroll Year in Peachtree, you want to finish payroll processing for 2000. You should check employee background information, wage information, and tax information. Printing W-2s should be the last task you perform for 2000 so that you can be sure that the information on the forms will be accurate.

If you have adjustments or fringe benefits that should be reflected on W-2s, you can include them in the last payroll of the year, or you can run a separate payroll. We recommend that you try to include them in the last payroll of the year. See Chapter 9 for information on setting up and paying bonuses.

Accounts Payable

In addition to printing 1099s before closing the payroll year, the end of the year is a good time to consider identifying any vendors with whom you no longer do business and marking them inactive in the Maintain Vendors window. You also should review open purchase orders and close any that you know you won't fill, making them candidates for purging.

Inventory

There are no special year-end procedures for Inventory in Peachtree; however, many businesses perform a physical inventory count at this time of year. Peachtree's Physical Inventory List contains space for you to enter actual counts, which makes taking physical inventory easier.

Be sure to print an Inventory Valuation Report after you adjust your quantities to the physical count.

Accounts Receivable

In Accounts Receivable, you simply need to clean up your files. You should review customers and, in the Maintain Customers/Prospects window, mark inactive those with whom you no longer do business. Review open quotes and sales orders and close any that you know you won't fill, making them candidates for purging. You should also review your Accounts Receivable aging report for possible bad debts and write off any amounts that you know you won't collect.

Job Cost

Job Cost, by its very nature, doesn't run on a calendar or fiscal year basis — Job Cost helps you track costs and revenues over the life of a project. Therefore, Job Cost has no end-of-year procedures other than standard housekeeping. You should review existing jobs and mark appropriate ones as inactive using the Maintain Jobs window.

Account Reconciliation

We recommend reconciling your December bank statements before you close the fiscal year to make reconciled checks and deposits candidates for purging; unreconciled transactions remain in the system.

General Ledger

You'll probably want to wait to close the Fiscal Year until you've had time to make year-end adjustments — and you get those from your accountant after he or she has prepared the income tax return for the business. You also should review your Chart of Accounts for accounts you're no longer using — and mark those accounts inactive.

As a point of interest, even though Peachtree purges inactive transactions, Peachtree retains enough information to produce comparative financial statements.

Closing the payroll year

Remember to back up before you start this process!! Peachtree asks you to back up during the process, but we really think you should do it now.

Even if your company's fiscal year doesn't match the calendar year, Payroll always operates on a calendar year basis. Therefore, sometime in January, 2001, after you have performed your last payroll for 2000, confirmed that your payroll data is complete, and printed your W-2s, you are ready to close your payroll information for 2000.

You won't be able to cancel this process after the first screen.

Follow these steps to close the payroll year:

1. **Choose Tasks⇨System⇨Close Payroll Year.**

   Peachtree displays a dialog box suggesting that you make a backup of your data before you close.

2. **Click the Continue command button to continue closing the year, because you backed up before you started this process.**

   If you have not yet printed W-2s or 1099s, Peachtree prompts you to print them before you continue. You should print W-2s or 1099s before continuing with payroll closing. Also, you *must* print any unnumbered (unprinted) checks before closing the payroll year.

   Peachtree begins the closing process and displays the Close Calendar Year dialog box, showing the new payroll calendar year you are about to start (see Figure 18-7).

Figure 18-7:
The sample company operates in the year 2003, so the new payroll year will be 2004.

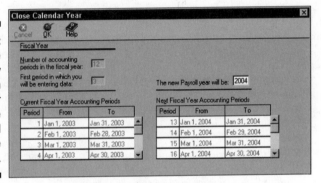

3. **Click OK.**

   Peachtree completes the closing process. You are now ready to enter payroll information into the next year.

Closing the fiscal year

Again, remember to back up before you start this process. Please.

If you have made all adjustments for the current year, you need to close the fiscal year in Peachtree. You should close the fiscal year *after* you have entered all adjustments for the fiscal year. That you'll postpone closing the fiscal year for quite a while is very likely. In fact, if your fiscal year matches the calendar year, you probably won't close 2000 any earlier than March, 2001.

Before Peachtree will let you close, you must not have any purchases that are "Waiting on a Bill" from the vendor in the year that you want to close. Typically, you will have received all bills by the time you want to close the fiscal year, but, if you haven't, you should change these transactions. Choose Tasks⇨Purchases/Receive Inventory. Then, click the Edit button. Open a Purchase that contains a "Y" in the Waiting column. Remove the check and post the transaction.

To close the fiscal year, follow these steps:

1. **Choose Tasks⇨System⇨Close Fiscal Year.**

   Peachtree displays a dialog box suggesting that you make a backup of your data before you close.

2. **Click the Continue button because you backed up before you started the process.**

   Peachtree asks whether you want to print reports.

3. **Click Yes.**

   Peachtree displays a list of suggested reports to print — this dialog box looks just like the dialog box you see if you print reports when changing an accounting period. After you finish printing, Peachtree continues the closing process by displaying a message telling you the number of the Retained Earnings account that will be updated during the closing process.

4. **Click OK.**

   After updating the Chart of Accounts and clearing history, Peachtree displays the Close Fiscal Year dialog box, showing you the first period into which you will be entering data (see Figure 18-8).

5. **Click OK.**

   Peachtree asks whether you want to purge.

6. **Click No.**

   Peachtree finishes the closing process. You can click Yes and begin the purge process, but you also can purge information at anytime (not just when you're closing a year) as you can find out in the next section. So, we broke up the discussion.

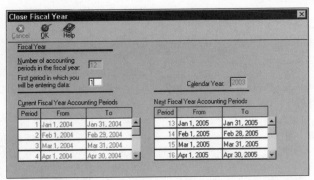

Figure 18-8:
The dialog
box you see
when
Peachtree is
about to
close the
fiscal year.

Purging

Purging can take quite a long time, depending on the size of your data, the speed of your computer, and the age of the transactions you choose to include in the purge. Peachtree's purge process doesn't have a limit to the number of passes it makes, or the time it takes to go through the journal file. We strongly recommend that you start this process before leaving for the night or weekend.

If your Peachtree journal file is large, you may want to purge every month. To determine the size of your journal file, choose Help⇨File Statistics and look at the Size in Kbytes column for the Jrnl Rows file. If this file is larger than 5000KB (5 meg), then you will probably want to purge in small increments.

Peachtree purges two types of data:

- ✔ **Transactions:** Quotes, invoices, sales orders, receipts, purchases, purchase orders, payments, paychecks, and general journal entries from previous years that are no longer needed.

- ✔ **Inactives:** Customers, vendors, employees, inventory items, jobs, phases, cost codes, and general ledger accounts that have been marked as Inactive on the Maintain screens.

If you plan to purge Inactives, you should also purge transactions because Peachtree won't purge Inactives if any transactions apply to them.

You can automatically start the purging process as you close the fiscal year, or you can purge at any time.

Back up before you start purging. Really. We mean it.

Follow these steps:

1. **Choose Tasks⇨System⇨Purge Old Transactions/Inactives.**

   Peachtree prompts you to make a backup.

2. **If you didn't back up before you started this process, choose Backup; otherwise, choose Continue.**

   Peachtree asks whether you want to print reports before purging. If you choose Yes, Peachtree displays a list of reports that you can print — just like the list you see when changing the accounting period. When you finish printing or if you choose No, Peachtree continues with the purge process and displays the first window of the Purge Guide, where you can select expired quotes and purchase and sales orders that were not converted to purchases or invoices to purge (see Figure 18-9).

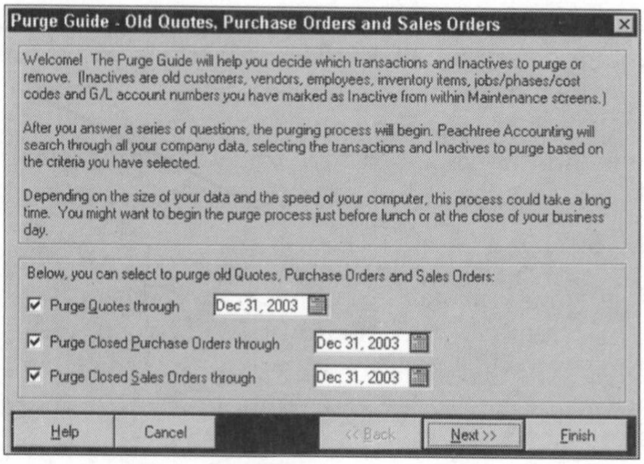

Figure 18-9:
Identify quotes, sales orders, and purchase orders to purge.

3. **Set an ending date.**

   We suggest that you keep one year of history — for example, when you close 2000, purge stuff older than January 1, 1999.

4. **Click Next.**

   If you're using Peachtree Complete Accounting, two windows appear, providing you with the opportunity to identify tickets that you want to purge. The first window lets you identify, based on dates, tickets you've used or don't intend to use (tickets for employees who don't get paid based on tickets, nonbillable tickets, and vendor tickets). The second window, which closely resembles the first window, allows you to identify tickets to purge, again based on dates, that are unused but available for use — specifically, unused tickets for employees you do pay based on tickets.

5. Check appropriate boxes to identify tickets you want to purge and set ending dates for each box.

If you're using any other version of Peachtree, you won't see these windows.

6. Click Next.

The Purge Guide allows you to set dates for old transactions and Audit Trail records (see Figure 18-10).

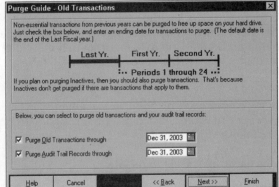

Figure 18-10:
Select old transactions and audit trail records to purge.

7. Click Next.

The Purge Guide allows you to specify whether you'll be using Account Reconciliation. If you choose Yes, the Purge Guide displays another window, in which you identify the accounts you intend to reconcile. After you identify the accounts you intend to reconcile, the Purge Guide allows you to establish the date of the oldest transaction you want to keep. Peachtree purges all unreconciled transactions dated earlier than that date.

8. Click Next.

The Purge Guide asks whether you intend to use reimbursable expenses. If you choose Yes, the Purge Guide displays a window in which you identify the jobs for which you plan to use Reimbursable Expenses. In the next window, the Purge Guide asks you to set a date for the oldest reimbursable expense you want to keep for the selected jobs.

9. Click Next.

The Purge Guide displays a window in which you can choose to purge inactive G/L account numbers, customers/prospects, vendors, employees/sales reps, inventory items, or jobs/phases/cost codes.

10. **Click Finish.**

    Peachtree displays a summary window showing your selections.

11. **Click Begin Purging.**

    Peachtree purges and completes the closing process.

Some important notes about purging

Sometimes, after purging, you'll find information still in the system that you think should have been purged. Peachtree follows some rather extensive rules when selecting information to purge. As a result of these rules, you will probably find a lot of information still in the system that you think should have purged. We call anything Peachtree leaves in your database a "saved" transaction.

Rather than list all the rules Peachtree follows, we summarize briefly, and we refer to the date you specify while setting up a purge as *the purge date*. Peachtree saves the following:

- All transactions dated after the purge date
- All payroll checks in the current year
- Purchases and sales that are not completely paid as of the purge date
- All cash receipts or disbursements applied to a saved invoice or purchase
- All purchases and sales that are related to saved cash disbursements or cash receipts
- Sales orders and purchase orders used by saved invoices or purchases
- Inactive jobs with saved transactions that refer to the inactive job

Chapter 19

Managing the Money

In This Chapter

▶ Understanding the Managers

▶ Using Peachtree Today

Accounting for the money is really only half the battle . . . managing the money is the rest. In addition to helping you account for your money, Peachtree contains some tools that help you manage your money . . . and in this chapter, we explore them.

Meet the Financial Manager

Peachtree's Financial Manager can give you a "quick" view of your financial picture. It displays some key ratios and key balances in an overview fashion that can help you check the pulse of your business without analyzing reports.

Business Summary

Choose Analysis⇨Financial Manager to display the window you see in Figure 19-1. Peachtree displays, by default, the Business Summary view, which contains four panes of financial information presented as percentages.

Ratios by themselves are meaningless; you need to compare the ratios to either historical data for your company or other companies in your industry. You may want to take a look at Leo Troy's Almanac of Business and Industrial Financial Ratios 2000 (you can purchase the book from www.amazon.com).

Financial analysts and bankers calculate dozens of ratios to help them understand the financial picture of a company — and Peachtree provides some of the more basic ones in the Business Summary, using information you can find on your income statement and balance sheet.

Figure 19-1:
The
Business
Summary
displayed
in the
Financial
Manager
focuses
primarily on
key ratios
in your
business.

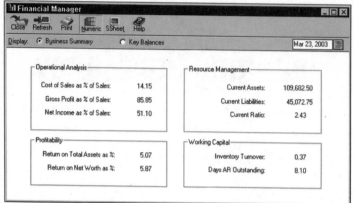

The numbers you see in the four panes of the Business Summary are percentages, and we describe ratios here; you must multiply the result of all the following calculations by 100 to adjust for percentages. Remember that high school math? (Ugh!)

Operational analysis

To calculate the Cost of Sales as a Percentage of Sales, Peachtree uses your income statement and divides Total Cost of Sales by Total Revenues. The higher the ratio, the more it costs you to make your sales — reducing your gross profit.

To calculate Gross Profit as a Percentage of Sales, again, Peachtree uses your income statement and divides Gross Profit by Total Revenues. This ratio plus the previous ratio will sum to 100%, so, you can expect that a lower ratio will indicate that your cost of sales is high.

To calculate Net Income as a Percentage of Sales, Peachtree again uses your income statement and divides Net Income by Total Revenues. This ratio takes into consideration both your cost of sales and your operating expenses; a higher ratio means that you've kept your expenses down.

Profitability

To calculate Return on Total Assets as a percentage, Peachtree uses both your income statement and your balance sheet and divides Net Income on your income statement by Total Assets on your balance sheet. If the resulting ratio is high, either you have a high profit margin or you turn over your assets quickly.

To calculate Return on Net Worth as a percentage, Peachtree again uses both your income statement and your balance sheet and divides Net Income by Total Equity (or Capital). The higher the ratio, the better, because it indicates you're making more money on the money you invested.

Resource management

In this section, Peachtree lists your Current Assets and your Current Liabilities (both found on your balance sheet) and then calculates the Current Ratio by dividing Current Assets by Current Liabilities. The Current Ratio gives you a measure of your ability to cover your debts with your assets in case of an emergency. A number less than 1 indicates that your assets would not cover your liabilities.

Working capital

To calculate Inventory Turnover, Peachtree uses both the income statement and the balance sheet and divides Total Cost of Sales by Inventory. This ratio helps you measure how long items remain in inventory before you sell them. A higher number indicates that you keep items in inventory longer.

Days A/R Outstanding represents the average length of time (in days) your receivables remain outstanding. To calculate Days A/R Outstanding, Peachtree first divides Total Sales by the number of days in the period — call the result "Sales Per Day." Then, Peachtree divides Average Accounts Receivable for the period by Sales Per Day to determine the average number of days receivables remain outstanding.

Key Balances

This window (see Figure 19-2) provides key balances for certain balance sheet accounts and, in the Operations section, you see a summarized version of your income statement. Click the Key Balances button to switch to this view.

While viewing either the Business Summary or the Key Balances, you can click the S.Sheet button in the window to have Peachtree display corresponding monthly values.

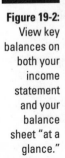

Figure 19-2:
View key balances on both your income statement and your balance sheet "at a glance."

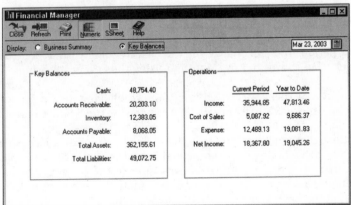

Understanding the Cash Manager

"I *really* need to know how much cash I'm going to have at the end of the month." Have you heard yourself say that? Let Peachtree's Cash Manager do the math for you.

The Cash Manager window, shown in Figure 19-3, shows you the company's expected cash balance for a particular date, taking into consideration sales you'll collect, payments you'll make, payroll you'll meet, and any cash adjustments. To open this window, choose Analysis⇨Cash Manager.

If you use batch posting, you need to post before using the information in this window to get an accurate picture of your cash position.

Figure 19-3:
Use the Cash Manager to predict your cash balance on a particular date.

	As of Date: 4/23/03	Due By: 4/30/03	Due By: 5/7/03	Due By: 5/14/03	Due By: 5/21/03
	Starting Cash:	48,754.40	52,338.44	52,338.44	46,469.27
Add:					
	Sales To Collect:	17,521.26	0.00	0.00	0.00
	Cash Adjustments (+):	0.00	0.00	0.00	0.00
	Total Available:	66,275.66	52,338.44	52,338.44	46,469.27
Less:					
	Payments To Make:	8,068.05	0.00	0.00	0.00
	Payroll To Pay:	5,869.17	0.00	5,869.17	0.00
	Cash Adjustments (-):	0.00	0.00	0.00	0.00
	Ending Cash:	52,338.44	52,338.44	46,469.27	46,469.27

To calculate the first "Starting Cash" balance, Peachtree sums the balances in all accounts you defined as "cash" accounts in your Chart of Accounts. All subsequent starting cash balances equal the ending cash balance from the prior period. You can change the forecast frequency from its default of "Weekly" to "Biweekly" or "Monthly" using the Forecast list box.

You can view this information in a graph by clicking the Graph option button. Or, you can switch to a spreadsheet view using the S.Sheet button.

Suppose that you think you're going to be able to close a large deal that you've been working on — and you'd like to see what the cash picture will look like if you do close the deal. Or suppose that you *might* buy a truck during the time period and you'd like to include the effects of the down payment in the Cash Manager. You can include these "what if" scenarios in the

Cash Adjustments lines. To add cash to the picture, double-click the Cash Adjustments (+) line. To subtract cash from the picture, double-click the Cash Adjustments (–) line. After you double-click, a window appears in which you can record an adjustment.

To subtract cash, record the adjustment as a positive, not a negative, number.

Using the Payment Manager

The Payments Manager can help you select bills to pay and pay bills. When you open the Payment Manager window by choosing Analysis⇨ Payment Manager, you see the window shown in Figure 19-4.

Even if your business operates on a cash basis, you'll see bills in this window.

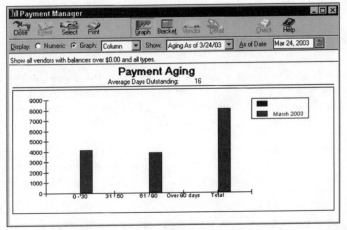

Figure 19-4: This graph presents a picture of the total amount you owe based on the age of the bills.

You can view the information numerically by clicking the Numeric option button. You typically set the As of Date to "today," but you can change it, too. Initially, the Show list box date matches the As of Date; however, you can change the Show date to compare last month to this month or this month last year to this month this year.

Suppose that you want to see the details that comprise the 61-90 day bar. Double-click the bar to see a window like the one shown in Figure 19-5.

Place a check next to bills that you want to pay and click the Check button at the top of the window. Peachtree allows you to select a form and print checks for the selected bills.

Click here to print checks

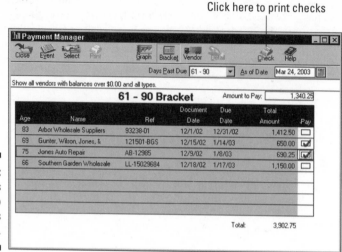

Figure 19-5:
Use this
window to
select bills
to pay.

Using the Collection Manager

Managing Accounts Receivable can be critical to the survival of your business. If you don't collect money that your customers owe you in a timely fashion, you don't have enough money to buy the things you need to continue your business — and the cash flow crunch could squeeze you out of business.

From the Collection Manager window, shown in Figure 19-6, you can monitor your receivables and even create collection letters to send to your customers. Choose Analysis⇨Collection Manager to open this window.

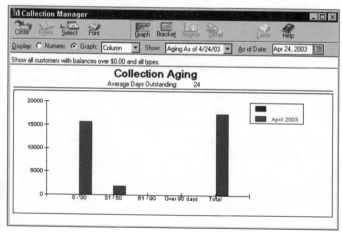

Figure 19-6:
Use the
Collection
Manager to
help you
manage
accounts
receivable.

The Collection Manager works a lot like the Payment Manager; you can view the information numerically and you can change the dates you're viewing. And, if you double-click a bar on the chart, you can view details of the invoices that are past due for that period. In the Collection Manager window, you can select invoices about which you want to send collection letters. When you click the Letter button at the top of the window, Peachtree permits you to select a letter format. The letter formats range from gentle reminders to firm requests for payment. You can view the text for each letter format by clicking the Design button in the window where you select the letter format.

Peachtree treats collection letters as forms; therefore, you can modify the various collection letters the same way you modify other forms. You can find the collection letters by opening the Select a Report window for Accounts Receivable and looking for a folder called Collection Letters.

See Chapter 14 for more information on customizing forms and collection letters.

Looking at Peachtree Today

Peachtree Today is new in Version 8.

You probably noticed that a browser page appeared when you first opened your company in Peachtree. The browser page displays "Peachtree Today" for you. You can think of Peachtree Today as an information center for your company. Each time you open Peachtree, by default, you see the Welcome page (see Figure 19-7) of Peachtree Today, which contains topics that will help you use Peachtree. The topics work like Web page links; click one to display the information on that topic.

If you close Peachtree Today and want to reopen it, click the Today button that appears in the bottom-right corner of the Peachtree window.

On the My Business page, shown in Figure 19-8, you can find a quick snapshot of major items of interest, such as sales invoices and vendor bills overdue by 10 days or more, and an interesting graphic that shows your net income for the current period. You also can customize this page to display the balances and the budget variances of accounts you select. And, you can print certain reports, such as the General Ledger Trial Balance, directly from this page.

When you click the My Resources link, Peachtree prompts you to sign onto the Internet unless you have a "full-time" connection. After you sign on, a page like the one shown in Figure 19-9 appears, which contains news and services particularly interesting to Peachtree users.

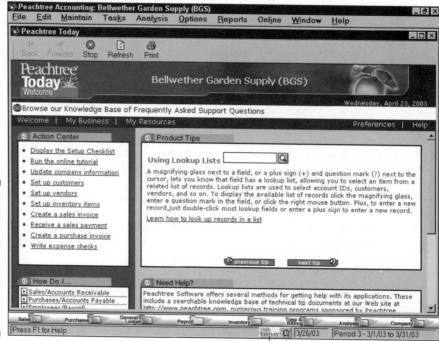

Figure 19-7:
You can find product tips and help on the Welcome page of Peachtree Today.

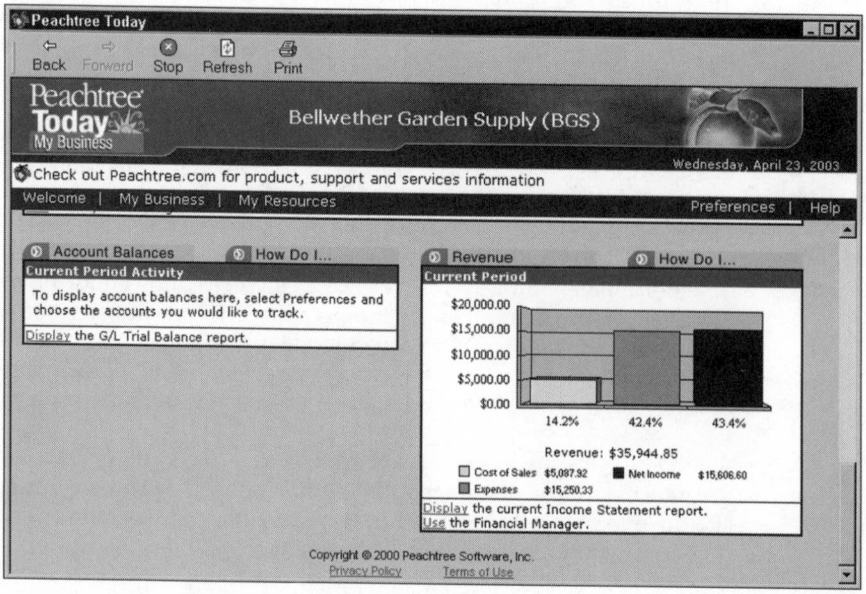

Today button

Figure 19-8:
View a snapshot of your company on the My Business page.

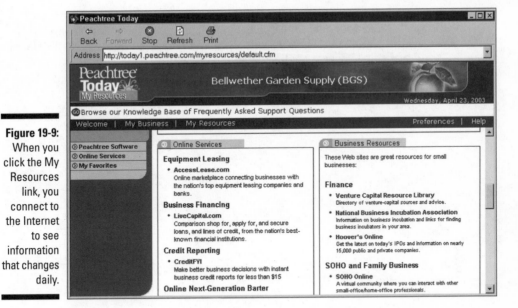

Figure 19-9:
When you
click the My
Resources
link, you
connect to
the Internet
to see
information
that changes
daily.

When you click Preferences, you see a page similar to the one shown in Figure 19-10. On the Preferences page, you can specify the behavior of Peachtree Today — including whether it appears each time you open your company. If you *don't* want to see Peachtree Today each time you open your company, remove the check that appears in the Start Up section at the bottom of the General Preferences page.

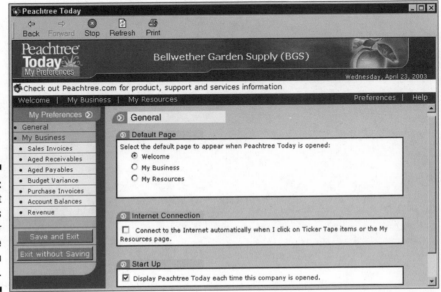

Figure 19-10:
Set
preferences
for
Peachtree
Today from
this page.

To set preferences for the other Peachtree Today pages, click links that appear on the left side of the page under Preferences and make changes as necessary. For example, to monitor account balances, click Account Balances and place checks next to the accounts you want to monitor.

Chapter 20

Peachtree in Real Life

. . . .

In This Chapter

▶ Dealing with customer prepayments

▶ Making a prior year company

▶ Moving to a new computer

▶ Handling retainage

▶ Organizing employee loans, garnishments, and other odds and ends

. . . .

*W*e felt strongly that this book wouldn't be complete if we didn't provide you with some solutions to some common situations that arise. In fact, we worked really hard to make room for these "real-life situations."

Handling Customer Prepayments

Under certain conditions, your customers may pay you before you actually deliver the goods or services you promise. For example, in the building business, customers often provide down payments that builders use to purchase construction materials. Some service businesses request retainers before performing work. In these cases, you are accepting money that is a liability to your business, and you must account for it as a liability until you deliver the promised goods or services.

Deposits and *prepayments* are, by definition, payments received before goods or services are delivered. Your method of accounting — cash or accrual basis — has no bearing on how you handle these prepayments. Prepayments from customers are actually your liabilities. Because you have received the money before you supplied the goods or services, you now have an obligation to the customer to complete the transaction. Deposits are unearned revenue.

First, you need a G/L account in which to record customer prepayments when you receive them. To handle customer deposits, from the Maintain Chart of Accounts window, set up "Customer Deposits" as an "Other Current Liability" type account. (See Chapter 3 to review adding accounts.)

Second, set up a nonstock class inventory item for Deposits. Use the Customer Deposits G/L account you created for all three G/L accounts (Sales, Salary/Wages, and Cost of Sales). See Chapter 11 to review setting up inventory items. When you receive a prepayment from your customer, create a receipt to track the deposit:

1. **Choose Tasks➪Receipts to display the Receipts window.**

2. **Enter the deposit ticket ID, customer ID, reference #, date, payment method, and cash account as you normally enter receipts.**

   Refer to Chapter 8 for details on entering receipts.

3. **On the Apply to Revenues tab, enter a quantity of 1; then, from the Item drop-down list, select Deposits.**

4. **Enter the amount of the deposit.**

5. **Click Post to save the transaction.**

This transaction debits Cash and credits Customer Deposits. The balance sheet shows the Customer Deposits account and the Cash account increased by the amount of the prepayment.

After you perform the work, you want to send your customer an invoice. Create an invoice for the customer, but add a final line item on the invoice showing a quantity of –1 with an Item Deposits for the amount of the prepayment (see Figure 20-1). If the amount of the invoice you create equals the amount of the prepayment, the customer owes you nothing; however, if the invoice amount exceeds the prepayment amount, the customer really does owe you money — the difference between the invoice amount and the prepayment amount.

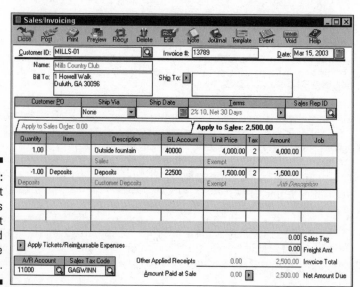

Figure 20-1: The deposit reduces the amount owed against the invoice.

Be sure to enter a negative quantity (–1) on the invoice, but use a positive number for the unit price amount. Peachtree automatically converts the total amount to a negative number. When you receive the balance due from the customer, create another receipt. The amount that appears in the Receipts window is the remainder of the invoice amount.

Creating a Prior Year Company

Chapter 18 shows you how to close and purge a fiscal year. When you do so, the transactions and reports are no longer accessible. Before you close your year, you should create a prior year company so you can print reports, look for transactions, and so on. The big picture? You create a backup of your existing company, create a new, empty company, and then restore the backup into the new, empty company.

Follow these steps *before* you close the fiscal year.

1. **Open your company in Peachtree.**

2. **Change your accounting period to the last period in the year you want to close.**

   For example, if your fiscal year is the same as a calendar year and you're closing fiscal year 2000, then change to period 12, which would be December 2000. Chapter 18 shows you how to change your accounting period.

3. **Choose File⇨Backup and click Backup Now.**

4. **In the File Name text box, type an appropriate name such as** FY2000 **if you're closing fiscal year 2000.**

5. **Under Save In, select the C drive again so that the backup is saved in the root (C:\) directory on your C drive. Click Save to continue backing up.**

   When the backup is complete, you need to create a new company.

6. **Choose File⇨New Company and create a new company called FY2000 or something that indicates the prior year; enter only a company name and then continue through the setup by clicking Next in all subsequent windows.**

   Refer to Chapter 2 to set up a new company.

   It does not matter what options you select because these settings will be overwritten by restoring the FY2000 backup.

   After you set up the new company, restore the backup data from the prior year company.

7. **Choose File⇨Restore to display the Restore window.**

8. **Under Look In, select the C drive.**

9. **Select the FY2000.ptb (or whatever you named the backup file) backup and click Open.**

10. **When the restore is complete, choose Maintain⇨Company Information and change the name of the company to something really obvious like FY2000 Company Data.**

    This step makes the second copy of your company appear as a separate name in the Open Company window.

You can now open your regular current company by choosing File⇨ Open Company. When you need to refer to the prior year company, you can find it in the Open dialog box.

Moving Peachtree to a New Computer

If you need to move Peachtree to another computer, you need to reinstall the Peachtree program and current tax tables. Then you can copy the company data folders and any customized forms to the new computer.

To determine the name of your company data folder, open the company in Peachtree, then choose Help⇨File Statistics. At the top of the dialog box that appears, you'll see Data File Statistics for *xxx* where *xxx* is the company data folder name. That's the folder you want to copy to the new computer. It's usually located in the Peachw folder.

You also want to copy customized forms. For customized forms, look in the Peachw folder. All form files end in the .frm extension. The first three characters of the filename indicate the type of form; for example, INV means invoice while PRC means payroll check. The last five characters in the filename are numbers. Any number less than 1000 is a customized form. Any number greater than 1000 is a predefined form that's installed with the Peachtree program. Table 20-1 lists a few examples:

Table 20-1	**Sample Form File Names**	
Filename	*Type of Form*	*Source*
APC00001	Accounts Payable Check	Customized
APC01043	Accounts Payable Check	Peachtree
INV00000	Customer Invoice	Customized
PRC00101	Payroll Check	Customized
STM01031	Customer Statement	Peachtree

Handling Retainage

Suppose that, in your business, you get paid for part of a job at the beginning of the job and get paid for the rest when the job is completed. If you work this way, you have *retainage,* and you need to know how to correctly bill the customers and to track both billed and unbilled amounts owed to you.

You need only one extra account on your balance sheet — an account called Retainage Receivable. Choose Maintain⇨Chart of Accounts. In the Maintain Chart of Accounts window, provide an account number appropriate to the asset section of the Chart of Accounts, name the account, and make it an Other Current Asset account.

Suppose that the terms of your contract specify that you will earn $10,000 and you'll get paid 90 percent at the beginning of the job, with 10 percent, or $1,000, being held as retainage. You need to prepare an invoice for $9,000 and account for the $1,000 being retained by the customer:

1. **Choose Tasks⇨Sales/Invoicing to display the Sales/Invoicing window and select the customer for whom you need to prepare the invoice.**

2. **In the line item section of the invoice, create two lines.**

3. **Fill in the total sale amount ($10,000 in our example) and post the line against an income account.**

4. **On the second line, post the retainage amount as a negative number to the Retainage Receivable account.**

   This transaction credits an income account for $10,000, recognizing the revenue you will generate from the contract. It also debits Accounts Receivable for $9,000, the amount the customer owes immediately, and Retainage Receivable for $1,000, the amount the customer will pay when the job is completed.

When the customer pays you for the original invoice — $9,000 in this example — record the receipt the same way that you would record any receipt in the Receipts window. When you finish the job, you need to bill the customer for the final amount — the retainage amount of $1,000 in this example. Record an invoice, posting the line item for the retainage amount against the Retainage Receivable account (see Figure 20-2). As a result of this invoice, Peachtree debits the Accounts Receivable account and credits the Retainage Receivable account, reducing the amount of retainage the customer owes.

To use the following method to track retainage, we suggest that you use an invoice number for the retainage bill that is the same as the original invoice number, followed by an R.

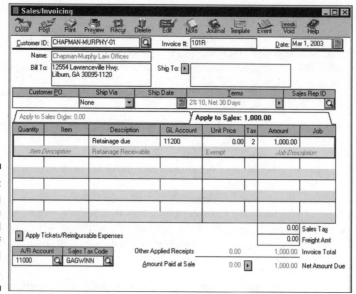

Figure 20-2:
Recording
the invoice
for final
payment of
retained
money.

When the customer pays this bill, record the receipt the same way you would record any receipt in the Receipts window.

To help you identify clients who have unbilled retainage amounts, we suggest that you take advantage of Peachtree's Account Reconciliation feature, which allows you to reconcile *any* account, not just bank accounts:

1. **Choose Tasks⇨Account Reconciliation to display the Account Reconciliation window.**

2. **Select the Retainage Receivable account.**

   Notice that some amounts appear in both the top and the bottom portions of the window — note that the Vendor/Payee at the top and the Description at the bottom are the same. The entry at the bottom of the window occurred when you prepared the original invoice that held back the retainage amount. The entry in the top portion of the window occurred when you billed the retainage.

3. **When you see a pair of like entries, check them off as we've done in Figure 20-3, because they represent billed retainage amounts.**

   You don't need to enter the Statement Ending Balance, because you don't have a statement; the Unreconciled Difference should always be zero, because you're checking off matching entries in both the top and bottom of the window.

4. **When you finish marking off matched pairs, click OK.**

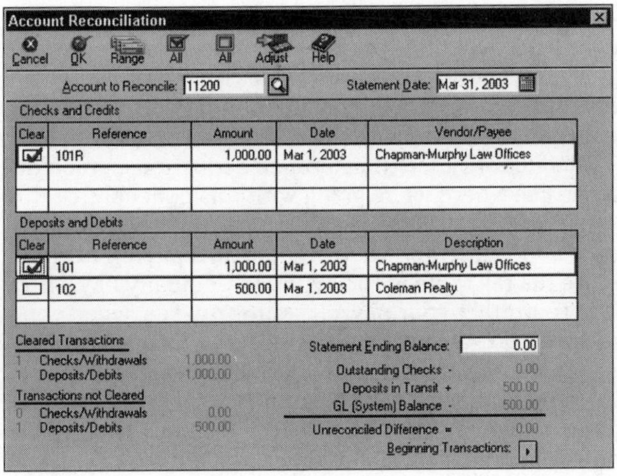

Figure 20-3:
Matching
retainage
amounts to
help identify
billed
retainage.

Use the Account Reconciliation Other Outstanding Items report to identify the clients and retainage amounts you didn't mark off in Account Reconciliation. These are the amounts that you have not yet billed. Choose Reports⇔Account Reconciliation and highlight the Other Outstanding Items report. On the Filter tab, choose the Retainage Receivable account. When you print the report, you'll see only retainage amounts that you haven't yet billed.

Real-Life Payroll Situations

There are dozens of "real life" payroll situations, so we picked the ones we figure occur most frequently and therefore would be of the most use to you. In the pages that follow, we show you how to set up some common payroll deductions and taxes.

Payroll deductions, in general

For all payroll deductions, you need at least two elements: the payroll field for the deduction and a general ledger account that you tie to the field. Because you assign a general ledger account to a payroll deduction, we usually walk you through setting up first the general ledger account and then the deduction.

In many cases, you also need a third element: a payroll tax table to calculate the amount of the deduction. And, you assign a payroll tax table to a deduction. So, when a deduction requires a payroll tax table, we walk you through setting up the general ledger account and then the payroll tax table. Last, we show you how to set up the deduction.

"But, what does a payroll tax table have to do with a deduction?" you ask. Well, Peachtree uses tax tables to calculate more than just federal, state, or local taxes due. The name "payroll tax table" is somewhat of a misnomer, because these "tax tables" store calculations that you need for payroll — even if the calculation is not for a tax. You can set up payroll tax tables to calculate 401(k) deductions, health insurance deductions, union dues deductions — you can see where we're going with this concept.

Remember one important fact when you create a payroll tax table for your own use: Create the tax table in the Maintain Company Payroll Tax Tables window. Why? To protect your payroll setup. You see, when you subscribe to Peachtree's payroll tax table update service, Peachtree will *replace* the tax tables you see in the Maintain Global Payroll Tax Tables window. But it won't touch the tax tables you see in the Maintain Company Payroll Tax Tables window. If you store your calculations in the Maintain Global Payroll Tax Tables window, your calculations will be wiped out when you update payroll tax tables at the end of the calendar year.

Finally, you also need to define the elements of Adjusted Gross Income to Peachtree to make Peachtree calculate payroll deductions or additions correctly. You find out how to define the elements of Adjusted Gross Income later in the chapter.

Employee loans

Suppose that you loan money to an employee. You can set up a payroll deduction so that the employee can repay the loan from his paycheck. And, depending on the repayment amounts, you can either manually enter the repayment amount on each paycheck or Peachtree can automatically deduct a fixed amount from each paycheck until the loan is repaid.

The general ledger

You need at least two elements for a payroll deduction: the general ledger account and the deduction. For the employee loan, you really don't need the third element — the payroll tax table.

To track a loan, set up an "other current asset" account on your Chart of Accounts, called Employee Loans or Employee Advances.

If you intend to loan more than one employee money, we suggest that you use Peachtree's masking feature and set up individual accounts for each loan that would roll up into the Employee Advances account. For example, if you created 14100 for your Employee Advances account, the account number for a loan to Dorothy Beckstrom might be 14100-01, and the account number for a loan to Elliot Adams might be 14100-02. See Chapters 3 and 16 for information on masking.

Writing a loan check

When you write the check for the employee's loan, use the Payments or the Write Checks window. You don't need to set up the employee as a vendor; simply type the employee's name in the Pay To The Order Of box. On the Apply to Expenses tab of the Payments window, fill in the employee's loan account as the G/L Account. Or, at the bottom of the Write Checks window, supply the employee's loan account as the Expense Account.

The payroll field for repaying the loan "manually"

You need to use the "manual" repayment method if the repayment amounts differ from paycheck to paycheck.

Set up a payroll deduction for the loan by following these steps:

1. **Choose Maintain⇨Default Information⇨Employees. Scroll to the bottom of the EmployEE Fields tab to add a field called Loan (see Figure 20-4).**

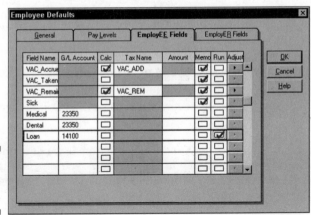

Figure 20-4: Setting up a payroll field.

The name you type in the Field Name column will appear on the paycheck stub.

2. **In the G/L Account field, select the main account you set up for employee loans — 14100 in our example.**

3. **Place a check in the Run column so that Peachtree will maintain a running total for the deduction even when you close the payroll year.**

4. **Click OK.**

5. **Choose Maintain⇨Employees/Sales Reps and display the information for the employee to whom you are making the loan.**

6. **On the EmployEE Fields tab, remove the check from the STD column (see Figure 20-5).**

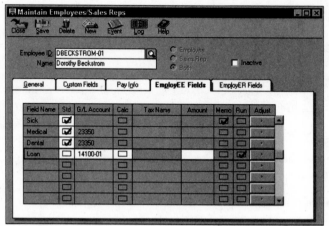

Figure 20-5:
Make
changes for
employees
who don't
use the
standard
defaults.

7. **Change the G/L Account to the account for the employee.**

8. **Click Save.**

When you create a paycheck for the employee, fill in the repayment amount as a negative number.

The payroll field for repaying the loan "automatically"

If you can divide the loan amount into equal installment payments, then you can let Peachtree automatically record the loan payment on the employee's paycheck.

Set up the general ledger account and the deduction as we describe in the previous section. However, when you edit the employee's record in the Maintain Employees/Sales Reps window, also fill in the loan repayment amount as a negative number on the EmployEE Fields tab.

Garnishments

Occasionally, you need to hold back money from an employee's check as a legal garnishment. *Garnishments* are another form of payroll deduction similar to employee advances; however, garnishments typically use all three elements of the payroll deduction. For the general ledger account, use an "other current liability" account in the case of a garnishment instead of the "other current asset" account you set up for an employee loan. You also need to set up the payroll deduction, and you'll probably use a payroll tax table to calculate the garnishment amount. Later in the chapter, you see some examples of setting up payroll tax tables.

Different states have different requirements for garnishments; the garnishment might be a percentage of adjusted gross pay or a percentage of net pay. Check with your accountant to determine the correct way to calculate the garnishment.

Health insurance

For health insurance deductions, you need two elements: the general ledger account and the payroll deduction. But health insurance deductions come in two basic types: after-tax deductions (standard plan) and before-tax deductions (cafeteria plan). And, for cafeteria plans, you need to take an extra step and exclude the field when Peachtree calculates taxes.

You, as the employer, must pay the amount you deduct for health insurance to the insurance company that supplies the plan. Therefore, the amount is a liability to you, and you need to set up an "other current liability" account in your Chart of Accounts.

You set up the health insurance deduction the same way that you set up the deduction for an employee loan. On the EmployEE Fields tab of the Employee Defaults dialog box, type a name that doesn't contain spaces for the health insurance deduction. Remember that the name you type will appear on paycheck stubs. Supply the liability account for health insurance.

You handle this next part the same way you handle employee loans, as we describe in the previous section. If you deduct the same amount for most employees, enter the amount in the Amount column as a negative number. To supply amounts for employees who don't pay the standard amount, open the Maintain Employees/Sales Reps window and select the employee. Click the EmployEE Fields tab and remove the check from the STD column for the health insurance deduction. Then supply the appropriate amount as a negative number in the Amount column (refer to Figure 20-5).

A new payroll field can affect the calculation of existing payroll fields. Whenever you add a tax-sheltered deduction or an addition that is taxable, you need to click the Adjust button for *other payroll fields* that are affected by the new field. For example, suppose that an addition field — perhaps an automobile benefit — is subject to Social Security and Medicare. You need to click the Adjust buttons for Social Security and Medicare and check the Use box for the new addition field to make sure that Peachtree includes the addition field when calculating adjusted gross wages for Social Security and Medicare.

Tax-sheltered deductions — like a health insurance deduction for a cafeteria plan — are typically deducted from Gross Pay before calculating taxes. So, you need to click the Adjust buttons next to Federal Income Tax, Social Security, Medicare, as well as any state and local taxes. In the Calculate

Adjusted Gross dialog box, shown in Figure 20-6, you need to check the Use box next to the health insurance deduction. Then Peachtree will subtract the health insurance deduction from gross pay before calculating taxes. If you're not sure whether a deduction is taxable, check with the plan administrator.

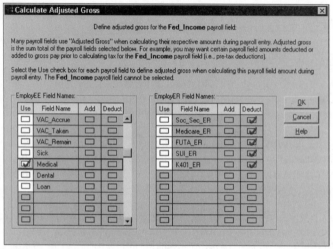

Figure 20-6: Selecting the payroll elements Peachtree should include when calculating Adjusted Gross Income.

You'll find ADJUSTED GROSS in the formulas of many payroll tax tables. When you use one of these payroll tax tables, you need to identify the fields that Peachtree should include when calculating ADJUSTED GROSS to make Peachtree actually calculate something. You identify these fields by clicking the Adjust button next to the new field you're adding and then checking the Use box next to the fields that Peachtree should add or subtract when calculating ADJUSTED GROSS. As a rule, whenever you create a payroll field for which you don't supply an amount in the Amount column, you should always click the Adjust button for the new field and check the Use box for the Gross field. The Gross field is the first field in the left column — you can't see it in Figure 20-6. A formula that includes ADJUSTED GROSS in its calculation makes Peachtree actually calculate something; if the formula doesn't include ADJUSTED GROSS, you won't hurt anything.

Union dues

Deducting union dues from an employee's paycheck can be tricky simply because so many different ways exist to calculate union dues. In this section, we examine how to set up payroll to calculate and deduct union dues, and examine four different ways of calculating the amount:

✔ Deducting a flat amount per month

✔ Deducting a number of hours' pay per month

✔ Using an hourly rate based on hours worked

✔ Using a percentage of gross pay

To calculate union dues, you need all three elements of the payroll deduction: the General Ledger account, the Payroll field, and the payroll tax table to calculate the union dues amount.

As an employer, you handle union dues deductions the same way you handle federal income tax deductions — you collect the money due from the employee and turn it over to the proper authority. So, you need a liability account on your Chart of Accounts that you'll use to track the amount of union dues collected that must be paid to the union. Choose Maintain⇨Chart of Accounts to display the Maintain Chart of Accounts window. Supply an Account ID and description — we called ours Union Dues Payable — and, for the Account Type, choose Other Current Liabilities, and then save the account.

Setting up a payroll tax table

For most union dues calculations, we think you'll find it easiest to use payroll tax tables to calculate the amount to deduct from an employee's paycheck. Follow these steps:

1. **Choose File⇨Payroll Tax Tables⇨Edit Company to display the Maintain Company Payroll Tax Tables window (see Figure 20-7).**

2. **Enter an ID for the tax table; we called ours Union 03.**

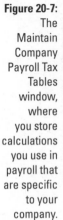

Figure 20-7:
The Maintain Company Payroll Tax Tables window, where you store calculations you use in payroll that are specific to your company.

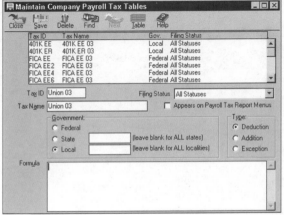

3. **Enter a name, making sure that you add to the end of the name a space and the last two digits of the year for which the tax table will be applicable. We called ours Union 03 again.**

4. **Even though the Government box has nothing to do with union dues, select State or Local in the Government box.**

5. **Enter the appropriate formula for the calculation you want Peachtree to make (see the next section).**

6. **Click the Save button to save the tax table.**

Figuring out what goes in the Formula box

The information in the Formula box will change, depending on how you need to calculate union dues. And many of the formulas we show you use EMP_SPECIAL1_NUMBER or EMP_SPECIAL2_NUMBER. These two values represent variables that you set for individual employees; to understand the formulas better, we show you where you set these values before we dive into the formulas:

1. **Choose Maintain⇨Employee/Sales Rep to display the Maintain Employees/Sales Rep window and select an employee.**

2. **On the General tab, in the Withholding Information section in the bottom-left corner of the window, scroll down until you see Special 1 (see Figure 20-8).**

3. **In the Additional Withholding column, type the value for EMP_SPECIAL1_NUMBER.**

   If you're supplying a percentage, make sure you type the percentage as a percentage. If the percentage is 2.65%, type 2.65; don't type .0265, which is the rate, not the percentage.

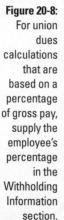

Figure 20-8:
For union dues calculations that are based on a percentage of gross pay, supply the employee's percentage in the Withholding Information section.

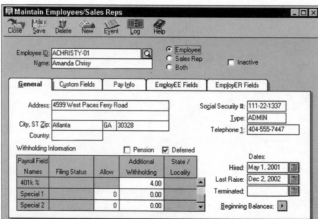

If the formula you use requires different rates for each employee, the formula will reference EMP_SPECIAL1_NUMBER or EMP_SPECIAL2_NUMBER, and you'll need to enter each employee's rate in the employee's record. If, however, the formula you use calls for the same rate for each employee, you should substitute that rate in the formula for EMP_SPECIAL1_NUMBER or EMP_SPECIAL2_NUMBER.

To calculate union dues for hourly employees as a percentage of adjusted gross pay, use the following formula for both salaried and hourly employees:

```
ANSWER = -ADJUSTED_GROSS*EMP_SPECIAL1_NUMBER/100
```

If you need to calculate union dues based on a number of hours worked, use the following formula for hourly employees, where Regular, Overtime, and Special are the pay levels you set up in your company:

```
ANSWER = - (REGULAR+OVERTIME+SPECIAL)*EMP_SPECIAL1_NUMBER
```

If you pay your employees a salary instead of an hourly wage, use this formula, where pay periods are biweekly and include 80 hours. If you pay some employees weekly, some biweekly, and some semi-monthly, you'll need separate tables. In the "weekly" table, change 80 to 40; in the semi-monthly table, change 80 to 88:

```
ANSWER = -80*EMP_SPECIAL1_NUMBER/100
```

If all salaried employees pay the same percentage, you can substitute that percentage for EMP_SPECIAL1_NUMBER/100 in the formula.

Suppose that you must deduct an amount equal to two hours of pay per month for an hourly employee. In the following formula, you enter the annualized amount you need to deduct in the Special 1 field in the Withholding section on the General tab in the Maintain Employees/Sales Reps window (refer to Figure 20-8). Peachtree will prorate the annualized amount so that the correct amount is deducted from an employee's paycheck based on the frequency you pay. For example, if an employee earns $10/hour, union dues would be $20 for the month or $240 for the year — and that's the number you'll enter in the Special 1 field. If you pay your employees weekly, you'd want to deduct $4.62 per paycheck. Using the PRORATE function tells Peachtree to divide the annualized amount ($240 in our example) by the number of pay periods in the year (52 in our example) to determine the amount to deduct per pay period.

```
ANSWER = -PRORATE(EMP_SPECIAL1_NUMBER)
```

If you must deduct a flat amount — say 5 cents per hour — based on the number of hours worked, use the following formula:

```
ANSWER = -(REGULAR+OVERTIME+SPECIAL) * .05
```

where Regular, Overtime, and Special are the pay levels you set up in your company.

If you must deduct a flat amount per month, regardless of the number of hours the employee works, you don't need to set up a payroll tax table. Instead, calculate the total amount due for the year and divide that number by the number of pay periods in the year. When you set up the deduction, you'll supply that number.

Creating the payroll deduction for union dues

You create the payroll deduction for union dues on the EmployEE Fields tab of the Employee Defaults dialog box, using the same steps that you used to create the deduction for health insurance. Remember that the name you type will appear on paycheck stubs. Supply the liability account for union dues and, if you created a payroll tax table to calculate union dues, place a check in the Calc column. The Tax Name column will become available and you'll be able to select the payroll tax table that you created. Last, be sure to click the Adjust button and select the elements of pay that Peachtree should include in ADJUSTED GROSS when calculating union dues. At a minimum, check the Use box next to Gross.

If you didn't create a payroll tax table to calculate the union dues deduction, supply the liability account for union dues, but don't place a check in the Calc column. If most employees pay the same amount for union dues, type that amount in the Amount column, remembering to supply the amount *per pay period*. Peachtree will assign the amount you type in the Maintain Employee Defaults dialog box to *all* employees. You handle employees who don't pay the standard amount in the Maintain Employees/Sales Rep window by selecting the employee and clicking the EmployEE Fields tab. Then, remove the check from the STD column and type the amount per pay period that you want to deduct for the selected employee in the Amount column.

Showing employer contributions on paycheck stubs

Suppose that you want to display the employer's contribution on the employee's paycheck stub. No problem. In fact, although we use union dues as the example, you can display *any* employer contribution to *any* program on the employee's paycheck stub.

By default, the paycheck stub shows only the information that appears on the EmployEE tab of the Employee Defaults dialog box. But employer's contributions appear on the EmployER tab of the Employee Defaults dialog box. To make an employer contribution appear on the paycheck stub, you create a field on the EmployEE tab for the field, and, to avoid affecting the employee's paycheck, make the field a memo field.

Remember that you use the memo field *in addition to* (not "instead of") the EmployER field.

By the way, you use a memo field to track tips on employee paychecks.

Employer contributions to benefit plans are handled as liabilities on the balance sheet. As such, to calculate correctly, the formula you use usually generates a negative value. If you don't mind showing the contribution as a negative value on the employee's paycheck stub, you can use the same formula for the memo field as you use for the employer's contribution. However, you may prefer to show the contribution as a positive number on the check stub — so that the employee doesn't mistakenly think you deducted the money from his paycheck. In this case, create another formula that mirrors, exactly, the employer contribution formula; however, make sure that you

- ✔ Remove the negative sign from the portion of the formula that calculates the deduction
- ✔ Set up the formula type as an Exception rather than a Deduction

Don't forget to click the Adjust button for the new memo field and make sure that you include the same fields when calculating the memo field that you included when calculating the actual employer contribution.

Adding a 401(k) plan to an existing company

Okay, you've been using payroll for a while now, and your company decides to implement a 401(k) plan. In this "real-life" situation, we're not going to walk you through setting up a 401(k) plan, because you have the Payroll wizard to help you set up.

However, the Payroll wizard assumes that you want to assign contribution percentages individually to each employee in the Maintain Employees/Sales Reps window. If your employees' contribution rates vary greatly, then you really don't have much choice. Choose Maintain⇨Employees/Sales Reps. On the General tab, scroll down in the Withholding Information section until you see 401k% and supply the employee's contribution percentage. If an employee doesn't participate in the plan, leave his rate at 0%.

However, suppose that most of your employees contribute the same percentage, and only a few contribute a different percentage. You can save yourself some work by changing the 401K EE tax table that Peachtree creates to calculate the 401K contribution using the percentage that most employees contribute. That way, you'd only need to set up specific percentages for those employees who contribute the "different" rate — let Peachtree use a default rate that matches the rate contributed by most employees:

1. **Choose File⇨Payroll Tax Tables⇨Edit Company.**

2. **Highlight the 401K EE tax table and add three lines. Place these lines either at the very top of the tax table or immediately below the first line of the tax table that specifies the limit ($10,000.00 in the example).**

   To add lines below the first line, place the insertion point at the end of the first line and press Ctrl+J to start a new blank line. Make sure you include a semicolon at the end of each line you add.

3. **In the first line you add, type in the fixed percentage used by most employees — in our example, we made the percentage 2%.**

   ```
   E=2%;
   F=EMP 401K NUMBER%:
   G=If (F=(0),E,F);
   ```

4. **After you add these three lines, edit the line that contains the information for the variable A and replace EMP_401K_NUMBER% with G.**

   The line should look like this:

   ```
   A=G*ADJUSTED_GROSS;
   ```

Using this method, you edit *only* the records of employees who don't use the standard rate and employees who don't participate in the 401(k) plan. For the employees who *don't* use the standard rate (2% in our example), choose Maintain⇨Employees/Sales Reps. On the General tab, supply the correct rate in the 401k% field in the Withholding Information section. For the employees who don't participate in the 401(k) plan, open the same window and click the EmployEE Fields tab; then remove the check from the STD column next to the K401 payroll field.

The modifications to the 401K EE payroll tax table that we suggest change the way Peachtree calculates the 401(k) contribution. Using our modifications, Peachtree first checks the rate in the 401k% field in the Withholding Information section on the General tab of Maintain Employees/Sales Reps. If an employee's rate is 0, Peachtree uses the default rate specified in the formula stored in the 401K EE payroll tax table — in our example, 2% — to calculate the employee's 401(k) contribution. If, however, Peachtree finds a percentage in the 401k% field in Maintain Employees/Sales Reps, Peachtree uses that percentage to calculate the 401(k) contribution.

Multiple state withholdings

If your business is located on the border of a state, you might employ people who live in both the state in which your company is located and in the neighboring state. In this case, your payroll is affected at two levels:

✔ Typically, you need to pay state unemployment insurance (SUI) for only the state in which your business is located.

✔ You must deduct correct state income taxes for employees based on where *they* reside, *not* based on the state in which your business is located.

Look first at SUI. When you set up Payroll, Peachtree automatically created a payroll field for state unemployment insurance for the state in which your business is located. Peachtree makes the calculation for each state based on the employee's state of residence. So, you need to edit your payroll setup to tell Peachtree to include all employees, regardless of their residence, when calculating state unemployment for your company's state. Follow these steps:

1. **Choose File⇨Payroll Tax Tables⇨Edit Company to display the Maintain Company Payroll Tax Tables window.**

2. **Highlight the state unemployment tax table; typically, its name is comprised of your two-letter state abbreviation and the characters SUI.**

   The state unemployment insurance tax table for Florida would be FLSUI.

3. **In the State box, delete the characters that represent the two-letter abbreviation for your state.**

4. **Click the Save button to save the tax table.**

Next, you need to make sure that Peachtree uses the correct state unemployment insurance tax table. Follow these steps:

1. **Choose Maintain⇨Default Information⇨Employees.**

2. **Click the EmployER Fields tab.**

3. **Highlight your state unemployment insurance tax table.**

4. **In the Tax Name box, replace **SUI ER with your state's payroll tax table — in our example, you'd replace **SUI ER with FLSUI.**

5. **Click OK.**

Last, you need to make sure that all employees' records use the correct state.

1. **Choose Maintain⇨Employees/Sales Reps to display the Maintain Employees/Sales Reps window and select an employee.**

2. **On the General tab, check the Withholding Information table and make sure that the state code matches the state in which the employee resides.**

Local taxes

During initial payroll setup, you have the opportunity to set up local taxes as well as state taxes. But suppose your employees live in a variety of localities instead of just the locality in which your business is located. You need to set up additional tax tables for other localities and assign them to the appropriate employees.

The process will remind you of setting up payroll for multiple state withholdings. First, make sure you have an "other current liability" account set up in your Chart of Accounts. Then, confirm that you have a Local tax payroll field set up and assign it, if necessary, to the correct box on the W-2.

1. **Choose Maintain⇨Default Information⇨Employees to display the Employee Defaults dialog box.**

2. **Click the EmployEE Fields tab.**

3. **If you don't find a "Local" field, on a blank line, type Local and assign it to the appropriate "Other Current Liability" account.**

4. **Click OK to save the field.**

5. **Reopen the Employee Defaults dialog box.**

6. **On the General tab, click the W-2s button. In the Assign Payroll Fields for W-2s dialog box that appears, assign Box 21 to the Local payroll field you created.**

Next, set up additional local tax tables by following these steps:

1. **Choose File⇨Payroll Tax Tables⇨Edit Company.**

   Peachtree displays the Maintain Company Payroll Tax Tables window.

2. **Enter a tax ID — in Florida, it might be something like FLLIT (FL for Florida, and LIT for Local Income Tax).**

3. **In the Tax Name box, enter the Tax ID and follow it with the last two digits of the current year — something like FLLIT 00 for 2000.**

4. **Set the Government type to Local. In the Local box, type a name for the locality (you have up to 15 characters).**

5. **In the State box (above the Local box), type the two-letter abbreviation for the state.**

6. **In the Formula box, type the formula for your state. Remember to place a semicolon (;) at the end of every line except the last line and press Ctrl+J to start a new line.**

The last line should begin with ANSWER = . A local tax formula might look something like this, and you'd change the percentage amount in the first line to match the percentage for your local tax:

```
PERCENT = .7:
ANSWER = - PRORATE ((ANNUAL (ADJUSTED_GROSS)) * PERCENT%)
```

7. Click the Save button to save the tax table.

Last, make sure that you assign each employee to the correct local tax. Follow these steps:

1. Choose Maintain⇨Employees/Sales Reps and select an employee.

2. On the General tab, check the Withholding Information table and make sure:

- The State/Locality box for the State field contains the two-letter abbreviation for the state in which the employee resides.

- The State/Locality box for the Local field contains the name of the locality you supplied in Step 4 above when you created the payroll tax table.

3. Click the EmployEE Fields tab and find the Local payroll field.

4. Remove the check from the STD column and place a check in the Calc column.

5. Select the payroll tax table you created in the previous steps.

6. Click the Adjust button for the Local field and place checks in the Use boxes for all fields you want Peachtree to include when calculating Adjusted Gross Income. At a minimum, place a check in the Use box next to Gross and ask your accountant about the others if you're unsure.

7. Click Save.

Chapter 21

Keeping Your House Safe

. . . .

In This Chapter
- ▶ Backing up and restoring data
- ▶ Password-protecting your data
- ▶ Using the audit trail

. . . .

A business has a lot at stake with Peachtree data; after all, it holds the financial picture of the business. In this chapter, we show you how to protect that data. You discover how to protect your data from computer failure as well as from unauthorized entry. We even show you how to play detective and "snoop" on what others are doing to your financial data. We won't provide the detective hat, overcoat, and spyglass. Those you'll need to provide for yourself.

Backing Up Your Data

You know the dumb (but popular) little saying, "Doodoo Happens." (That's not exactly how it goes, but you get the idea.) Well, it's true. Things happen. Now we don't mean to sound pessimistic here, but computers do fail, data gets deleted or corrupted, and disasters like fire or theft occur.

Well, you can always get another computer and reload Peachtree, but for millions of dollars, you cannot buy all that work you've put into your Peachtree company. That's why backing up your company data files on a regular basis is important. You can then restore your data, if necessary.

By backing up company data within Peachtree Accounting, your company data files and customized forms are backed up using the Peachtree Accounting format. You can save your Peachtree Accounting backup to a diskette, a hard drive, or other mediums such as Zip drives, tapes, or recordable CDs.

If you choose to back up your company data to a tape device or recordable CDs, you must exit Peachtree Accounting and use the tape backup or CD program to copy company files. To make backups to those mediums, refer to the CD or tape instruction manual.

You should establish a regular policy for backing up your data. Backups are the only way to guarantee the safety of the accounting records you create in Peachtree Accounting. Without backups, you run the risk of losing weeks, months, or even years of work. Do you really want to take that kind of risk?

The general rule is that if you used Peachtree that day, back it up that day. Backing up data doesn't take long, and in case of a catastrophe, you'll be glad you did. Disks are inexpensive, even Zip disks, especially when compared to the costs of reconstructing and reentering data.

In Table 21-1, we show you an ideal plan for backing up. That's the one we really wish you would do. However, we're also realistic. We also show you an absolute minimum strategy for backing up in Table 21-2. If you don't follow Plan A (the ideal), at the very least, follow Plan B (the minimum). Believe us — you won't regret it. Backing up is the cheapest form of insurance you can have.

When we refer to backup disks, remember these can be floppy diskettes, Zip disks, tapes, or recordable CDs.

Table 21-1	Plan A: An Ideal Backup Strategy
Number of Disks or Tapes	**Backup Plan**
Ten daily disks	Back up onto a different disk(s) each day (Monday through Friday) for two weeks then begin again with the same set of disks.
Twelve monthly disks	At the end of each month, back up to one of these disks. Keep the monthly disks off site.

Table 21-2	Plan B: The Minimum Backup Strategy
Number of Disks or Tapes	**Backup Plan**
Five daily disks	Use one disk for each day of the week and then start reusing them again the following Monday.
Two monthly disks	At the end of each month, back up to one of these disks. Again, alternate them. For example, use one disk in January, and then use the second disk in February. Reuse the January disk in March. Keep the monthly disks off site.

Label each disk with the day of the week.

To back up your Peachtree data and customized forms, use the following procedure:

1. **Choose File➪Back Up or press Ctrl+B to display the Back Up Company dialog box.**

   No other users can be accessing Peachtree during the backup process.

   Click the Reminder check box if you want Peachtree to prompt you to back up in a specified number of days. When the specified number of days have elapsed since your last Peachtree Accounting backup, Peachtree displays a reminder message when closing the company or exiting the program.

   In a moment, Peachtree suggests a name for the backup file, but first, Peachtree wants to know whether it should include the company name as part of the backup filename. We recommend that you *do* include it if you have multiple companies. That way, you won't be able to confuse the backups of each company. If you do want to include the company name as part of the backup, click the check box next to the option.

2. **Click the Back Up Now button to display the Save Backup As dialog box.**

3. **In the File name text box, type a filename for the backup set or leave the one Peachtree suggests.**

   Peachtree backup files use the *.ptb file extension. If you elect not to include the company name as part of the backup filename, Peachtree includes the letters BU as part of the filename. (In case you're wondering, BU stands for *backup*.)

4. **From the Save in list box, choose a location for the backup set.**

   We recommend backing up to a floppy disk (the A: drive), a zip disk, or a different computer.

   For data protection, don't back up the Peachtree data to the same hard drive where the current data resides. If the hard drive crashes, you'll have two sets of unrecoverable data and that won't do you one bit of good.

5. **Click the Save button.**

   Peachtree displays the estimated size in megabytes (MB) of your backup, or if you're backing up to a floppy disk, Peachtree displays the estimated number of diskettes.

6. **Click OK.**

   If you're backing up to diskettes, Peachtree prompts you to insert the first and subsequent diskettes, as needed.

7. **Click OK.**

   The system displays the backup progress.

Depending on the quantity of data and the speed of your computer, the backup process may take several minutes to complete. Don't interrupt the process. Interrupting the backup process may corrupt the data.

If you're backing up to floppy disks, you'll probably need to erase those disks before you use them again. Refer to your Windows documentation for procedures on erasing floppy disks.

If you are backing up to a Zip disk, at some point the disk becomes too full to hold another backup, so you'll want to erase the oldest backup file. Refer to your Windows documentation for directions on deleting files.

Restoring Information

We sincerely hope you never ever have to restore your data. If you do, it probably means something really bad happened and we just don't wish those kinds of incidents to materialize.

But if it does . . .

You'll be so glad you read this chapter and found out how to back up and restore your data.

If you backed up company data using an alternate utility (for example, a tape program), you must use that program to restore your company data.

No other users can be accessing Peachtree during the restore process. Use the following steps to restore your data:

Data entered after the backup date is lost.

1. **Open the company you want to restore.**

2. **Choose File⇨Restore to display the Open Backup File dialog box.**

   Peachtree displays the Open Backup File window, as shown in Figure 21-1.

Figure 21-1: Click a backup filename.

3. **Click in the Look in drop-down box to choose the location of the Peachtree backup file.**

4. **Click the name of the backup file you want to restore.**

   Peachtree backup files use the *.ptb file extension.

5. **Click the Open button to begin the restore process.**

6. **Click OK to continue past the warning message to display the Restore Options dialog box.**

   Version 8 can restore both data and customized forms or restore these items individually.

   What data gets restored? Peachtree works differently from some of the accounting programs you may have used. When you restore data, you'll be restoring ALL the information previously backed up; all the receivable, payroll, payable, inventory, and job cost information together. Everything. The process replaces all the current data files with those that have been previously backed up. You cannot restore individual files because each file relates to another. You can however, restore your customized forms, such as invoices or checks, separately from your data.

7. **Click the options to be restored and then click Restore.**

Peachtree displays the progress of the restoring data files. If you restore data from diskettes, Peachtree prompts you to insert any subsequent diskettes as needed.

Depending on the quantity of data and the speed of your computer, the restore process may take several minutes to complete. Don't interrupt the process. Interrupting the restore process may corrupt the data.

Securing Your Data from Prying Eyes

Because accounting data is highly sensitive and confidential, you may want to prevent unauthorized persons from accessing your data. Peachtree includes a security system that allows you to set accessibility parameters for each user you identify. Peachtree security uses User IDs and passwords.

Setting up users

Peachtree Accounting can allow tailored access for different individuals. With the security feature activated, Peachtree requires each user to enter his or her ID and password before opening and working with company data. With the correct user ID and password, users can access the areas of the program to which they have rights.

If you choose to set up users, you must set up at least one user with access to the Maintain Users window. Typically, this user is considered a system administrator who has the access rights to all Peachtree features, including setting up and maintaining company users and their passwords.

Setting up users requires single user access. While setting up users, no other users can be using Peachtree.

To set up users, follow these steps:

1. **Choose Maintain⇨Users.**

   With the first user ID created, Peachtree displays an information box.

2. **Click OK to close the information message.**

   Set up the system administrator first.

3. **In the Maintain Users dialog box, enter a unique ID for the first user.**

   Typically, you use the first name or initials, or in the case of the administrator, try something like *admin* for the user ID.

4. **Enter a password for the user.**

   This is the user's secret code to access Peachtree. The password can be 13 alphanumeric characters. Do not use the slash (/) key as part of the password.

   Both passwords and User IDs are case sensitive and must be unique. Two users cannot have the same password.

5. **Click Save.**

   With the first user ID created, a message box displays.

6. **Click OK to close the message box.**

   Don't lose the password! If you do lose your user ID or password and no one else can open the Peachtree Accounting company, there is no "back door" way for you to access the passwords. You'll need to back up your data and send it into Peachtree Technical Support for them to locate the information. This process can take several weeks!

7. **To enter additional users, click the New button.**

8. **Enter the next user ID and its corresponding password.**

   From here, you can then customize the rights for each user (see the next section) or click the Close button to close the Maintain User dialog box.

Customizing user rights

When setting up users, you can select an access level for each program area for an individual user. For example, if you have a clerk who mainly makes accounts receivable entries, you may want to restrict that clerk from accessing payroll or general ledger information. Perhaps you have a person who receives inventory, but you want to restrict him or her from editing the information after it has been entered, or from printing inventory valuation reports.

By customizing the user rights, you give each user specific access. The rights vary depending on the feature. You can allow a user no access at all to the feature, or you can allow only the ability to view the data. From there, you can also allow the user to view and add to the data. Or, you can allow the user to add to or edit the data; finally, you can provide full rights, which allows the user to view, add, edit, or erase data.

The security we describe here is for Peachtree Complete Accounting. If you're using Peachtree Accounting, your choices are limited to setting security selections for an entire module (A/R, A/P, P/R, and so on).

With the exclusion of the system administrator (the first user you set up), by default, Peachtree provides each user full access to all areas of Peachtree except access to Maintain Users.

We recommend that you have only one administrative user with access to the Maintain Users window. This setup will prevent multiple users from accessing other users' passwords, changing other users' records, or inadvertently erasing users.

To quickly restrict access to a primary program area, such as Payroll, select a control level in the Summary tab of the Maintain Users dialog box. For example, in Figure 21-2, we restrict all rights to Payroll by clicking the Summary tab and selecting No Access from the Control drop-down list.

Click in the Control box to display a drop-down list.

Figure 21-2:
The user named Bob will not be able to access any feature of Payroll.

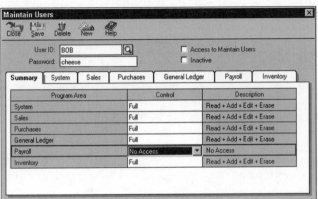

Program Area	Control	Description
System	Full	Read + Add + Edit + Erase
Sales	Full	Read + Add + Edit + Erase
Purchases	Full	Read + Add + Edit + Erase
General Ledger	Full	Read + Add + Edit + Erase
Payroll	No Access	No Access
Inventory	Full	Read + Add + Edit + Erase

To be more specific in user accessibility, you can click a specific area tab and set restrictions:

1. **Click the tab for which you want to set restrictions.**

   Peachtree displays a list of the program areas.

2. **To expand the list of program areas in the grid, double-click the triangle to the left of the program area.**

   The access choices vary depending on the feature. For example, if you click the Sales tab and open the Control list for Receipts, you'll find that you can choose Full, No Access, Read, Add, or Edit. But if you open the Control list for Master Lists under the Reports program area, you can choose only Full or No Access. In Figure 21-3, the user named Alex can enter or view Inventory transactions, but cannot edit or erase them.

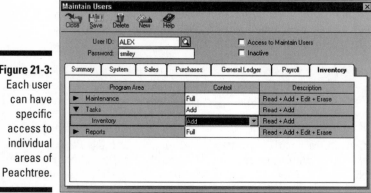

Figure 21-3:
Each user can have specific access to individual areas of Peachtree.

3. **Click Save.**

   Any changes you make take effect the next time you open the company.

Removing users

When users leave or change positions, you can stop them from accessing Peachtree data. You have the option of deleting users or inactivating them. Inactivating users leaves them in the user ID profiles, but disables their access. Deleting users erases their user IDs and passwords.

To remove a user, choose Maintain⇨Users to display the Maintain Users window. Enter or look up the user record you want to remove and then check the Inactive check box or click OK to delete the user.

If multiple users still exist and you attempt to delete the only administrative user with access to Maintain Users, Peachtree displays an error message. You cannot remove the administrator user until you have removed all other user records.

Any changes you make take effect the next time you open the company.

Logging on as a user

Once user ID's are assigned, when you or, if you're on a network, anyone on your Peachtree network tries to open your Peachtree company files, Peachtree prompts you for a user ID and password.

Enter your user ID in the User ID box and then enter your password in the Password box. Press Enter.

Remember that user IDs and passwords are case sensitive.

The user ID system works like this: Say you give user Bob no access to payroll, but user Alex does have payroll access. No matter whose computer Bob uses — his own computer or Alex's computer — he will not have access to payroll when he logs on as Bob.

Using the Audit Trail Report to Track Actions

Peachtree includes an audit trail security feature that tracks when a person enters new data, maintains (edits) existing data, and removes data. The audit trail provides accountability of users, discourages users against fraudulent activity or mistakes, and tracks transaction history. The Audit Trail report traces all activity and adjustments; from this report, you may find that transactions were completed without your knowledge.

The Audit Trail feature is available only in versions of Peachtree Complete Accounting. It is not available in Peachtree First Accounting or Peachtree Accounting.

Turning on the audit trail

Before you can begin using the Audit Trail report, you need to tell Peachtree Accounting to begin tracing your steps:

Choose Maintain⇨Company Information to open the Maintain Company Information dialog box. Then click the Use Audit Trail check box and click OK.

If you have not set up users with password protection, a message displays suggesting that you do so to personalize audit trail activity. We recommend that you set up users as described earlier in this chapter. Peachtree can associate the user currently working in the Peachtree Accounting company with the data being entered or maintained, consequently providing a more comprehensive audit trail.

If you activated the Audit Trail feature and implemented password security, you should limit access to the Maintain Company Information window to one or two users. This action can prevent other users from inadvertently removing Audit Trail functionality to enter or maintain company data in a fraudulent manner.

Viewing the Audit Trail report

The Audit Trail report displays the date and time a Peachtree action took place as well as who did it and what he or she did.

To view the Audit Trail Report, choose Reports⇨Company to display the Select a Report dialog box and then double-click the Audit Trail Report to display the report on-screen.

Like other Peachtree reports, you can customize the Audit Trail report. See Chapter 15 for instructions on customizing reports.

By default, this report displays only the transactions that took place on the current date, but you can click the Options button to select a different time frame. You can even specify the user ID you want to review.

Part IV
The Part of Tens

The 5th Wave   By Rich Tennant

"I'm not sure — I like the mutual funds with rotating dollar signs although the dancing stocks and bonds look good too."

In this part . . .

Move over David Letterman. Your competition is here. *Not!* Our top ten lists aren't as funny as yours, but they clearly serve a practical purpose.

This part provides remedies to common Peachtree error messages; offers locations of helpful Web stuff and lists ways to keep your typically very solemn accountant happy. Don't you just love it when your accountant is happy?

Chapter 22

Ten or So Common Peachtree Messages (and What You Can Do about Them)

In This Chapter

▶ Surviving and mastering common errors

Sometimes computer programs just don't act the way you'd like them to act. At any moment in time, error messages may pop up, throwing most people into a near state of panic.

This may sound a little strange, but frequently when error messages occur, simply exiting Peachtree and restarting your computer fixes the problem. Always try shutting down your computer before any other step. If the problem remains after restarting your computer, then look at this chapter or contact technical support for a better resolution.

Although most error messages are easy to fix, if an error occurs due to data problems, you may need to run a program called Integrity Check. Contact Peachtree or your Peachtree consultant *before* you attempt to run Integrity Check. You may notice we didn't even include the instructions for running Integrity Check anywhere in this book. We did that on purpose!

Here's a valuable piece of advice: Don't run Integrity Check unless you *really* know what you're doing and ALWAYS make a backup before you run the program. We don't mean to scare you, but trust us on this one . . . we learned it the hard way.

Period Changed to ## Due to Unposted Entries There

Our clients call us about this error message more than any other. This error occurs when you're trying to change your accounting period and means that Peachtree didn't get one or more transactions posted properly. Usually, but not always, the error occurs if you interrupt Peachtree's posting process. You can repair the problem by changing to a batch posting method, unposting all journals, then reversing those steps by posting all journals and changing back to a real-time posting method.

To correct the error, follow these steps (if you already use the batch posting method, skip Steps 1–4 and 9–12):

1. **Choose Maintain⇨Company Information to display the Maintain Company Information dialog box.**

2. **Click the arrow next to Posting Method to display the Posting Method dialog box.**

3. **Change the Posting Method to batch posting and then click OK.**

4. **Click OK again to close the Maintain Company Information dialog box.**

5. **Choose Tasks⇨System⇨Unpost to display the Unpost dialog box.**

6. **Click OK.**

   Peachtree begins the unposting process. Be patient. Depending on the volume of transactions and the speed of your computer, the unposting and posting process could take a few minutes.

   When Peachtree completes the process:

7. **Choose Tasks⇨System⇨Post to display the Post dialog box.**

8. **Click OK.**

9. **Choose Maintain⇨Company Information to display the Maintain Company Information dialog box.**

10. **Click the arrow next to Posting Method to display the Posting Method dialog box.**

11. **Change the Posting Method to real-time posting and then click OK.**

12. **Click OK again to close the Maintain Company Information dialog box.**

    Now you'll be able to change your accounting period.

Not a Valid Date in This Period

This error occurs when you attempt to enter a transaction with a date in a prior period. Peachtree allows you to date a transaction within or ahead of the current period, but gives you this error message if you attempt to create and post a transaction behind the current period. You have three choices at this point:

- ✔ Change the accounting period to the period in which you need the transaction posted.

- ✔ Go ahead and post the transaction with a date in the current month, then edit the transaction in question and put a prior period date on it. Peachtree gives you a warning message that you're modifying a transaction that's not in the current period. Click Yes, and Peachtree posts the transaction in the previous period. This method is our personal favorite and will work with all types of transactions except General Ledger or Payroll Transactions.

- ✔ Leave the transaction dated in the current period. (Not recommended.)

This Report Contains No Data

First, make sure that you have the correct date specified on the report you're attempting to print.

Second, this message may display when you select a single ID using the "Automatic Field Completion" feature. To prevent this from happening, use the lookup list and select the customer by double-clicking.

Third, this message displays if you select a "type" such as customer type or vendor type, and don't use an exact match of the types you entered.

The Record You Are Trying to Access Is Currently in Use

This error, which also includes the phrase "Please try again when it is available," occurs when you attempt to select, use, or modify a customer, vendor, item, employee, job, and so on when you or another user has the respective Maintain window open. In order to access the record in question, the user who has the maintenance window open needs to close it.

Your Security Settings Do Not Allow ERASE Access to This Area of Peachtree Accounting

The message occurs when you attempt to delete a transaction, but do not have user rights to perform such a task. Your Peachtree administrator can change user rights through Maintain Users.

No Forms to Print

Peachtree displays this message in a couple of different situations:

- ✔ **If you try to print forms such as invoices or checks and Peachtree determines no transactions meet the requirements you specified.** For example, you tell Peachtree to print invoices, but no invoices exist without an invoice number. (Remember that Peachtree chooses invoices or checks that need to be printed if they don't have a reference number.)

  Sometimes Peachtree displays the "No forms to print" message if, when you created these transactions, you dated them for a future date, say for example, tomorrow. Unless you change the Last Date for the form in the About To Print dialog box, Peachtree assumes you want to print only the forms dated today or earlier.

- ✔ **If you try to reprint a customer statement after updating the customer file.**

The Transaction Refers to a Non-Existing Invoice

You might receive this message when you try to erase or edit a customer receipt or a vendor payment. The message occurs when someone edits or erases an invoice (sales or purchase) that had a receipt or a payment associated with it. The link originally established between the amount received or paid and the invoice becomes broken, and Peachtree cannot locate the original transaction. Someone may have deleted the invoice, changed the invoice number, or changed the customer (or vendor) ID.

To correct the error, follow these steps:

1. **Write down information on the customer or vendor causing the error, including the ID and the invoice number referenced in the error message.**

   Be sure to make note of the invoice number *exactly* as Peachtree references it in the error message.

2. **Choose Tasks⇨Sales/Invoicing if the error refers to a customer, or choose Tasks⇨Purchase/Receive Inventory if the error refers to a vendor.**

3. **Recreate the missing customer or vendor invoice using the *exact* same invoice number referenced in the error message.**

4. **Post or save the invoice.**

   Peachtree now allows you to edit or erase the customer receipt or vendor payment.

After you erase the receipt or payment, you can erase the invoice you just entered. If necessary, you can now re-enter the receipt and apply it to the proper invoice.

This Program Has Performed an Illegal Operation

First of all, you haven't done anything illegal. Rest assured, you don't have to live in fear that the software police are going to knock at your door and haul you away to jail (or the hoosekow, as Grandma called it).

Frequently, programs just decide they won't play nice any more, so you see this error message. There are too many reasons to list that can cause a program to crash, but usually, you can just restart the program. If that doesn't work, reboot your computer and then start the program. If *that* doesn't work, try reinstalling the program, and if that *still* doesn't work, you need to contact the software manufacturer or a consultant.

GL Does Not Foot

This message occasionally appears when you attempt to print a General Ledger report. To correct the error, you need to access and run Peachtree's Integrity Check and run the Data Sync Test for COA/Journal.

Don't run Integrity Check unless you *really* know what you're doing. We suggest you contact Peachtree or your Peachtree consultant *before* you run Integrity Check and *always* make a backup before proceeding.

Users of Version 7 or earlier: If you still get the error message after running the integrity check, exit Peachtree. Locate and delete a file called SORTJOB.DAT. (Do not delete any other files!) The file is located in your Peachtree company data folder. When you restart Peachtree, the file will recreate itself.

Could Not Find The xxx Single (or Married) Calculation

This message occurs when you're trying to generate a paycheck and the payroll tax tables have not been updated. Update the tax tables as covered in Chapter 18.

File System Error 11 or 35

This message usually appears if you're on a network and the network has lost connection to the Peachtree data file location or lost mapping to a network drive. It can also occur if you move your Peachtree data files to a different drive or folder. If it occurs because of a network issue, contact your network administrator.

If you've recently moved the Peachtree data files, you need to modify Peachtree's .ini file (pronounced inny). You need to know the location of the Peachtree data files before you can modify the .ini file.

1. **Open the Windows Explorer program, locate the Windows folder, and locate the following file:**

   For any Peachtree Version 6 — PAW60.ini

   For any Peachtree Version 7 — PAW70.ini

   For Peachtree Complete Accounting Version 8 — PCW80.ini

   For Peachtree Accounting Version 8 — PAW80.ini

   For Peachtree First Accounting Version 8 — PFA80.ini

2. **After you locate the correct .ini file, double-click the filename to open it in the Windows Notepad program.**

3. **Look for the line that reads:** DATAPATH=

4. **Change this line to the correct Peachtree data directory.**

   For example, suppose that you originally stored the Peachtree data files on your hard drive and you moved them to the network drive F: into the ACCTG folder.

   The datapath line in the .ini file would originally read something like this: DATAPATH=C:\PEACHW.

   After you modify the line to the preceding scenario, it would read DATAPATH=F:\ACCTG.

5. **Choose File⇨Save.**

6. **Choose File⇨Exit.**

7. **Restart your computer.**

I/O Error in File xx

This error can appear when you use Peachtree on a network; generally, you can trace it to operating system or hardware problems. First, make sure you are using a stable operating system, such as Windows 98 (Second Edition), Windows 2000, or Windows XP, which help prevent applications from stepping on each other by managing the memory used by each program. Also avoid mixed brand network cards, faulty cables, and badly fragmented disks. All of these can lead to a high rate of database errors in Peachtree and you can virtually eliminate the errors by eliminating the culprit.

Chapter 23

More Than Ten Things You Can Get from the Web

In This Chapter

▶ Surfing and finding helpful, interesting, and fun Web sites

*I*f your business does not yet have Internet access, we suggest that you check it out and get online. You can find an entire world of information only a few mouse clicks away.

What are you waiting for?

Please keep in mind that this was a tough chapter to write. There are so many wonderful Web sites to choose from and only room enough to list a few.

Peachtree Software

www.peachtree.com

Well, of course we'd suggest this Web site. Peachtree has lots of information accessible from its Web site. From Peachtree's Web site, you can search through the PeachFact Knowledgebase for answers to many frequently asked questions or click Contact Us and send suggestions and enhancements for the future versions of Peachtree. (They really do listen to what the users want!)

How about subscribing to Peachtree's free e-mail newsletter, Netsource Newsletter? You'll find it full of tips and informative articles about Peachtree.

Discover Peachtree's Online Services — a relatively new collection of services designed to assist you with various business needs. Although the online services change periodically, here is a list of the services available at the time we wrote this book:

- ✔ **CreditFYI:** Make better business decisions with instant business credit reports, which include credit ratings and historical highlights.

- ✔ **LiveCapital.com:** Comparison shop for, apply for, and secure loans, lines of credit, equipment leases, and more from many of the nation's best-known financial institutions.

- ✔ **NationTax Online:** Prepare, file, and pay your state and local sales and use taxes through an automated Web-based filing process.

- ✔ **OneCore.com:** See an alternative to traditional business banking.

- ✔ **WebEx:** Meet and collaborate with others at any time, from anywhere. Share documents, software applications, even your entire desktop, live over the Web. (We used WebEx while writing this book. It's really cool!)

- ✔ **works.com:** Get volume purchasing power on 20,000+ business products.

- ✔ **World Wide Wallet Merchant Services:** Accept credit cards if you have a Web store.

In the appendix, we discuss additional services with which Peachtree 2002 integrates.

Hungry Minds, Inc.

www.dummies.com

or

www.hungryminds.com

Just in case you missed the commercial announcements we plugged in this book, we're going to give you one more. Visit Hungry Minds's Web sites to purchase additional copies of this book and check out all the other great *For Dummies* and Hungry Minds books available.

Obviously, we're not too proud to beg.

Peachtree Users Forum

www.peachtreeusers.com

An online user group for Peachtree. Use the free online support in the Peachtree discussion forums (message boards). Share tips, questions, answers, and comments about Peachtree accounting software. Also, learn how to add value to Peachtree with Peachtree add-on products. Some are free!

Peachtree Newsgroup

`alt.comp.software.financial.peachtree`

If you have access to newsgroups, here's a newsgroup devoted exclusively to Peachtree users. Ask questions and have them answered by other Peachtree users.

The (Infernal) Internal Revenue Service

`www.irs.gov`

Visit the IRS Web site for all the forms and publications you may need, such as the Circular E, Schedule C, or Form 1040. You can also find taxpayer help and information on electronic services such as e-filing.

Just for fun, check out the Tax Stats, which consists of data compiled from all kinds of returns and sorted in a variety of ways. The IRS groups statistics together by various topics and downloads them in a Lotus 1-2-3 or Microsoft Excel format.

Inside Peachtree

`www.insidepeachtree.com`

Okay, we admit it. We're a little biased about this one because Elaine writes most of the articles for Inside Peachtree for Windows, a monthly online newsletter designed to help you use Peachtree more efficiently. The publication tries to address the ways people can use Peachtree to handle real business situations. An annual subscription fee provides 12 issues and other benefits such as:

- A "user-to-user forum" where users can pose questions and other users may supply answers or try to help.
- E-mail notification when a new issue is posted. You can then view and print the current issue.
- The ability to view and print back issues.

It's money well spent.

Small Business Administration

```
www.sba.gov
```

America's 23 million small businesses employ more than 50 percent of the private workforce, generate more than half of the nation's gross domestic product, and provide the principal source of new jobs in the U.S. economy.

The U.S. Small Business Administration provides financial, technical, and management assistance to help Americans start, run, and grow their businesses. With a portfolio of business loans, loan guarantees, and disaster loans, the SBA is the nation's largest single financial backer of small businesses. Last year, the SBA offered management and technical assistance to more than one million small business owners and played a major role in the government's disaster relief efforts by making low-interest recovery loans to both homeowners and businesses.

Checks and Forms

```
www.deluxeforms.com
```

For more than 80 years, Deluxe Forms has supplied businesses with business checks and forms that work seamlessly with Peachtree software. When ordering, reference this book and discount code R03578 to receive an additional 20 percent off your first order.

*Note: You can find additional information on forms for Peachtree Software from Peachtree's Web site (*www.peachtree.com*). While you can't actually purchase the forms from the Web site, there is a phone number you can call to place your order.*

Microsoft Corporation

```
www.microsoft.com
```

You'll find Microsoft.com an informative site that provides product updates, hardware drivers, corporate news, training information, and most importantly, access to the Microsoft Knowledgebase, where you can find solutions to problems you may have with Windows and other Microsoft products.

You can also locate information on Microsoft Office, Small Business Edition, which includes add-ons for Peachtree. See a description at www.microsoft.com/office/smallbiz/SmallBizTour.htm?.

You'll also find information about Peachtree add-ons in the appendix.

United States Postal Service

`www.usps.gov`

From this government Web page, you can find a Zip code, calculate postage rates, order stamps, and have other shipping supplies delivered to your door. In addition, you can track and confirm delivery of mail and find out about USPS products and services.

Buy Postage Online

`www.stamps.com`

A relatively new concept is the ability to download and print postage from your laser or ink-jet printer. With your PC, printer, and an Internet connection, you have unlimited access to postage from your desktop 24 hours a day.

Download Shareware

`www.download.com`

Sponsored by CNET news, this site has all the best downloadable shareware and freeware for PCs, Macs, Linux, and PDAs. Other computer users develop shareware files and offer them to you to try them out for free. If you decide you like a product, you pay a minimal fee to register it.

You can also find tips, product reviews, newsletters, and even an auction site where you can buy or sell just about anything!

Just for the Fun of It

`www.funnymail.com`

Has the computer got you down? Are you feeling major stress and need a break? Check out this site for jokes, puzzles, cartoons, games, sounds, and just plain fun. Each joke is rated on a scale similar to the movie ratings. Lighten up a little!

When You're Bored . . .

www.quizland.com/cotd.htm

Now that you've mastered working with Peachtree Accounting, you'll probably find yourself with spare time on your hands. If you like crossword puzzles, visit this Web site and play the crossword puzzle of the day.

Chapter 24

Ten Do's (and Don'ts) to Make Your Accountant Love You

Most small businesses have an outside CPA firm to handle issues such as filing corporate taxes or auditing the business. Elaine's accountant is her brother, so he *has* to love her. But you may not be lucky enough to have a relative who will forgive everything, so here are some ways to help you and your accountant get along much better!

Because we're not accountants, we contacted a variety of CPA firms in our area with clients using Peachtree. The suggestions you see in this chapter came straight from the horses — excuse us, accountants — mouths.

Do Communicate with Your Accountant

Keep the lines of communication between you and your accountant open. We placed this one first for a reason. Talk to your accountant before you convert to Peachtree. Taking advantage of his or her experience with Peachtree can often save you hours of work.

Just because you're now using Peachtree doesn't mean you won't need your accountant. You may not need his or her services as frequently or in as much detail as before you began using Peachtree, but you still need your accountant's advice and you'll probably want him or her to file your corporate taxes and give you end-of-year adjustments.

As the old saying goes . . . don't burn your bridges. . . .

Do Use the Same Version of Peachtree

If your accountant also uses Peachtree (and many accountants do), make sure that both of you are using the same version of Peachtree. Periodically, the accountant will come and back up your Peachtree data to a disk, then take it to the office and restore it. This allows your accountant to print his or her own reports and to more closely analyze your day-to-day transactions.

If, for example, you are on Version 8 and your accountant uses Version 7, the accountant wouldn't be able to restore the data to his or her computer. Not being able to restore the data means the accountant has to recreate your business transactions from scratch and you *know* what that means — a MUCH larger bill to you!

Another example is if you use Peachtree Complete Accounting and the accountant uses Peachtree Accounting. Make sure you have the same software version as your accountant.

Do Use the Same Chart of Accounts

This one is especially important if your accountant doesn't use Peachtree or if he or she doesn't back up data from your PC and restore it on the office PC.

Make sure that you have the same account numbering system as your accountant. Your referring to an account as one number and the accountant referring to it as a different number could cause errors and a great deal of confusion.

For example, suppose that you use the account number 61500 as Automobile Repairs and Maintenance, but to your accountant, account number 61500 is Meals and Entertainment. In the month of July, you had to have a new transmission installed in your company car and the bill was $3,000, so you record the $3,000 to account 61500. Your accountant posts this amount to his or her account 61500 and all of a sudden you have a $3,000 meals and entertainment expense! (Which, by the way, is not entirely deductible on your tax return, so you lose some of the expense deduction to which you really were entitled.)

Keep the lines of communication open and make sure you and the accountant are comparing apples to apples when referring to an account number.

Don't Edit After Closing a Period

Oh, boy! This one is *really* a sore spot with the bean counters. Because Peachtree doesn't officially have closing of accounting periods, going back and editing a prior period transaction is very easy. That's not necessarily a bad thing as long as your accountant hasn't come in and picked up your data. After your information has been transferred to the accountant, if you change (or delete) a prior period transaction, the accountant's information is out of date.

"Okay," you say, "this doesn't affect me because my accountant doesn't come in until the end of the year to pick up my data." Well, here's another reason. Suppose you've printed your monthly reports and filed them away. If you edit a transaction, your filed reports are all wrong.

We'd like to give you a real example. A client printed payroll reports on a monthly basis and filed them in a binder. At the end of the quarter, when she ran her 941 report, she noticed the figures didn't match her previously printed reports. It took a lot of investigation to discover that she had changed a transaction *after* she printed her reports, therefore making the report out of sync with the current Peachtree information.

Do Delete Sparingly

Although Peachtree is very flexible about allowing you to delete unwanted transactions, deleting transactions makes accountants flinch. In most cases, *especially* if the transaction you want to get rid of occurred in a prior month, issue a credit or reversing transaction. Don't delete it. You have a much better audit trail and that keeps everyone happy.

Don't Adjust Customer or Vendor Balances through the General Ledger

The balance on the A/R Aged Receivable Report should match the accounts receivable figure on the balance sheet. Along the same line, the A/P Aged Payables Report balance should match the accounts payable figure on the balance sheet.

If the amounts on your Accounts Receivable (or Accounts Payable) aging reports are incorrect, adjust the figures from the A/R or A/P module. You may need to issue a credit, receipt, or payment to clear a transaction, but never adjust the balance through a General Ledger journal entry.

Don't Change the A/P Account When Entering a Purchase

If your business is cash basis, then you can just read on and skip this item. This suggestion only applies to you if your business is accrual-based.

Some users get confused when looking at the Purchases/Receive Inventory window and they see the box for the A/P account. This box is asking for your Accounts Payable account number, *not* the expense account number you're using for this transaction. Changing the A/P account not only makes the current transaction post to the wrong account, but also changes the default account number for future transactions.

We know we told you in Chapter 5 that while you can change the A/P account, typically, you don't, but because this situation happens quite often, we felt the need to repeat it.

Don't Change the A/R Account Number When Generating an Invoice

The same rule as the preceding item also applies to accounts receivable. Make sure the G/L account number referenced in the Sales/Invoicing A/R account box is the accounts receivable account, not the sales account.

Don't Make Any Adjustments to Balances through Retained Earnings

Many clients, when they need to make an adjusting entry and don't know where else to put it, have a tendency to post the adjustment to the retained earnings account. Don't. If you have an item in question, post it to a suspense account, then ask your accountant where you really should put the transaction, and edit it accordingly.

Seldom should there be any reason to make an adjusting entry to retained earnings. If you're not sure, ask your accountant.

Do Print the Journals

Accountants *love* the word journal. Anything journal. Cash receipts journal, purchase journal, payroll journal, Crazy Larry's love journal. Well, maybe not the last one. Anyway, make your accountant see hearts and flowers by printing Peachtree's journals for him or her. Their favorite report is not exactly called a journal, but it's a combination report of all the other journals. It's the General Ledger report. I know, that's a big report — but you do want your accountant to love you, don't you?

Appendix

New Features in Peachtree 2002

•••

*P*eachtree 2002, the successor of Peachtree 8, was released in July 2001. In this appendix, we highlight the new things you can expect from Peachtree 2002.

Interface

In the main Peachtree window, the Online menu is now the Services menu.

There are some cosmetic changes to Peachtree's interface; for example, in various Task and Report windows, you'll find drop down toolbar buttons (see Figure A-1). Notice that the toolbar buttons have changed slightly and been repositioned:

Figure A-1:
Task window toolbar buttons have changed names and moved around, and some buttons include a new drop down arrow.

- ✔ The Edit button has been replaced by the Open button — and the Open button appears in a different position than the Edit button appeared.

- ✔ The Post button (for those who use real-time posting) has been replaced by the Save button — and the Save button appears in a different position than the Post button appeared.

- ✓ A Row button enables you to add and remove rows from your transaction.

- ✓ A New button clears the contents of the window so that you can start a new transaction.

In appropriate Task windows, you can click the drop down arrow for the Open or the Save buttons to select or save a memorized transaction.

You also can maximize several of the Task windows, such as the Purchases window, the Sales/Invoicing window, and the Quotes window.

The interactive period and date buttons shown in the lower right corner of the main window are a really nice touch (see Figure A-2). You can now click these buttons to change the period or today's date.

Transaction notes

In Peachtree 2002, you can record both notes that will print and notes that won't print — so that you can create reminders to yourself about various transactions. You store these notes from any Accounts Receivable or Accounts Payable transaction window by clicking the Notes button on the toolbar of the window. In Figure A-3, you see the Internal Note tab of the Note window that we opened from the Sales/Invoicing window.

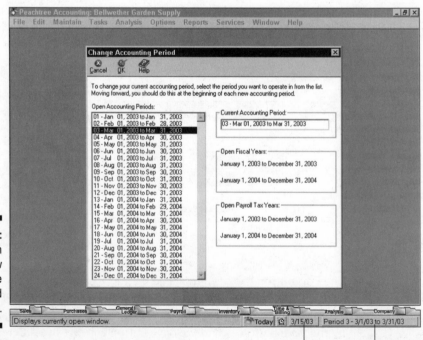

Figure A-2:
It's much easier now to change the date and period.

Today's date   Period

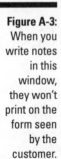

Figure A-3:
When you
write notes
in this
window,
they won't
print on the
form seen
by the
customer.

Fast add

Peachtree 2002 uses information you provide in various Task menu windows to create a new vendor or customer "on the fly". For example, suppose that you supply a vendor ID that doesn't exist in your Peachtree company as you complete a check in the Write Checks window. When you click the Save button, Peachtree will display the message that you see in Figure A-4. If you click the Fast Add button, Peachtree will store a record for the vendor, including the ID, vendor name, and address information; Peachtree will also assign the account on the check to the vendor as the default Purchase account.

Figure A-4:
Peachtree
prompts you
to "fast
add"
unknown
vendors and
customers.

Note: While you can't "fast add" employees, general ledger accounts, inventory items, or jobs, you can set them up "on the fly" in any Task window. When you enter an employee, general ledger account, inventory item, or job that you haven't set up yet, Peachtree displays a dialog box similar to the one shown in Figure A-4, but it doesn't contain the Fast Add button. Instead, you click the Set Up button. What's the difference between "fast add" and "set up"? When you click Fast Add, Peachtree uses the information you supplied in the Task window and saves it in the appropriate Maintain window. When you click the Set Up button, Peachtree opens the appropriate Maintain window to enable you to fill in the details. After you save and close the Maintain window, you'll see that the Task window contains all the necessary information.

Drill down

You can drill down from the Receipts and Payments windows to associated invoices and purchases so that you can easily view and edit the invoice or purchase against which you posted the receipt or payment you're viewing. As you pass the mouse pointer over the invoice or purchase, the mouse pointer changes to a magnifying glass (see Figure A-5). Double-click, and Peachtree opens the invoice or purchase in the appropriate window.

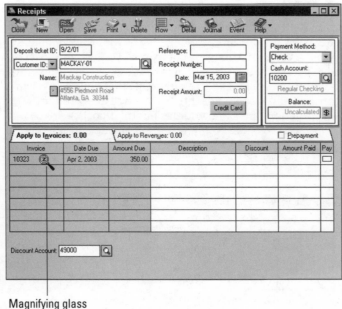

Figure A-5:
Drill down
from a
receipt to an
invoice.

Magnifying glass

More e-mail and Web site addresses

In Peachtree 8, you could store e-mail and Web addresses in the Maintain window for customers and vendors. In Peachtree 2002, you can store e-mail addresses for employees; in the Maintain Company Information dialog box, you can store an e-mail and Web address for your company (see Figure A-6). You can add this information to invoice and statement forms by customizing them.

You can e-mail an alert to any e-mail address stored in your Peachtree company (see Figure A-7). For example, if an inventory item falls below the minimum quantity on hand, you could e-mail the vendor, perhaps to prompt the vendor to get in touch with you to place an order.

Be aware that Peachtree 2002 automatically turns on event tracking, even if you previously had turned it off. Since the event log can become huge and slow down Peachtree's performance significantly, you may want to turn off event tracking again. To do so, follow these steps:

1. **Choose Tasks⇨Action Items.**

    The Action Items window appears.

2. **Click the Option button on the toolbar.**

    The Action Items and Event Logs dialog box appears.

3. **Select the Transactions tab and remove the check marks from all the boxes in the Create Event column (shown in Figure A-8).**

    Event tracking is now once again turned off.

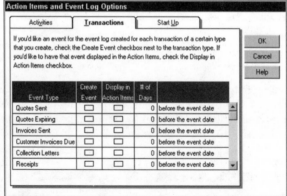

Figure A-8: Avoid generating extra transactions with the Transactions tab.

Choosing a form to print

If you choose to print a form or check from a Task window, you'll see a new dialog box (see Figure A-9) that enables you to use the form you used last time or select from all the available forms.

New inventory item pricing

Peachtree 2002 allows you to store up to ten sales prices for each item and base the sales prices upon a calculation (see Figure A-10). When creating the calculation, you can use the current price or the last cost as the foundation of the formula, and you can increase or decrease the price by a percentage or an amount.

Figure A-9:
You can use
the same
form you
used the
last time you
printed or
you can
choose
another
form.

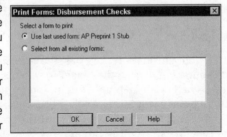

Figure A-10:
Set up to ten
sales prices
for an
inventory
item, and
base the
prices on a
calculation.

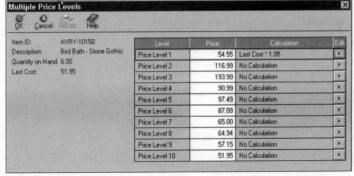

New in Accounts Receivable

You'll find three new features that affect Accounts Receivable.

"Out of Stock" warning

Previously, when you tried to sell an item you didn't have in stock, you got an out of stock warning in the Sales/Invoicing window only. Starting in Peachtree 2002, when you try to sell an item you don't have in stock, an "Out of Stock" warning appears in the Sales Order window and in the Sales/Invoicing window.

Print Receipts

In prior versions of Peachtree, you could not print Receipts. In Peachtree 2002, there is a Print button in the Receipts window, enabling you to print Receipts.

Print deposit slips

You can now create and print a deposit ticket report based on receipts entered through the Receipts window. To open the Select for Deposit window (see Figure A-11), choose Tasks⇨Select for Deposit. You no longer need to remember to assign the same Deposit Ticket ID to each receipt you intend to include in a particular bank deposit. Instead, you can use the Select for Deposit window to group the receipts so that they match the way that you actually deposit receipts at the bank — and make Account Reconciliation easier. Note that Peachtree calls it a deposit ticket, but it does not contain the bank routing information needed to get the money in your account. You might ask your bank if you can simply attach the report to a deposit slip to save you time and effort.

Figure A-11:
Use the Select for Deposit window to create a deposit ticket report.

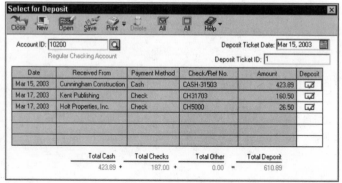

By default, the receipts that appear in the Select for Deposit window are those receipts that you enter without assigning a Deposit Ticket ID in the Receipts window. If you assign a Deposit Ticket ID to a receipt in the Receipts window, you can edit the deposit in the Select for Deposit window by clicking the Open button and then choosing Print. Peachtree produces a report that lists each item in the deposit; you can attach the report to a bank deposit ticket to supply the details of the deposit.

Peachtree will suggest Deposit Ticket ID numbers from either the Receipts window or the Select for Deposit window. You can control this behavior from the Pay Methods tab of the Customer Defaults dialog box (see Figure A-12). If you choose the Select for Deposit window, Peachtree will not suggest a Deposit Ticket ID as you enter receipts in the Receipts window, and all receipts you enter will appear in the Select for Deposit window. If you choose the Receipts window, Peachtree will behave as it always has behaved — it will suggest a Deposit Ticket ID number for each receipt as you enter it in the Receipts window; it will group receipts with the same Deposit Ticket ID number into one deposit in both the Select for Deposit window (when you click the Open button) and in the Accounts Reconciliation window.

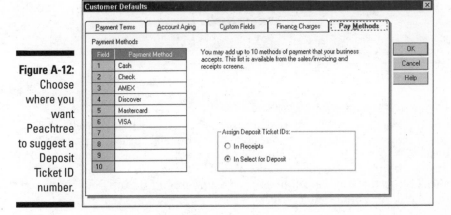

Figure A-12:
Choose where you want Peachtree to suggest a Deposit Ticket ID number.

New in Accounts Payable

You'll find two enhancements that affect Accounts Payable.

1099 enhancements

In Vendor Defaults, you can set each general ledger account's treatment of 1099 transactions. The defaults work in conjunction with the 1099 setting in Vendor Defaults window (choose Maintain⇨Default Information⇨Vendors and then click the 1099 Settings tab). By default, each GL account is set up so that Peachtree uses the settings in the Vendor Defaults window (see Figure A-13). However, you can override those settings for specified general ledger accounts and have Peachtree calculate 1099 payments using contractor payments credited to those accounts. This feature comes in very handy for those contractors whom you sometimes reimburse for expenses.

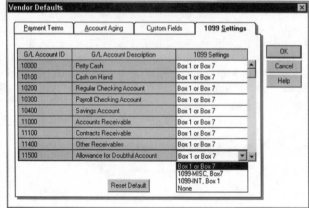

Print purchase details on checks

Up until Peachtree 2002, you had access to check forms that printed the ID you assigned to the purchase, but none of the details. For a long time, Peachtree users have wanted the ability to print the details of a purchase on the check stub the vendor receives. Well, Peachtree 2002 contains two new check forms that enable you to do just that: MultiP AP 1 Stub Detail form and the MultiP AP 2 Stub Detail form.

New in Payroll

In Peachtree 2002, if you don't subscribe to the Payroll Tax Table service, you cannot open the Global Tax Table window. Do not fear, however, if you have updated global tax tables manually in the past, because there is nothing stopping you from saving tax tables for FIT, Social Security, Medicare, and others in the Company Tax Table window. Just be sure to copy down your formulas before you upgrade to Peachtree 2002.

Data Verification

Peachtree 2002 contains a Data Verification tool that helps you analyze and possibly repair your data, should it become damaged. Before you use this feature, be sure to make a backup and contact your Peachtree Support representative.

Year End Wizard

The new Year End Wizard guides you through the process of closing the year, making that process easier.

Optional integrated additions and online services

Peachtree 2002 also offers some additional integrated products and online services, for which additional fees apply.

Crystal Reports for Peachtree

Approximately six months after Peachtree 8 was released, an update became available that enabled you to use Crystal Reports for Peachtree with Peachtree 8. Peachtree 2002 also works with Crystal Reports for Peachtree, which you can buy from www.peachtree.com.

You can contact Diane Koers, co-author of this book, at dkoers@home.com for custom-designed reports using Crystal Reports for Peachtree.

Peachtree Credit Card Service

With the Peachtree Credit Card Service you can accept, authorize, and process credit card transactions online from inside your Peachtree company. If you choose to use Peachtree's merchant services, you can accept credit cards for payments with no need for a credit card swipe terminal. All funds collected from credit card payments are deposited directly into your business bank account.

Peachtree WebsiteTrader Service

Peachtree WebsiteTrader helps you take advantage of e-commerce capabilities on a Peachtree-hosted Web site. You can accept orders directly from your Web site with options for calculating sales tax and selecting shipping methods. Orders received on your Peachtree-hosted Web site can be easily brought back into your Peachtree Accounting as new Sales Orders. You can build your Web site for free using tools contained in Peachtree 2002, but charges apply for Web-hosting services.

Peachtree Web Accounting

Keep your eye on this up-and-coming fee-based service that permits you (or your accountant) to view and enter Peachtree transactions on the Web from any computer and then synchronize Web-entered data with your Peachtree company on your local computer. At the present time, the transactions you can enter are limited, but watch for expansion in this area.

Internet Postage Service

Save time in your daily correspondence and shipping by buying and using stamps online from within Peachtree. This service is available through a partnership with Stamps.com.

Index